PORTLAND

Fairgoers appear ghostlike due to the long exposure time required for this 1905 photo of the Lewis and Clark Exposition at night. Courtesy, Oregon Historical Society (OHS)

PORTLAND
GATEWAY
―TO THE―
NORTHWEST

CARL ABBOTT

Pictorial Research by Ted Van Arsdol
"Partners in Progress" by Richard Pintarich

Produced in Cooperation with the
Portland State University Foundation

Windsor Publications, Inc.
Northridge, California

Windsor Publications, Inc.—History Book Division

Publisher: John M. Phillips
Editorial Director: Teri Davis Greenberg
Design Director: Alexander D'Anca

Staff for Portland: Gateway to the Northwest

Senior Editor: Pamela Schroeder
Picture Editor: Julie Jaskol
Director, Corporate Biographies: Karen Story
Assistant Director, Corporate Biographies:
    Phyllis Gray
Editor, Corporate Biographies: Judith Hunter
Editorial Assistants: Kathy M. Brown, Patricia
    Cobb, Lonnie Pham, Patricia Pittman,
    Deena Tucker
Design and Layout: J.R. Vasquez

Honorary Advisors

The publisher wishes to acknowledge the following
individuals who lent valuable assistance in the
preparation of this volume:

Philip Bogue
Howard Hubbard
Leigh D. Stephenson
A. Roger Pease
David S. Belles
George H. Fraser
Robert D. Scanlan
Louis Scherzer
Caroline Stoel
Joseph C. Blumel

Library of Congress Cataloging in Publication Data

Abbott, Carl.
    Portland: gateway to the Northwest.

    Bibliography: p. 265
    Includes index.
    1. Portland (Or.)—History. 2. Portland (Or.)—
Description. 3. Portland (Or.)—Industries.
1. Title.
F884.P857A32   1985   979.5'49   85-9520
ISBN 0-89781-155-0

Facing page: *Skidmore
Fountain has been one of
the city's favorite land-
marks since its completion
in 1888. Increasing num-
bers of people have visited
the fountain on S.W. First
Avenue since the opening
of the Saturday Market
and restoration of the New
Market building, both
nearby. Courtesy, Barbara
Gundle*

Endpapers: *Portland in
1861 enjoyed a lovely and
active riverfront according
to this lithograph "drawn
from nature" by Grafton T.
Brown. Courtesy, Amon
Carter Museum, Ft.
Worth, Texas*

CONTENTS

Willamette Falls, fifteen miles above Portland, was a barrier to transportation on the Willamette River. The Hudson's Bay Company established a trading post at this popular fishing place in 1829. A townsite was laid out in 1842. (OHS)

PROLOGUE: GATEWAY TO THE NORTHWEST

Our great-great grandparents were quick to give full credit to divine providence for the growth of their cities. The Creator, said one early Chicagoan, had marked the inevitable destiny of that city by rolling back the waves of Lake Michigan. The great bend of the Missouri River seemed a heaven-sent guarantee for the success of Kansas City. Armchair geographers were confident that the falls on the Mississippi assured the future of St. Paul.

In the case of Portland, the general idea was clear enough. There seemed to be no doubt that a major center of commerce would develop *someplace* along the lower valley of the Columbia River between the Cascade Mountains and the Pacific Ocean. The only problem was exactly *where* that place would be. It was not until 1843 and 1844—after fifty years of Anglo-American exploration and thousands of years of occupance by Native Americans—that a permanent settlement was founded at what has now become the middle of downtown Portland.

More than any of its West Coast rivals of Seattle, Tacoma, San Francisco, or Los Angeles, Portland is indeed "the city that gravity built," to repeat the phrase of historian Glenn Quiett. It lies at the center of a great lowland crossroad that the forces of geological change have stamped into the mountains and plateaus of western America. From north to south, more than two-

thirds of the population of the Pacific Northwest and all but one of its major cities are found along a 500-mile trough between the volcanic peaks of the Cascades and the string of coastal mountains that extends from the redwood country of northern California to the spine of Vancouver Island. South of the Columbia, the Willamette River flows through the heart of the trough. Further north, the Cowlitz River extends the lowland through Washington State to Puget Sound and the Strait of Georgia. The string of cities runs from Eugene, Salem, and Portland in Oregon, through Olympia, Tacoma, Seattle, and Bellingham in Washington to Vancouver and Victoria in British Columbia.

The Columbia River crosses the lowland axis after breaking through the Cascade range 160 miles from the Pacific. East of the mountains, the river drains an Inland Empire that is larger than all of New England. As soon as the Columbia's existence was known, it entered the dreams of eastern Americans as the sure route to the western coast—the "North American road to India," in the words of Missouri Senator Thomas Hart Benton.

Later boosters talked as if the divine hand not only had pointed out the general location for the metropolis of Oregon but had actually staked the exact site. In sober fact, as we have said, it took explorers and pioneers half a century to hit on the precise spot for Port-

land.

The English-speaking discoverer of the Columbia River was the American trader Robert Gray, who entered the mouth of the river in May 1792 but showed no interest in venturing upstream into the interior. It was left to Lieutenant James Broughton of the British navy, sailing with Captain James Vancouver on the expedition that first mapped Puget Sound, to become the first European actually to explore the lower Columbia. In October 1792, he took the 135-ton *Chatham* across the dangerous Columbia bar and spent three weeks exploring the river in small boats. He reached the Sandy River and claimed the region for England. Although he noted the confluence of the Willamette, he was more interested in enjoying the scenery and bestowing the name Mt. Hood on the region's most prominent peak.

A decade later, Meriwether Lewis, William Clark, and their handful of companions on their famous transcontinental expedition of 1804-1806 missed the mouth of the Willamette River not once but twice. On their way downstream to the Pacific in November 1805, they recorded several islands along the south shore of the Columbia but failed to notice the mouth of the Willamette. On its return after a winter at Fort Clatsop near present-day Astoria, the expedition reached the Quicksand (Sandy) River before Clark doubled back with a Cushook Indian guide to find the "Moltnomar" or "Multnomah" river, his term for the Willamette. On the morning of April 3, he paddled as far as the bluff now occupied by the University of Portland, where the river turned east-southeast to swing around Swan Island. As Clark recorded in his journal, he turned around in a thick mist "being perfectly satisfied of the size and magnitude of this great river which must water that vast tract of Country between the western range of mountains and those on the sea coast."

One reason that Clark and other explorers failed to remark on the site that was to become the heart of Portland was because the location was relatively unimportant to Native Americans. When European and American fur traders began to arrive in the Pacific Northwest at the end of the 1700s, Chinook-speaking peoples dominated the lower Columbia west of the Cascades from its mouth to the falls at The Dalles. The Lower Chinooks, among whom Lewis and Clark spent the winter of 1805-1806, lived around the wide Columbia estuary. The Upper Chinooks lived in small bands along the middle stretch of the river. Their greatest concentration was on Sauvie Island and along the adjacent Oregon shore, an area dominated by a subgroup known as the Multnomahs. Lewis and Clark counted 2,400 people on the island and

Captain Meriwether Lewis, shown here circa 1810, and Captain William Clark headed the army exploring party down the Columbia River past the mouth of the Willamette in 1805. This was the first recorded visit of an American to the vicinity, although trading ships had stopped along the coast. (OHS)

Left: *The Multnomahs were Indians residing on and adjacent to Sauvie Island, near the mouth of the Willamette River. This tribe member, Old John, owned an iron skillet said to have been given to him by white men, possibly Lewis and Clark.* (OHS)

Above: *With information gathered from Indians, Captain William Clark drew the first map of the Willamette River. He also traveled up the river a short distance from the Columbia in 1806. Clark reported that the Multnomah Indians lived on Wappato Island (now Sauvie Island).* (OHS)

another 1,800 nearby on the south shore. Six years later, British fur trader Robert Stuart reported a population of about 2,000 for the island itself. By piecing together the reports of different travelers, we can now locate more than fifteen separate villages on Sauvie Island and immediately across the Columbia, the Willamette, or Multnomah Channel.

Twenty-five miles up the Willamette were other Indians who also spoke Chinook dialects. The Clackamas groups were the largest, with perhaps a dozen villages. Smaller bands included the Cushooks and Chahcowahs, who clustered below the falls at the present Oregon City, where it was easy to take salmon out of the Willamette and Clackamas rivers. Above the falls to the south, the Willamette Valley was occupied by the Kalapooias, a people distinct from the various branches of Chinooks. They were divided into at least a dozen bands with defined territories. Closest to present-day Portland was the Tualatin band in what is now Washington County.

Compared to Native Americans in many other parts of the continent, the Chinooks along the lower Columbia lived a relatively rich and easy life. Lewis and Clark remarked on the special fertility of the Columbia Valley in the vicinity of Portland. The Multnomahs, Clackamas, and other groups in this Portland basin fished for salmon, sturgeon, and smelt; hunted migratory birds and deer that thrived in the riverside woods and clearings; gathered nuts and berries; and dug wappatoo roots out

Captain Robert Gray of Boston discovered the mouth of the Columbia River in 1792, as depicted here. The Willamette River and other important tributaries of the Columbia remained unknown. Courtesy, Oregon State Transportation Department

of the mud of the marshes with pointed sticks. The abundance of wappatoo on Sauvie Island gave the island its first name and supported an especially dense population that was quite possibly larger than is found there now. Cedar logs washed loose from the mountains provided the materials for dugout canoes, cooking utensils, and longhouses made of planks lashed to a framework of poles and posts. Usually erected over a shallow pit, the plank lodges might reach 100 feet in length, with woven tule mats subdividing the interior space.

For travel to seasonal hunting and fishing grounds, the Chinook bands used temporary shelters of poles covered with mats and hides.

Chinook settlements ranged from clusters of a few small houses to substantial villages with hundreds of residents. Each village was an independent entity, bound together by complex kinship ties and represented by one or several headmen. Although the Chinook-speaking villages acknowledged some common connection, each was closer to an extended family than a unit within

an organized tribe. Villages were built to last for years, not for decades or centuries, for the abundance of resources made it easy to move from one spot to another within a band's general territory.

In the economy of the Chinook bands, the centers of trade were the mouth of the Columbia and the future site of The Dalles, where Celilo Falls marked a break in navigation on the river. Where the Columbia met the sea, they traded with other coastal tribes and, after the visits of Robert Gray and James Broughton in 1792, with European and American sailing ships. The Dalles was the dividing point between the lush coastal lands and the dry ranges and plateaus of the interior. It was also the boundary between the lifestyle of the northwest coast and that of inland tribes such as the Shoshonis, Paiutes, and Nez Perce. Both before and after the arrival of British fur traders, the break in navigation on the Columbia made The Dalles a natural market, as well as "a general theater of gambling and roguery" in the critical view of one trader. The Multnomahs and other tribes near the lower Willamette lived along the artery of trade but controlled neither of the key points of exchange.

The Chinooks were natural trading partners for American and British fur companies. The initial commerce was carried on by both "King George's men" and "Boston men"—English and American merchants who took two years to make a round-the-world circuit with stops at the northwest coast, the Hawaiian Islands, and China. The heyday of maritime commerce to the Columbia lasted from 1792 until the War of 1812. Thereafter attention was focused on transcontinental trade. New Yorker John Jacob Astor organized the Pacific Fur Company in 1810 and planted the trading post that evolved into the city of Astoria at Point George on the south bank of the Columbia. Three years later, he sold out to the North West Company, a Montreal-based firm that renamed the post Fort George and dominated the fur trade of the Columbia Basin until 1821.

In turn, the North West Company was absorbed by its powerful rival, the British Hudson's Bay Company. Fort George was soon reduced to a lookout post to report on possible competition,

and the Hudson's Bay operations moved to Fort Vancouver, built in 1825 on the north shore of the Columbia seven miles upstream from the Willamette. Under the leadership of Dr. John McLoughlin, chief factor for the Hudson's Bay Company in the Oregon Country, it was the focal point of a Columbia Basin trading network extending hundreds of miles into the interior.

Fewer than thirty years after the Lewis and Clark expedition brought back reports of the Chinooks and Kalapooias and less than a decade after the building of Fort Vancouver, disease vir-

tually exterminated the population of northwestern Oregon. The spread of the Anglo-American trading system opened the possibility of both immediate economic gains and ultimate catastrophe for the Indians. The "Cold Sick" or "Intermitting Fever" appeared in the Chinook and Kalapooia villages in 1829 and raged for the next three years. Circumstantial evidence suggests that the disease may have been malaria brought in from the tropics by traders, although a form of influenza is another possibility. The disease was at its worst around Fort Vancouver and Sauvie Island. Eu-

Parts of old Fort Vancouver, headquarters of the Hudson's Bay Company in the Northwest, have been restored at Vancouver, near Portland. Among these is the blacksmith shop, where tools similar to those of frontier times are made for the nearby trader's store. Courtesy, Ted Van Arsdol

ropean observers estimated death rates that ranged from 50 percent to the appalling 90 percent reported by John McLoughlin of the Hudson's Bay Company. Observed from the outside and in retrospect, the Cold Sick was a tragedy whose human cost we can scarcely reckon.

The first Caucasian settlers who filled the void left by the virtual destruction of the native population also ignored the site of Portland. Fort Vancouver continued to be the major British settlement in the Portland area and hummed with activity that deeply impressed occasional visitors. Fort William, a rival trading post built on Sauvie Island by the independent American fur trader Nathaniel Wyeth, lasted only two years, from 1835 to 1837, before the Hudson's Bay Company took over the abandoned site

as a dairy farm. Hall J. Kelley, an eccentric New Englander who dedicated his life to fervent boosting of the Oregon Country, proposed to the general public the establishment of a "commercial town ... about two miles square" at the juncture of the Willamette and Columbia. According to his crudely sketched plat, the city was to run across the North Portland peninsula from Smith Lake and the Columbia Slough to the St. Johns neighborhood of present-day Portland. We are scarcely surprised that the proposal sank without a trace, since Kelley had picked the site years before his own brief and highly unsuccessful visit to Oregon in 1834 and 1835.

Early traders and settlers who followed the Willamette upstream from Fort Vancouver in the 1830s or early

1840s had their eyes on the falls or the interior valley beyond. Their diaries and reports usually ignored or dismissed the first few miles of the river, where Portland was eventually to be built. The banks were either low and swampy, or else too thickly wooded for quick and easy cultivation. Philadelphia physician and naturalist John Townsend summed up the common reaction when he wrote that "there is not sufficient extent unincumbered, or which could be fitted for the purposes of tillage in a space of time short enough to be serviceable; others are at some seasons inundated, which is an insurmountable objection."

Indeed, the first large European settlements along the Willamette itself were both upstream from the site of Portland. Retired employees of the Hudson's Bay Company, mostly French Canadians, had begun to settle and cultivate the "French Prairie" in 1829. By 1840-41, the community had grown to more than sixty families who could worship in a new Roman Catholic church and sell their surplus wheat to Fort Vancouver through a small warehouse and landing at Champoeg, twenty-five miles above the Willamette Falls. A second settlement formed at the base of the falls where John McLoughlin and Methodist missionaries contended for control of what seemed to be the natural location for a major town. Rival development efforts started in 1840 and 1841. By the winter of 1842-1843, the new community of Oregon City had made a significant impression on the wilderness, with more than thirty buildings, a gristmill, and a growing competition for building lots. It was the first destination for most of the participants in the swelling American migrations that had brought over 800 new settlers to Oregon in 1843 and about 1,200 more in 1844.

Into the early 1840s the history of Portland is, in short, a story of near

misses. The Chinooks preferred to live at Sauvie Island and the falls of the Willamette and traded at the mouth of the Columbia and The Dalles. The Hudson's Bay men operated out of Fort Vancouver with a satellite settlement at Champoeg. Missionaries followed the Indians into the Willamette Valley and up the Columbia, while American settlers made Oregon City their first real town. The site of Portland, meanwhile, remained at the start of 1843 what it had been before—a small clearing of an

A somewhat fanciful 1846 illustration shows sailing ships at the great river of the West, the Columbia. Vessels sometimes encountered difficult conditions crossing the river bar before proceeding upriver to Fort Vancouver or into the Willamette, where several towns were vying for prominence. Courtesy, Reverend C.G. Nicolay's The Oregon Territory

acre or so made by trappers and Indians traveling between Fort Vancouver and Oregon City. It served as a sort of early rest area where travelers could rest or cook a midday meal on the thirty-mile trip. Jesse A. Applegate later described the site he had visited as a boy in 1843:

We landed on the west shore, and went into camp on the high bank where there was little underbush ... No one lived there and the place had no name; there was nothing to show that the place had ever been visited except a small log hut near the river, and a broken mast of a ship leaning against the high bank. There were chips hewn from timber, showing that probably a new mast had been made there .... We were then actually encamped on the site of the city of Portland, but there was no prophet with us to tell of the beautiful city that was to take the place of the gloomy forest.

Lieutenant Henry J. Warre of the Royal Engineers, on a reconnaissance of Oregon for the British, sketched the new American settlement at Oregon City. He arrived with Lieutenant Vavasour in 1845 and started on the return trip in the following spring. (OHS)

CHAPTER I
STUMPTOWN

The Pacific Northwest was an international trouble spot in 1845. Political control of the Oregon Country—what is now Idaho, Oregon, Washington, and British Columbia—had been in dispute since the eighteenth century. England and the United States had pushed Russian claims north to Alaska and Spanish claims south to California in the first quarter of the nineteenth century and had then settled down to a diplomatic marathon that lasted from President to President and Prime Minister to Prime Minister. Along the lower Columbia, both sides traced their claims to the 1792 voyages by Gray and Boughton.

Tension had mounted rapidly with the Presidential campaign of 1844, when the issue of American control of Oregon helped to put Democrat James K. Polk in the White House. The growing American settlements along the Willamette and Columbia rivers were upsetting the delicate balance of commercial interests worked out by the men of the Hudson's Bay Company, and the British government correctly feared that Polk would cancel the joint occupancy agreement that had given citizens of both nations free access to Oregon since 1818.

The Northwest was a North American hot spot with its own set of spies and agents. The British military command in Canada dispatched Lieutenants Henry Warre and M. Vavasour from Montreal in 1845 for a military reconnaissance of Oregon. They traveled openly under the joint occupancy agreement in the guise of "private individuals, seeking amusement." Their real job was to spy out possibilities for coastal defenses, sea batteries, and river fortifications in case Britain decided to hold the territory against the Americans. Their report from Fort Vancouver in October 1845 counted the surviving Chinooks, Kalapooias, and Klickitats; described the American settlements; and suggested that a small British force stationed at Oregon City "would overawe the present American population" of 300. The only other settlement they noted on the lower Willamette was one family at Linnton.

Warre and Vavasour's second report on June 16, 1846, mentioned a new town. "Since the summer," they wrote their superiors, "a village called Portland has been commenced between the falls and Linnton, to which an American merchant ship ascended and discharged her cargo, in September." After struggling with their canoes through high water and willow swamps and camping on muddy beaches for more than a year, the two British officers were impressed by dry land. "The situation of Portland is superior to that of Linnton, and the back country of easier access. There are several settlements on the banks of the river, below the falls, but the water, covering the low lands during the freshets render them valueless for cultivation, and but few situations can be found adapted for building on."

Neither the British travelers nor the handful of Portlanders knew that exactly three days after Warre and Vavasour sealed their second dispatch, the United States Senate would make their mission

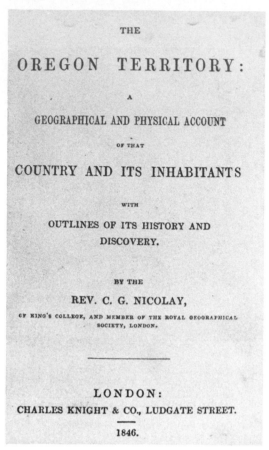

THE

 OREGON TERRITORY:

A

GEOGRAPHICAL AND PHYSICAL ACCOUNT

OF THAT

COUNTRY AND ITS INHABITANTS

WITH

OUTLINES OF ITS HISTORY AND
DISCOVERY.

BY THE

REV. C. G. NICOLAY,

OF KING'S COLLEGE, AND MEMBER OF THE ROYAL GEOGRAPHICAL
SOCIETY, LONDON.

LONDON:

CHARLES KNIGHT & CO., LUDGATE STREET.

1846.

Far left: Peter Skene Ogden was prominent among Hudson's Bay Company leaders when Great Britain claimed the land on the north bank of the Columbia, opposite today's Portland. Ogden led hardy groups of traders from Fort Vancouver to the Snake River country to trap and trade for furs. (OHS)

Left: Books and articles helped build interest in the relatively unsettled Pacific Northwest in the decade or so before Portland was established. This book reported that the Willamette settlement was flourishing, and begins "to wear some little appearance of civilization." Courtesy, The Oregon Territory

irrelevant by ratifying the Anglo-American Oregon Treaty. The compromise boundary was the 49th parallel from the Rocky Mountains to Puget Sound, and from there around the south end of Vancouver Island and through the Strait of Juan de Fuca to the open Pacific. The future states of Idaho, Washington, and Oregon became the undisputed territory of the United States.

Portland was two and a half years old when the new treaty officially made it an "all American" town. The burgeoning settlement was the result of a bright idea by a drifter named William Overton. Overton had spent two years off and on in Oregon before he spotted the clearing along the west bank of the Willamette. In November 1843 he showed the site to Asa Lovejoy, an Oregon City lawyer, and the two became co-owners of the 640 acres that would become

downtown Portland when they filed a claim with the settlers' provisional government at Oregon City early in 1844. Lovejoy took a half-interest in the property when he agreed to pay the 25-cent filing fee with the provisional government. The men were claiming presumptive title, awaiting official acquisition of the territory by the United States and a procedure for distributing land to Oregon pioneers.

Portland's founding fathers quickly lost interest in their land speculation. Overton left Oregon to try his fortunes in California and, in the spring of 1844, sold out to Francis Pettygrove, a leading Oregon City merchant, for a $50 grubstake. Later that year, Pettygrove and Lovejoy hired a man to enlarge the clearing at the Willamette and build a cabin; he soon complained that the mosquitoes were so thick he couldn't work outside and that fleas made the inside of the cabin just as intolerable.

The next year brought the property both a name and a survey. But for the toss of a coin the town would have been called Boston, not Portland. Co-owner Asa Lovejoy was from Massachusetts and held a degree from Amherst College; he liked the idea of owning half of "Boston." Pettygrove hailed from the state of Maine and wanted to name the town "Portland." They "snapped up a copper," to use Lovejoy's words, and Pettygrove won the toss. That same year the speculators hired surveyor Thomas Brown to stake out blocks and lots so they could sell their property to new settlers. The original plat was two blocks deep and eight wide, bounded by Front, Second, Washington, and Jefferson streets. There were eight 50-by-100-foot lots on each small block.

Though Portland seemed well on its way to becoming a real community, Lovejoy, like his former partner Overton, soon lost interest in the townsite. Beckoned by a career in politics, Lovejoy decided in November 1845 that his future lay at Oregon City, the territorial capital, and sold his half interest to Benjamin Stark, cargomaster on the bark *Toulon*. Stark had traded with Pettygrove in the New York-to-Portland trade. Since Stark spent most of his time sailing back and forth to Oahu, finally settling down to a prosperous life in San Francisco, Pettygrove found himself responsible not only for the name but for the future of Portland.

What historian Eugene Snyder has called "Portland's Pettygrove period" lasted for two years of steady but unremarkable growth. Before the summer of 1846 was over, about sixty residents lived in Portland's first dozen or fifteen houses. James Terwilliger shoed horses at First and Morrison. Daniel Lownsdale's tannery was out of town to the west, where a creek flowed from the hills past the present site of Civic Stadi-

Asa Lovejoy, one of Portland's founders, arrived in Oregon with Dr. Elijah White in 1842. He rode east with Marcus Whitman during Whitman's efforts to save the missions in Walla Walla Valley and at Lapwai in Idaho. Lovejoy also served in the Oregon legislature. (OHS)

um. The center of town was Francis Pettygrove's store and wharf at the foot of Washington Street. A rough and rutted wagon track ran from the wharf past Lownsdale's tannery to the "Twality Plains." Other settlers in this first year of city-building included merchant J.L. Morrison, physician and teacher Dr. Ralph Wilcox, sawmill operator John Waymire, and shingle-maker William Bennett.

By the next summer of 1847, the town had grown to about 100 inhabitants. J.Q. Thornton, an early Oregon judge, described the place as having "an air of neatness, thrift, and industry." Sophisticates from larger towns like Oregon City were not always so kind. Although the trees had been cleared from rights of way to show where the streets had been surveyed, many of the stumps remained. Some were whitewashed to prevent nighttime wanderers from tripping. It was hard for outsiders to resist the nickname "Stumptown."

California's Gold Rush brought both crisis and opportunity for Stumptown. The news of James Marshall's discovery of gold at Sutter's Mill near Sacramento arrived in Oregon in August. Thou-

primarily wheat, for the California market. The supplies were sent by ship down the Willamette and Columbia rivers, then down the coast to San Francisco. On one day in midsummer 1849, twenty ships were loading in the lower Willamette at the same time. The volume of Oregon exports increased by fivefold in that year.

One summer of trade does not make a city. "Why Portland?" was the question that every smart investor and newly arrived merchant should have asked at the beginning of 1850. Stumptown would only grow if it was based on a successful business foundation. Two "generations" of Portland promoters—Overton and Lovejoy, Pettygrove and Stark—had already given up on Portland to seek greener pastures. Half a dozen rival settlements along a fifty-mile stretch of the lower Willamette and Columbia offered serious competition, and fortunes changed fast on the frontier. Would Portland or Milwaukie be the metropolis of Oregon? Milton City or Oregon City? St. Johns or St. Helens or some site still unnamed?

The competition between Portland and its rivals in the early 1850s is a fairly typical chapter in the familiar story of American townsite promotion. As settlement moved west in the nine-

Left: "Beaver" coins, five- and ten-dollar gold pieces, were produced by pioneers in 1849 at Oregon City, and were circulated for several years along the Willamette River. They helped eliminate bartering and the use of gold dust as money. Gold for the coins came from California. (OHS)

Below: Daniel Lownsdale, who occupied land in what is now downtown Portland, was involved in a townsite venture with Stephen Coffin and William Chapman. Lownsdale, who arrived in Oregon Territory in 1845, also established Portland's first tannery. (OHS)

sands of Oregonians caught gold fever. They hurried south to reach the Sierras before the snows and to get a jump on the expected hordes of prospectors from the East. Among the gold-seekers were dozens of families from Portland. According to popular lore the town's population was reduced to a grand total of three people. Francis Pettygrove bartered his half ownership of Portland to Daniel Lownsdale, Portland's first tanner, for $5,000 worth of leather, and liquidated his other assets in Oregon before sailing to San Francisco early in 1849. There he sold Lownsdale's leather to '49ers at a healthy profit. People who stayed in Portland also made good money by supplying lumber and food,

teenth century, speculators rushed to claim every promising harbor, ford, and dry stretch of riverfront. A cynical British observer had previously described the process in the Mississippi Valley:

A speculator makes out a plan of a city with its streets, squares, and avenues, quays and wharves, public buildings and monuments. The streets are lotted, the houses numbered, and the squares called after Franklin or Washington. The city itself has some fine name, perhaps Troy or Antioch. . . . All this time the city is a mere vision . . . five hundred miles beyond civilization,

probably under water or surrounded by dense forests and impassable swamps.

This ambitious platting of towns occurred across the young United States. The towns that managed to attract more than a handful of settlers plunged into a struggle for reputation and trade. There were half a dozen aspiring Toledos in northwestern Ohio in the 1830s. Chicago had to contend with the ambitions of Waukegan. At the same time that Portland was scrambling for its future, Kansas City was fighting Atchison and Leavenworth to be the metropolis of the Missouri. A few years later, Den-

Because early businesses faced the Willamette River, the street parallel to the water was known as Front. Wagons carried loads along the muddy street in this 1850s scene showing a washhouse, the Union Hotel, and a foundry. (OHS)

21

ver would have to battle the claims of Auraria, Highland, Mountain City, Arapahoe City, and Golden. Closer to home, Portlanders would soon be able to watch Tacoma, Seattle, and Everett competing to be the major city and chief port on Puget Sound.

In Oregon, the ostensible issue in 1850 was the location of the "head of navigation," the point of closest access by ocean shipping to the agricultural riches of the Willamette Valley. As every sailor knew, there was actually no such definitive point. The head of navigation varied with the season, the length of the wharf, the type of ship, and the courage or foolishness of its captain. Every town could legitimately advance some claim to the title. The real question was which town had the most *push*—a wonderful word that meant ambition, boosterism, and canny entrepreneurship to our great-great grandparents.

Portland eventually took the prize, beating out its rivals to establish itself as the head of navigation, because it

had the most skilled and persistant promoters. Daniel Lownsdale had divided his share of Portland with two new partners during the course of 1849. Stephen Coffin of Maine, an energetic building contractor who had come to Oregon City in 1847, and William Chapman of Virginia, a lawyer who had made money in the California Gold Rush, provided ideas, energy, and capital. In the short space of 1850 and 1851, Portland's triumvirate provided three essentials that assured their town's permanent growth—dependable steamship service to California, the Great Plank Road across the West Hills, and promotion of the town in the form of the purple prose of the *Oregonian* newspaper.

A newspaper on the nineteenth-century frontier was vitally important, serving as a sort of urban identification card. Like a post office or a county courthouse, even a four-page weekly was accepted proof that a townsite was a going concern. It rankled and grated the city's leadership in the early months of 1850 that Portland merchants had to advertise their wares in Oregon City's *Spectator.* Chapman and Coffin remedied the situation by recruiting an unemployed editor with a battered hand printing press from San Francisco. Thomas Jefferson Dryer arrived in November, his equipment a month later. The first issue of the *Oregonian* appeared on December 4, 1850.

Dryer ran the paper for ten years. He advocated the Whig and then the Republican party, boosted the city of Portland, and used every printable insult in the language in feuds with Salem's *Oregon Statesman* and Portland's second newspaper, the *Democratic Standard,* which was published from 1854 to 1859. The typical weekly issue of the *Oregonian* in the 1850s was a combination of newspaper, *Reader's Digest,* and telephone yellow pages. The first page

Thomas J. Dryer founded the weekly Oregonian *in 1850. Ten years later he turned it over to Henry Pittock, who had started work there in 1853. Despite serious competition over the decades,* The Oregonian *survived as a daily and became Portland's main newspaper. (OHS)*

Peter H. Burnett promoted Linnton, northwest of Portland, as a future great commercial town in 1844 and 1845. Burnett, who helped organize the Oregon legislature, moved to California in 1848 and was elected governor there in 1849. (OHS)

"the farmers' railroad," easy for amateurs to build and almost as cheap as dirt in the states around the Great Lakes and in the Northwest where lumber was virtually free for the cutting.

The territorial legislature chartered the Portland and Valley Plank Road Company in January 1851. The organizational meeting was held in Lafayette, but Portland's "Big Three"—Lownsdale, Coffin, and Chapman—signed up to buy a third of the stock and the construction started southwestward from Portland. The route led up the ravine of Tanner Creek, over the Sylvan hill, and on to its final destination of Hillsborough. Work on the roadbed started in late summer. The first planks, from Portland's own steam sawmill, went down with great fanfare and suitable oratory on September 27, 1851. The company ran out of money after planking only a few miles of this first version of Canyon Road, but even the rutted track that continued into the rich agricultural lands of the Tualatin Valley made Portland the most accessible port for Washington County farmers, who shipped their abundant wheat to San Francisco.

Portland's plank road doomed the already fading hopes of the nearby town of Linnton. Its founders were Morton McCarver, a "compulsive town promoter" in the words of historian Malcolm Clark, Jr., and Peter Burnett, a frontier lawyer who had come to Oregon ahead of his creditors and who eventually became the first governor of the State of California. They had staked out the town in 1844 at the end of an old cattle trail that the Hudson's Bay men at Vancouver had used to move their cattle to summer pastures in the Tualatin country. The developers planned to turn the cattle trail into a real road, but in fact never did, and few farmers bothered to ship their wheat through the Linnton warehouse. The

carried short fiction, jokes, articles copied from Eastern papers, and the equivalent of today's wire service filler. The back page and one of the interior pages carried business cards and advertisements from firms in Portland, Oregon City, and more distant towns like Albany and Olympia in the Oregon Territory. The listings, which scarcely varied from month to month, functioned as a business directory. The other inside page contained editorials and "Latest News by the Mail" from San Francisco.

If the *Oregonian* gave Portland equal standing with Oregon City as an information center for the territory, then a few miles of unfinished plank road were enough for Portland to gain victory over the town's nearest rivals. At the start of the 1850s, Americans throughout the Midwest and South were seized by a mania for plank roads—highways with a surface of sawed planks spiked to wooden stringers. They were touted as

California Gold Rush took Linnton's last residents as they headed south to seek their fortunes, and the Portland plank road killed any hopes of the town's revival.

Cazeno or Baker's Landing or Springville—it took a while to settle on a name—was a slightly more successful town located a mile upstream at what is now the west end of the St. Johns Bridge. Washington County cut a road through the hills in 1852 to give wheat farmers and stockmen on its northern edge an alternative route to the Willamette. One result was a new community that grew up around the warehouse at the Willamette terminus of the road. This small settlement of Springville helped to fill ships that sometimes left Portland half empty. We have no population count, but it was important enough to be made a post office around 1860. By the early 1870s, however, the warehouse had burned and the town and its road had fallen out of use.

Milwaukie and St. Johns, located on the Willamette's east side, were on the wrong side of the river to profit from the development of Washington County agriculture. James Johns had claimed a square mile of land and laid out a town

directly across the river from Springville at the end of the 1840s. By 1851 his town of St. Johns had a dozen families, but it was too isolated to prosper. There was more uncleared forest than farmland on the east side of the river and therefore little business for the town. The "ferry" to Linnton was a rowboat. The settlement would have a renaissance as an independent port and city around 1900 but it was not a serious contender in the competition among the region's towns in the early 1850s.

The other east-side town of Milwaukie had been founded by Lot Whitcomb in 1848. Whitcomb built sailing ships to carry lumber to the California market at great profit, and published the *Western Star,* whose first issue went to press two weeks ahead of the *Oregonian.* He also built a side-wheeled steamboat named for himself. The *Lot Whitcomb of Oregon* went into service in February 1851 on a regular run to Portland, St. Helens, the mouth of the Cowlitz River,

Left: *Joseph Kellogg operated a shipyard at Milwaukie, a rival of Portland for preeminence on the Willamette. Milwaukie, on the river's east bank, began trading with California as gold fever began rising. Today, Milwaukie is a suburb of Portland. (OHS)*

Below: *Milwaukie had big hopes of developing into Oregon's leading city. The community was served by a pioneering newspaper, the* Western Star, *and the steamboat* Lot Whitcomb, *named for one of the town developers. (OHS)*

Cathlamet, Astoria, and back. The steamer had a 140-horsepower engine and made an impressive fourteen miles per hour. It was also painfully expensive to operate. By June, Whitcomb was forced to sell his namesake to a syndicate of Oregon City investors.

Milwaukie was a good place to load lumber but, like St. Johns, was isolated and inconvenient for Washington County wheat growers. Ships reached Milwaukie without trouble during the spring floods. During the winter of 1850-1851, however, one after another scraped bottom or bent a propeller on the Ross Island sandbar that lay between Portland and Milwaukie.

Captain John H. Couch, the New England seaman and merchant who had made Portland his base of operations in 1849, announced to the public that the river at Ross Island ordinarily had "only about four feet of water." He had himself ridden across on horseback at Ross Island and did not think that Milwaukie would ever overcome the handicap created by the shallows. Most embarrassing of all for Milwaukie, the editor of the *Western Star* (who had gained ownership when Whitcomb ran out of cash) moved his business to Portland, where he printed the first copies of the *Oregon Weekly Times* on June 5. "In removing from Milwaukie to Port-

land," he announced, "we have been guided by those considerations which govern all business men."

Portland's promoters matched their rivals sawmill for sawmill, editor for editor, and boat for boat. Coffin and Chapman had rounded up more than editor T.J. Dryer in San Francisco. They had also found the steamer *Gold Hunter,* which arrived in Portland from California on the first day of December 1850 after they convinced the captain to sail to Portland with the idea of selling an interest in the ship. The San Francisco owners wanted $60,000 in order to transfer control. Several citizens of Portland decided to invest in the steamer, with Coffin taking the largest share. The *Gold Hunter* was a side-wheeler like the *Lot Whitcomb*. It was only twelve feet longer but much broader, displacing 510 tons to the 300 displaced by the pride of Milwaukie. Most important, the *Gold Hunter* ran not just to Astoria but to San Francisco, giving Portland a sort of presumptive equality with the metropolis of the West. The *Gold Hunter* made only four round trips before past debts and old creditors surfaced in California and squeezed out the Portland owners.

Though the *Gold Hunter* was a financial failure it was a speculative success because its service from San Francisco prompted California merchants to say "Portland" when they meant "Oregon." This helped fend off Portland's last and potentially most serious rival, St. Helens. Historian Eugene Snyder has summarized the situation by stating that Portland fought two battles with St. Helens and its satellite of Milton City: "one battle was fought over the wagons; the other battle was for the ships." St. Helenites built a road over the Cornelius Pass in 1850, but Portland countered successfully with the Great Plank Road. In February 1852, the Pacific Mail Steamship Company announced that its California-Oregon service would terminate at St. Helens. Portland had not been chosen as terminus since the company was concerned about the sandbar at Swan Island, which threatened to hamper navigation at Portland just as the Ross Island bar had done at Milwaukie. Two years later, however, Portland's population of a thousand, and its plank road, proved too much for tiny St. Helens. And, with Portland still served by sailing ships and occasional steamers, the Pacific Mail found it hard to make full cargoes in St. Helens. At the start

of 1854, Pacific Mail advertised to San Franciscans that its Oregon service would terminate at Portland.

With transportation by land and water and a newspaper editor to tell the world about its increasing success as a trade center, it was time to turn the settlement of Portland into a city. The territorial legislature issued Portland's municipal charter early in 1851, incorporating 2.1 square miles of fir forest, stumps, and houses as the city of Portland. In the city's first election, held the same year, Portland's male citizens chose Hugh O'Bryant as mayor and five other residents as city councilmen to serve the fledgling metropolis. Their main function seems to have been to keep the city in business. During their first months in office they established systems for assessing property, collecting taxes, recording city finances, selling business licenses, recording their own deliberations, and conducting elections. The first bill paid from the city treasury came to $29.65 (three brass candlesticks at one dollar each and a box of whale oil candles). In 1854, the territorial legislature created a separate Multnomah County with Portland as county seat.

By the time such recognizable names as Josiah Failing and William S. Ladd begin to appear on the list of mayors (elected in 1853 and 1854, respectively), the city had started to keep the peace and to lift the residents out of the mud. There were ordinances for abating nuisances, licenses for vehicles, and a town jail. Ordinance No. 20 required that "all male persons over the age of 21 years" devote two days a year to work on street improvements, or pay an equivalent tax. A start was made at planking the most heavily used streets, which one visitor had described as mud and water mixed to "a very good batter." Wooden sidewalks prevented pedestrians from miring down alongside

Facing page, right: *Douglas firs, shown here in an illustration about 1855, were thick at the mouth of the Willamette River and in other places, reported surveyors for a Pacific railroad. Woods had to be cut away to make room for early Portland. Courtesy,* Report of Explorations and Surveys for Pacific Railroad, 1854-55, VI

Facing page, far right: *Josiah Failing opened a Portland store with his son Henry in 1851. The elder Failing, elected mayor in 1853, was also a promoter of schools and active in the Baptist Church.* (OHS)

look. Another woman commented tersely that Portland was "rather gamey."

Over the next decade, Portland's population nearly quadrupled, increasing from 805 to 2,874. Oregon grew even faster as immigrants filled the Willamette Valley and explored the mountains with an eye toward a mineral bonanza like that of California. The city's mix of population set it apart from the rest of the territory. The typical Oregonian in

the horses and wagons and let the ladies keep their skirts out of the deepest mud.

The town that Mayor O'Bryant and his successors tried to govern was more like a giant fraternity house than a real community. Three quarters of the 805 residents recorded in the 1850 census were male. Nine-tenths of all Portlanders in their twenties were men, attracted by jobs in road and building construction. When young Elizabeth Miller and four other schoolteachers from New England passed through town in 1851 on the way to new posts in Oregon City, Miller reported that "the one-sided community was exceedingly interested." She speculated that the entire population must have crowded the wharf for a

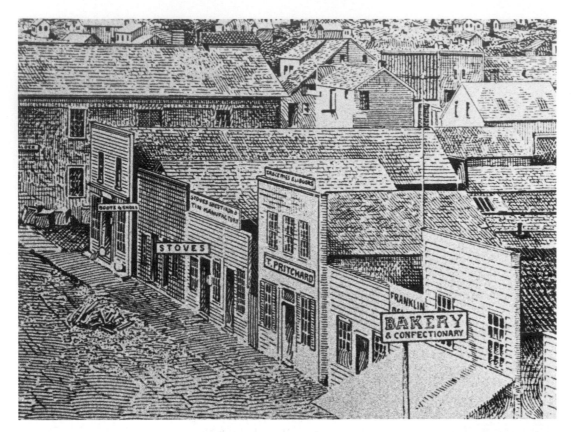

Left: *Plentiful trees near Portland provided timber for the first businesses and homes. Substantial stone and brick structures were to come later than 1854, the date of this drawing. Courtesy,* The Oregonian Souvenir

Below: *This sketch by Charles B. Talbot shows the log-cabin style of the first post office, established at S.W. Front Avenue and S.W. Washington Street in 1849. Thomas Smith was the first postmaster. (OHS)*

the early 1850s had come from states like Missouri, Illinois, Kentucky, and Indiana in the heart of the Mississippi Valley. In Portland, a much larger proportion hailed from New England and from New York, the number one state of origin. Together, Yankees and New Yorkers constituted more than a quarter of Portland's total population in its early decades. The states of the Northeast also supplied a disproportionate share of the city's business leaders, many of whom began their careers in the early 1850s as agents or correspondents for New York and Boston mercantile companies.

Portland served as the depot and general store for the growing Oregon population. Visitors usually began their descriptions of the city by tallying the number of businesses—eighteen "stores" in November 1850, thirty-five "wholesale and retail stores" in 1852, and a hundred shops by 1858. The census of 1860 counted 146 merchants,

ranging from local retailers to prosperous agents for large Eastern wholesalers such as Henry W. Corbett or the Failing family.

Portlanders strung their town along the river. In the first few years of development, any building more than 200 yards inland was likely to be hidden in the trees. Daniel Lownsdale had expanded the original survey with more than a hundred additional blocks in 1848, reserving two blocks as public squares between Third and Fourth streets and setting aside a narrow strip of eleven park blocks along the western edge of the city. In the long term citizens have been grateful for his foresight, but the earliest Portlanders continued to build on Front, First, and Second. If we can trust a view of the city drawn in 1858, woodcutters and sawmill owners had cleared the forest about half a mile back from the waterfront, leaving the straggling town exposed on bare ground between river and hills.

Business centered on the docks, warehouses, and waterfront stores. Four floors was the maximum and two floors the norm for the commercial buildings. The usual materials were locally sawed wood and white paint. Successful merchants followed the lead of Vermonter William S. Ladd, who had arrived in Portland in 1851 and who put up the city's first brick building to house his

Above: *Portland presented this view in 1858 as seen from the east bank of the Willamette. The gold rush to the Fraser River in Canada boosted business that year but the biggest gold excitement east of the Cascades took place in the 1860s. (OHS)*

Left: *Henry W. Corbett opened a general merchandise store in Portland in 1851. Later he entered the wholesale hardware business, became a financier, served as president of Willamette Iron and Steel Works and president of Portland Hotel Company, boosted street railway construction, and served in the U.S. Senate. Courtesy, H.W. Scott's* History of Portland, Oregon

mercantile business in 1853. Residents lived in old log cabins or new frame houses. The modern survivors of the first building boom are the Hallock and McMillan Building, erected in 1857 at the corner of Front and Oak, and the 1859 Delschneider Building half a block west on Oak, now handsomely restored.

In a city with few families, tax-supported schools were a hard sell to unmarried male voters. Transplanted New Englanders succeeded in organizing a public school district in 1851 and offered classes for two years, although *Oregonian* editor Dryer fulminated against spending a thousand dollars "for pedagogueing some dozen or two of children." The first schoolmaster not only taught school, but also unloaded ships, worked on the streets, and fought the shaking ague between terms. In 1854 the major educational institution in the city was the Methodists' Portland Academy and Female Seminary, but a reorganized district opened again in 1855 in rented space. Future mayor and Oregon governor Sylvester Pennoyer

taught in the new public school for six months until he established a law practice in Portland. There was another gap in public education in 1856 and 1857, but the first public school building, Central School, opened in 1858 at Sixth and Morrison, the present site of Pioneer Courthouse Square. By 1860, 272 students crowded into the three rooms of Central School, while an equal number attended several private schools.

Like every ambitious town on the Western frontier, Portland looked on every new building as a step from the log cabin to the metropolis. Portlanders were proud of public structures like the Central School and the city jail. Culture came to Portland in 1858 when the Willamette Theater opened on Stark Street. Traveling troupes of second-rate actors from San Francisco could now play to audiences of up to 600 rather than making do with second-story lecture halls or the Multnomah County Courthouse. Drinking, fighting, and horse racing were also high on the list of amusements.

Beards for men and lace collars for women were the vogue in the 1850s. One of the earliest pictures of the town's residents shows the first organized choir of the First Congregational Church in 1857. (OHS)

Stumps and a segment of remaining forest provided a primitive setting for Taylor Street Methodist Church. The boardwalk was an asset on wet, muddy days. The church, built between S.W. Second and Third avenues in 1849, was the predecessor of the First Methodist Church. (OHS)

More proper citizens in the 1850s could join the Sons of Temperance and pledge total abstinence from alcohol. They could attend Sunday services in a new Taylor Street Methodist Church after 1850, a new Congregational church in 1851, and a Roman Catholic church in 1852. Presbyterians and Episcopalians built their churches in mid-decade and Baptists at the beginning of the 1860s. The city's hundred or so Jews organized Congregation Beth Israel in 1858 and finished a synagogue in 1861.

By the end of the 1850s something about Portland set it apart from the rowdiest of the West's instant cities. There was money to be made here, but with none of the bonanzas of Nevada's Virginia City or Colorado's Leadville or the overnight fortunes of San Francisco. The New Englanders and New Yorkers who dominated the city's economy cannot be called complacent or sober, but they did treat their business lives as se-

rious business. They also propped open the door of opportunity for anyone who could help the city grow, whether U.S. born or immigrant from Europe. For example, Jewish immigrants like Bernard Goldsmith and Philip Wasserman started prosperous businesses in the 1850s and each later served two terms as mayor.

Few of Portland's city-builders wanted the life of Daniel Boone or Jim Bridger. They were true conservatives who wanted to reconstruct the society they had left behind while reserving a place for themselves at the head table. By the end of the 1850s, when the town was poised for a new surge of growth, Portlanders had organized a typically American community of churches and schools, government, politics, and fraternal organizations. To most visitors, Portland was a little island of New England on the western margin of the continent—handsome, energetic, steady, and homelike.

George H. Himes arrived in Portland in 1864 and became well-known as a printer. He kept a voluminous diary, started in 1866 as the longtime secretary of the Oregon Pioneer Association, and served as the curator and field secretary of the Oregon Historical Society beginning in 1898. (OHS)

CHAPTER II
ON THE EDGE
OF THE WEST

Portlanders have always lived on the edge of the West. The "real West" of Zane Gray and Louis L'Amour begins seventy-five or one hundred miles inland at The Dalles or Redmond and stretches across another 1,000 miles of sagebrush, and dry gulches, and Rocky Mountains to the high plains. The Oregon pioneers of 1844 and 1845 hurried through this area in their covered wagons heading for the green vision of the Willamette Valley. The Western interior is also the territory to which Portlanders turned back in the 1860s and 1870s to make their fortunes secure. Portland's success story is a chronicle of valley dwellers who learned to tap the wealth of the dry country without leaving the drizzle of their metropolis.

After the boom created by the Gold Rush to California, new discoveries of gold in the interior of the Northwest gave Portland its second and most essential spurt of growth. The boom of 1848-1849 and the benefits of victory over river-town rivals in 1850-1851 had faded by the middle 1850s. A national depression compounded problems at the end of the decade. Portland in 1860 was still economically dependent on San Francisco, prospering when Californians wanted Oregon wheat and suffering when the demand declined.

Mining booms in Idaho, Montana, and the interior of the Columbia River Basin provided Portland a strong impetus for growth. A gold strike along Idaho's Clearwater River in August 1860 was as fortuitous for Portlanders as it was for the prospectors. During the next four years, miners fanned out from Idaho's Orofino and Pierce City diggings to the Salmon River and Boise Basin, the Owyhee River on the present Oregon-Idaho border, Bannack City and Gold City in western Montana, and the Kootenay River just over the border in Canada. The old trading center of Walla Walla, Washington and the new town of Lewiston, Idaho were the final outfitters for the mines, but Portland was the supply base and jumping off point during these frenetic boom years. More than 15,000 people passed upriver through Portland in 1861, 24,000 in 1862, and 22,000 in 1863. The *Oregonian* reported gleefully that "rents are up to an exorbitant figure, many houses contain two or more families, and the hotels and boarding houses are crowded almost to overflowing. The town is full of people ... buildings are going up ... wharves stretching their proportions along the levees, and a general thrift and busy hum greet the ear."

Portland monopolized the growing business of the Inland Empire of the Pacific Northwest because of geography *and* because of the Oregon Steam Navigation Company (OSNC)—Oregon's first "millionaire-making machine" in the words of one early employee. The company's leading figure was John C. Ainsworth, a former Mississippi River

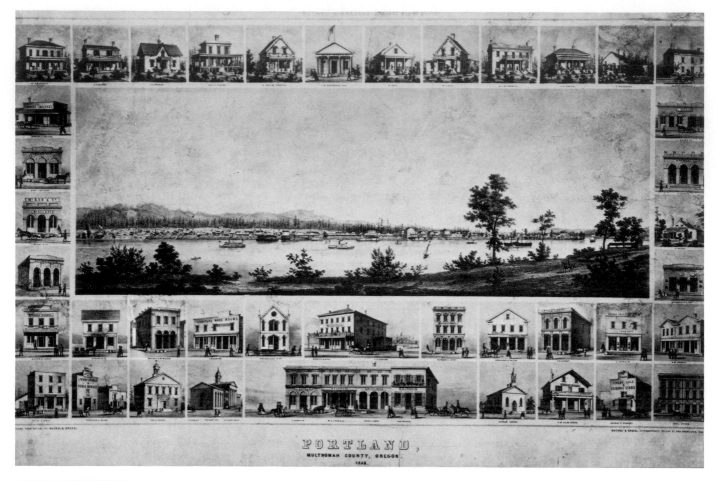

Above: *This 1858 lithograph by Kuchel & Dresel shows a wooded Portland sporting a few stone structures amid the wood-frame buildings. Courtesy, Stokes Collection, New York Public Library*

Left: *The Willamette Theater was bedecked in the national colors during somber rites for Brigadier General Edward R.S. Canby, commander of the Department of the Columbia. He was killed by Modoc Indians in 1873. An honor guard stood at attention in front of the building. (OHS)*

steamboat captain who had been the first master of the Milwaukie steamship, the *Lot Whitcomb.* He knew that navigation on the Columbia was interrupted by rapids at "the Cascades" and again by Celilo Falls at The Dalles. If Portland were to profit from the river, there would have to be something better than crude portages around both barriers. In 1860 Ainsworth formed the OSNC to unite the various businessmen who operated segments of the Columbia River route. The new corporation controlled improvements at both bottlenecks, operating a six-mile railroad on the north bank of the Columbia that carried traffic around the rapids at what is now the town of Cascade Locks and a fourteen-mile road that bypassed Celilo Falls at The Dalles. OSNC investors Simeon Reed, Robert R. Thompson, William S. Ladd and others who put up large chunks of capital learned the value of conservative management as they put profits back into the business, expanding and improving service. OSNC operated Columbia River steamers, wagon trains, stage lines, and connecting boats on the Snake River, Lake Pend Oreille, and the headwaters of the Missouri, establishing, within a few years, a powerful transportation monopoly.

Few residents of eastern Oregon,

Below, left: Steamboats from Portland could not pass the Cascades of the Columbia River, but a railroad provided a link to other craft just above the rapids. The river business bolstered Portland's prosperity. This ad is from the 1877 Portland Directory. (OHS)

Below: J.C. Ainsworth was a key figure in steam navigation development on the Columbia River. Courtesy, Portland, Oregon, Its History and Builders

OREGON
eam Navigation Co.

e Oregon Steam Navigation Company's Steamers

\EONTA" and "EMMA HAYWARD,"
(CAPT. JOHN WOLF),
ve PORTLAND Daily (Sundays excepted), at 5 A. M., connecting with the
CASCADE RAILROAD,
—AND—
teamers 'DAISY AINSWORTH' and 'IDAHO,'
Capt. JOHN McNULTY,
Arriving at the DALLES at 4 P. M. same evening.
'YAKIMA', 'TENINO', and 'ALMOTA',
ve CELILO on TUESDAY and SATURDAY (on arrival of the Morning
a from THE DALLES) for UMATILLA and WALLULA, proceed-
g as far as LEWISTON during high water in the Snake River.
FOR KALAMA AND ASTORIA,
Strs. 'DIXIE THOMPSON' **AND** 'BONITA',
Captains J. W. BABAGE and GEORGE A. PEASE,
ve PORTLAND at 6 A. M. daily, arriving at ASTORIA the same
day at 6 P. M.

eastern Washington, or Idaho had a kind word for the OSNC monopoly. They paid high tariffs on every cargo they imported or shipped out via OSNC. (Customers who paid in gold received a 30- to 50-percent discount over those who used paper money.) Rumor had it that the company paid for a new steamer with the profits from a single trip upriver from Portland to the gold mining country. Through the OSNC, pioneers and prospectors indirectly paid for the growth of Portland by generating the Ladd and Ainsworth and Reed fortunes. These investors would provide much of the capital for the city's railroads, factories, utilities, and real estate development.

The OSNC made Portland the true gateway to the Northwest, but the city would remain a second-class citizen in the commercial world as long as the latest news and mail arrived twice a month by steamer from the Golden Gate. In 1860 the California Stage Company cut the time in half when it signed a contract to carry the mail overland from Sacramento to Portland. Service began in September. The running time was seven days during an optimistically defined dry season from April through December. In mid-winter running time was twelve days as drivers contended with hub-deep mud, landslides, and sudden snows in the Siskiyous. By 1866, when Portland's Henry Corbett took over the route, the time in good weather was down to five and one-half days. In the years before railroads began to creep south, the stage line was essential in making Jackson and Douglas counties seem an integral part of Oregon.

In 1864, the telegraph replaced the creaking and bouncing stagecoach as the source of essential information. The California State Telegraph Company built a telegraph line north from Sacramento and Maryville to Yreka in

As one of the leading officials of Oregon Steam Navigation Company, Simeon G. Reed gained a fortune when the organization was sold to the Villard syndicate. He and his wife bequeathed money to fund a college, which was named in their honor. Courtesy, Portland, Oregon, Its History and Builders

Northern California in 1858. W.S. Ladd, S.G. Reed, H.W. Corbett, and A.L. Lovejoy incorporated the Oregon Telegraph Company in 1862 to make the connection to the California company. The Portland company's first load of wire sank in a shipwreck while being transported from San Francisco, but the company was able to string its line southward through Aurora, Salem, Corvallis, Roseburg, and on to California in 1863. The first dispatch from San Francisco arrived in Portland on March 8, 1864, with news that had been dispatched from New York just twenty hours before. The mayors of Portland, Oregon, and Portland, Maine exchanged congratulatory messages. Other lines connected Portland to Seattle, Walla Walla, and Boise before the decade was out. The rate for ten words to the east coast was $7.50—enough to feed a Portland family for a week or educate a public school pupil for a year.

Rails followed the roads and wires. Railroad building south from Portland confirmed the city's dominance in Oregon. It also shook the conservative Port-

land establishment by introducing them to Ben Holladay. An unscrupulous but highly successful businessman, Holladay had built the Overland Mail into the country's largest stageline in the 1860s. He had sold his company to Wells Fargo for $1.5 million in 1868 and turned his attention to railroad building in the Pacific Northwest. Proper Portlanders were fascinated by his success and repelled by his style of life. They whispered that he had populated his house with high-priced prostitutes and competed to find the right adjectives to describe him: vulgar, low, haughty, dictatorial, dishonest, and immoral were some of the favorites.

Holladay used the money from the sale of the Overland company to plunge into a struggle between rival railroad companies that wanted to build from Portland to California on opposite sides of the Willamette. The west side line was the Oregon Central Railway Company, backed by the Portland establishment of Reed, Corbett, and Ladd, who wanted to make sure that Willamette Valley trade poured directly into the city and added to the business of the

Above: *Smith's stage operating between Portland and Vancouver was typical of nineteenth-century transportation. Stagecoaches were displaced rapidly in Oregon when railroads were constructed. The rail lines also hurt steamboat business, but steamboats endured into the early 1900s. Courtesy,* The Columbian

Left: *Ben Holladay had already built a transportation empire in the West when he entered the railroad business in the Portland area in 1868. His methods aroused the ire of competitors and others. One typical critic described him as "rampaging, rapacious, ruthless." (OHS)*

Above: *Before building started, East Portland was a pastoral land, a semi-wilderness. Roads were poor and steamboats along the Willamette River were the easiest way to move in and out of the Portland area. (OHS)*

Left: *At Oswego, south of Portland, the Oregon Iron Company was the first plant on the Pacific Coast to manufacture pig iron in a blast furnace. Production started about 1867 and continued sporadically for a few years. The community is now Lake Oswego, a Portland suburb. (OHS)*

Oregon Steam Navigation Company. Holladay took them on by buying control of the east side line, which he named the Oregon and California Railroad Company in 1869. At stake were not only freight and passengers, but also a federal land grant of twenty square miles for every mile of track. It would go to the first railroad that finished twenty miles of operational track. His enemies later reported that Holladay spent $35,000 to bribe the state legislature to rescind a premature declaration in favor of the Oregon Central. However, he also had the drive and money to finish the necessary track and win the grant. By 1870, his Oregon and California Railroad bought out the defeated west side line.

As the Oregon and California Railroad (eventually absorbed into the Southern Pacific system) pushed slowly southward, Holladay put together a tottering transportation empire in Portland. He owned docks, warehouses, and steamships. He monopolized the local transfer of passengers and freight. Expecting that an east bank railroad would shift the city's economic center across the river and that a growing city would require the level lands of the east side, he built two hotels, grabbed a large chunk of the Northwest Portland waterfront, and laid out Holladay's Addition to East Portland in the present Lloyd Center area.

Portlanders tolerated Holladay's presence until 1874, when he came up nearly $500,000 short in interest payments on money borrowed from German investors for construction costs. Eastern

Left: *Construction began in 1869 on a post office and district court building, which opened in 1875. The building, once considered too far out of downtown, was surrounded in later years by businesses. Today it fronts on Pioneer Courthouse Square. Courtesy, Harper's Weekly*

Below: *This much traffic might not have been seen on the Willamette River on a typical day in 1882, but this illustration was good for promotional purposes for Portland. West Shore magazine artists recorded the city frequently before the advent of photography. (OHS)*

banker Henry Villard, a German-born newspaper man who was gaining a reputation as a shrewd businessman, investigated the viability of their investments for the German bondholders. In 1876, Villard bought Holladay out and laid the foundation of his own railroad kingdom. The Oregon and California Railroad was completed through Medford to California in 1883.

The growth of Willamette Valley farming was less spectacular than the Idaho gold rushes and less exciting than Ben Holladay's full throttle railroad career, but it provided a solid foundation for Portland's progress. Between 1860 and 1880, Oregon's improved farmland acreage increased by 150 percent; the production of wheat rose by 800 percent. Portland merchants began to ship grain directly to Liverpool, England at the end of the 1860s. Portland's foreign exports, mainly farm products, totaled $500,000 in 1870-1871 and reached $4 million by the end of the 1870s. The frontier was changing rapidly. One of the shrewdest observers of the mid-century American West was Massachusetts newspaper editor Samuel Bowles.

Bowles' 1865 account of his journey west, *Across the Continent*, is a classic description of the last frontier between the Rockies and the Pacific; his account of Portland summed up the city's expanding economic base:

Portland, by far the largest town of Oregon, stands sweetly on the banks of the Willamette ... Ships and ocean steamers of highest class come readily hither; from it spreads out a wide navigation by steamboat of the Columbia and its branches, below and above; here centers a large and increasing trade, not only for the Willamette Valley, but for the mining regions of eastern Oregon and Idaho, Washington Territory on the north, and parts even of British Columbia.

Portland's population was growing as fast as its trade. The 2,800 Portlanders of 1860 more than doubled by 1864; the census included 700 "floaters" in hotels and boardinghouses. In the Pettygrove and Coffin eras, everyone who counted in Portland knew everyone else. By 1863, however, the city was big enough to need the first annual city directory, published by former mayor S.J. McCormick. The population continued to grow to 8,300 in 1870 and 17,600 by 1880.

Railroads and steamers made Portland a center for ideas as well as commerce. At the end of the 1870s readers in the city and the greater Northwest supported a score of periodicals ranging from daily newspapers to scientific journals. Portland citizens dissatisfied with the weighty *Oregonian* could read the daily *Bee, Standard,* or *Telegram.* The weekly *Sunday Mercury, Sunday Welcome,* and *Sunday Call* (out of East Portland) supplemented the dailies. The *Pacific Christian Advocate* carried news to northwestern Methodists, the month-

Spires and church bells were features of the early city. This is Trinity Episcopal Church, constructed in 1872 at the corner of S.W. Sixth Avenue and S.W. Oak Street. Benjamin Stark donated a bell made from melted Spanish cannons. (OHS)

Left: *Oregonian Joaquin Miller published two books of poetry in Portland in 1868 and 1869 but earned no recognition. He finally found fame in London in 1871. The "Poet of the Sierras" is shown here at a chautauqua near Portland in 1906. (OHS)*

Below: *The Esmond Hotel, operated by J.H. Brenner at S.W. Front Avenue at S.W. Morrison Street, promoted itself in the early 1880s as Portland's leading hotel. The hotel claimed to be fireproof, and advertised bathrooms, "speaking telephones," and free coaches to meet passengers at steamboats and trains. (OHS)*

ly *Columbia Churchman* to Episcopalians, and the weekly *Catholic Sentinel* to Roman Catholics. There was a weekly *Willamette Farmer,* a monthly *Medical Journal,* and a semi-monthly *Journal of Education.*

The magazine *West Shore* (1875-1891) was the epitome of nineteenth-century geographic boosterism. Editor L. Samuel served up lavishly illustrated articles on the progress and possibilities of Portland and the Pacific Northwest. Stories of economic growth and pictures of new buildings and bridges had a wide appeal up and down the coast. The publication's subscription list grew from 9,000 in 1880 to 37,500 in 1890 before overextension put it out of business.

The founder and editor of the weekly

newspaper *New Northwest* (1871-1887) was Abigail Scott Duniway, who advocated women's rights, woman suffrage, "Eternal Liberty," and "Untrammeled Progression." The masthead spelled out Duniway's philosophy: "A Journal for the People, Devoted to the Interests of Humanity, Independent in Politics and Religion, Alive to all Live Issues and Thoroughly Radical in Opposing and Exposing the Wrongs of the Masses." Each weekly issue offered news on business and cultural events, descriptions of prisons and asylums, reports on Duniway's constant travels on the Western lecture circuit, and vitriolic editorials against the mossbacked opponents of female emancipation and social progress. There were also stories by famous writers like Mark Twain and Bret Harte and the serialized fiction that served as frontier soap operas. Duniway herself wrote seventeen serialized novels

during the paper's sixteen-year life. Behind the melodrama in such stories as *Madge Morrison: The Mollala Maid and Matron, Ethel Graeme's Destiny,* and the other stories were lessons about the problems of unloving and unequal marriages. Abigail Duniway certainly had one of the most energetic minds in late nineteenth-century Portland and quite possibly the brightest.

The Portland press served immigrants along with English-speaking residents. The *Deutsche Zeitung* after 1867 and the *Staats Zeitung* after 1877 kept alive the German language and supported Portland's German community on the Western frontier. New arrivals could put up at the *Deutsches Gast Haus* (also known as the New York Hotel), call on the German Aid Society, and drink lager brewed by a man appropriately named George Bottler. By 1880, several thousand German-Americans

Ship masts in the background denote the proximity of Willamette River business in the early 1880s. McCracken & Company, at left, was an importing and wholesale grocery business. At right is the office of Oregon Railway and Navigation Company, a major transportation firm of the era. (OHS)

supported four German-language churches and occasional stage performances in German.

The growth of Portland's black population from 16 to 147 during the 1860s was a more severe test for local tolerance than the immigration of easily assimilated Germans. In 1867, the school district and the courts refused to enter the four children of Maryland-born shoemaker William Brown in the all-white public schools. The *Oregonian* applauded the alternative—the appropriation of $800 for a segregated school that would enroll up to twenty-five black students between 1867 and 1872. But with the onset of a major national depression brought about by the Panic of 1873, the principle of segregation hardly seemed worth the cost and black students quietly enrolled in the regular schools. Black Portland staged an annual celebration of the anniversary of Emancipation in the 1870s but otherwise received little notice. They comprised only a small minority in the growing city. Judge Matthew Deady was satisfied to report in 1868 that they were "moderately thrifty and well conducted."

In fact, Deady was pleased with almost everything about his city. Writing a profile of "Portland-on-Wallamet" for the first issue of San Francisco's *Overland Monthly,* he described it as a "solid and reliable town." It would never be the center of fashion, he explained, but the blue river and the sublime Monarch of the Mountains, (Mt. Hood), glistening above the dark green forests forty miles to the east, were more than adequate compensation. Portland's good citizens, Deady told his readers, would "sleep sounder and live longer than in San Francisco." Oregon historian Francis Fuller Victor, who had lived in both California and Portland, shared Deady's assessment. She thought the Portland of 1871 "a cheerful-look-

Left: *Equal rights for women was the goal of Abigail Scott Duniway, who published* The New Northwest. *When the women's suffrage law was finally passed in 1912, Mrs. Duniway wrote the proclamation and was the first woman to register as a legal voter in Multnomah County.* (OHS)

Below: *German and Austrian culture was reflected in ads for a "chop house" and newspaper, appearing in McKenney's* Pacific Coast Directory, 1880-81. (OHS)

ing town . . . with handsome public buildings and comfortable, home-like dwellings." The well-to-do could pass their time with pleasure drives on the macadamized road that ran up the west side of the Willamette to the Riverside Race Course. And, wrote Victor, on sunny afternoons the "youth, beauty, and fashion of Portland" strolled the public squares opposite the courthouse to the bright music of brass bands.

One of the major functions of city government in those early years was to keep Portland pleasant for its business and professional families. One ordinance prohibited fast riding and driving "at a furious pace" anywhere east of Fourth Street and another banned horses and wagons from the sidewalks. An early version of the Oregon "bottle bill" made it unlawful "to throw, deposit, or leave any glass bottles or other glass vessels"

Brick buildings and ornate storefronts were replacing older wooden structures by the time of this parade in 1873. This view looks east on S.W. Morrison Street from S.W. Second Avenue, toward the Willamette River. A sign at the right advertises J. Kohn's "Clothing Palace." (OHS)

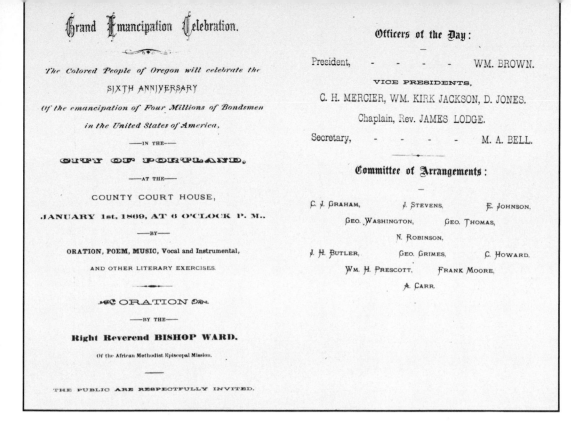

Grand Emancipation Celebration.

The Colored People of Oregon will celebrate the

SIXTH ANNIVERSARY

*Of the emancipation of Four Millions of Bondsmen
in the United States of America,*

——IN THE——

CITY OF PORTLAND,

——AT THE——

COUNTY COURT HOUSE,

JANUARY 1st, 1869, AT 6 O'CLOCK P. M.,

——BY——

ORATION, POEM, MUSIC, Vocal and Instrumental,

AND OTHER LITERARY EXERCISES.

ORATION

——BY THE——

Right Reverend BISHOP WARD.

Of the African Methodist Episcopal Mission.

THE PUBLIC ARE RESPECTFULLY INVITED.

Officers of the Day:

President, - - - - WM. BROWN.

VICE PRESIDENTS,

C. H. MERCIER, WM. KIRK JACKSON, D. JONES.

Chaplain, Rev. JAMES LODGE.

Secretary, - - - - M. A. BELL.

Committee of Arrangements:

C. J. GRAHAM, J. STEVENS, E. JOHNSON.
GEO. WASHINGTON, GEO. THOMAS,
N. ROBINSON,
J. H. BUTLER, GEO. GRIMES, C. HOWARD.
WM. H. PRESCOTT, FRANK MOORE,
A. CARR.

Left: Some former slaves migrated to Oregon following the Civil War. They gathered in 1869 to commemorate the Emancipation Proclamation, issued January 1, 1863, abolishing slavery in the Confederate States. The black population remained relatively small in Portland for many years. (OHS)

Left, below: New Market, built for Captain Alexander Ankeny, opened in 1872, with stalls for public markets on the first floor. A theater opened upstairs in 1875. In recent years, before restoration, the building was used as a parking garage. Now, after restoration, it houses restaurants and specialty shops. (OHS)

Below: Some lawyers' businesses must have been flourishing in the 1880s, judging from the fine residences occupied by J.W. Whalley (left) and M.W. Fechheimer, his partner (right). Home construction had not started on the hills in the background. (OHS)

in the streets; residents were to pick up litter to the mid-line of the street in front of their premises. The city encouraged the growing of shade trees and spent a substantial $32,000 to buy a forty-acre nucleus for Washington Park in 1871.

But Portlanders who ventured off their front porches in the "suburbs" west of Sixth Street could find a less sedate city if they knew where to look. Many theaters catered to the popular taste with "low grade minstrels and vulgar comedy." British visitor Wallis Nash in 1877 complained in a travel book he wrote that *Othello* fell flat

Far left: *Judge Matthew Deady, best known now for his two volumes of diaries,* Pharisee Among Philistines, *(edited by Malcolm Clark, Jr.) came to Portland in 1860 as an attorney, and served on the territorial supreme court. He was appointed a U.S. judge and served in that position until his death in 1893. Courtesy, H.W. Scott's* History of Portland, Oregon

Left: *Frances Fuller Victor lived in Salem and Portland and, beginning in the 1870s, wrote a series of books. Some of her work was included in Hubert Howe Bancroft's histories. Her biography of Joseph Meek was titled* The River of the West. *(OHS)*

compared with a "half hour of screaming farce" that followed. Thousands of patrons crowded into more than 200 saloons to drink, gamble, and try out Phelans Patent Billiard Tables. The Oro Fino saloon and theater at Front and Stark Street advertised "the choicest qualities of wines and liquors, ales, port, and fine cigars." The saloon belonged to James Lappeus, Portland's city marshal from 1859 to 1861 and chief of police from 1870 to 1877 and again from 1879 to 1883.

Law enforcement efforts expanded with the city. A part-time marshal was adequate to keep the peace at the beginning of the 1860s, but by mid-decade two paid deputies were hired, and a formal police force was established in 1870. Six officers covered three beats north of Oak, between Oak and Yamhill, and south of Yamhill. The officers' biggest responsibility in these early years was to run in drunks who threatened to tear up the town. With the police chief counted in their number, saloon owners and gamblers had less

trouble than they might otherwise have had. Portland's police were not noticeably energetic about enforcing the liquor and gambling laws. Saloon keeper Edward Chambreau later recalled of this era: "The first thing I did when I took charge of this 'Hell Hole' [Chambreau's saloon] was to *fix* the policeman on my beat." Economic growth, however, brought more opportunities for creative crime, as the Police Commission noted in 1874:

The number of arrests for 1873 are about double the number of any year prior to 1871 . . . . The perpetrators of housebreaking and highway robbery find this too hazardous to pursue, and have changed their occupations and found encouragement in a higher role . . . . A number of these dangerous characters are to be seen daily about our docks and custom house, placed side by side with many honest laborers, ready always to extend the hand of friendship to the

crews of newly arrived vessels, and to tender their services to show them "the sights about town"— through the "dives" where these characters and female "pals" do dwell. The sailor is easily imposed upon generally, and becomes an easy victim. His gold is soon gone ... and he is unable to tell by whom or how, for when it is done he is usually intoxicated, and thus the thieves escape detection and arrest. The great increase of our commerce has opened a wide field for the operations of these persons.

Portland's decision makers thought that jackrolled sailors and shanghaied crews were a small price to pay for commercial expansion. They also knew that the next necessary step in that growth was a direct transcontinental railroad connection. Hopes for such a connection rose in 1870 when the Northern Pacific decided to build down the south bank of the Columbia and engaged in a stock swap that made the Oregon Steam Navigation Company a wholly owned subsidiary. The same hopes fell with the financial crash of 1873, which drove the Northern Pacific into bankruptcy, brought the OSNC back to its original ownership, and stopped railroad construction on the Northern Pacific and other railroads for five years.

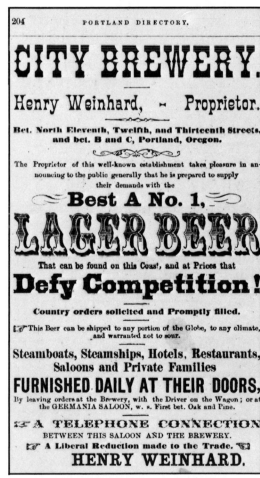

204   PORTLAND DIRECTORY.

CITY BREWERY.

Henry Weinhard, - Proprietor.

Bet. North Eleventh, Twelfth, and Thirteenth Streets, and bet. B and C, Portland, Oregon.

The Proprietor of this well-known establishment takes pleasure in announcing to the public generally that he is prepared to supply their demands with the

Best A No. 1,

LAGER BEER

That can be found on this Coast, and at Prices that

Defy Competition!

Country orders solicited and Promptly filled.

This Beer can be shipped to any portion of the Globe, to any climate, and warranted not to sour.

Steamboats, Steamships, Hotels, Restaurants, Saloons and Private Families

FURNISHED DAILY AT THEIR DOORS,

By leaving orders at the Brewery, with the Driver on the Wagon; or at the GERMANIA SALOON, w. s. First bet. Oak and Pine.

A TELEPHONE CONNECTION BETWEEN THIS SALOON AND THE BREWERY.

A Liberal Reduction made to the Trade.

HENRY WEINHARD.

Henry Villard filled the vacuum. He controlled Ben Holladay's system of Willamette Valley railroads and steamers after 1876. In 1879 Villard bought out the OSNC and formed the new Oregon Railway and Navigation Company, which included his entire network of Oregon rail and steamship compa-

nies. Portlanders who profited from the deal included OSNC founders Ainsworth, Reed, and Ladd plus later investors with names like Kamm, Lewis, Failing, and Corbett.

But Villard's greatest coup came in 1881. Raising eight million dollars from fifty capitalists, he gained control of the Northern Pacific and made himself the transportation magnate of the Northwest. While Portland businessmen lobbied the federal government to deepen the bar at the mouth of the Columbia, Villard tried to develop the city's railroad connections to the East. The main line of the Northern Pacific was finished at the end of the summer of 1883. A corporate peace treaty had already given the Union Pacific access to Portland over Northern Pacific tracks and the Northern Pacific reciprocal use of

UP tracks into Utah. When a Union Pacific branch reached the NP at Huntington, Oregon, in December 1884, Portland gained the advantages of service by two transcontinental railroads.

Henry Villard celebrated completion of the Northern Pacific by hauling four trainloads of dignitaries from the East, and bringing another train from San Francisco and Portland to the golden-spike ceremony at Deer Lodge, Montana. The eighty VIPs on the West Coast special could wander through four Pullman cars, two dining cars, and two commissary cars. A potpourri of diplomats, New York bankers, German financiers, Congressmen, and governors watched the driving of the golden spike (actually ordinary steel) late in the afternoon of September 8, 1883. Actually, the line had quietly opened to traffic in August, but trains had moved on a by-pass, leaving a 2,700-foot gap in the main line to be officially closed in front of General Ulysses S. Grant and hundreds of Crow Indians in full regalia at the Deer Lodge ceremony. It was the first step in a systematic publicity campaign that would bring investment and immigrants to the High Plains and Inland Empire through Northern Pacific agents in Liverpool, Hamburg, New York, Boston, Omaha, and Portland.

Villard, Grant, and the rest of the party pulled into east Portland several hours later than expected on the evening of September 10, 1883. The grand parade planned to celebrate the event was postponed until the following day but thousands of enthusiastic Portlanders still turned out along First Street to welcome the train. On the 11th, country people packed the ferries and crowded the roads into town. Restaurants served the throngs on double shifts at double time. The parade itself looped south on Fourth to Hall, gathered momentum back up Third to Burnside, and turned back on First to the Mechanics Pavillion where the Civic Auditorium now stands. Unlucky businessmen and their wives had to sit through the obligatory speeches, while the average Portlander got to enjoy the rest of the informal holiday in the bright sunshine. Board of Trade President Donald MacLeay expressed the reason for the excitement in one sentence: "We are now connected with the rest of the world."

Below: The Mechanics Fair Pavilion between Clay and Market on Third Avenue was built in 1879 for exhibitions and large public gatherings. U.S. Grant was honored at a reception there in 1879, and President and Mrs. Rutherford Hayes stopped at the pavilion a year or so later. The building was empty and dilapidated in this circa 1895 view. (OHS)

Facing page, far left: Henry Villard, railway promoter and financier, headed several Pacific Northwest transportation companies. In 1881 he was named Northern Pacific president, and in 1883 Portland welcomed him as a hero, after the "last spike" was driven in Montana, linking Portland with the East by fast transportation.

Facing page, left: This was one of three arches on S.W. First Avenue in 1883 commemorating completion of most of the Northern Pacific Railroad. Although the line was finished only to central Washington Territory, it linked up with other rail lines, giving Portland access to the East. (OHS)

"One seeing Portland for the first time will be surprised to find how well-built it is," reported Harper's Weekly *in 1889. This engraving from the well-read magazine showed imposing storefronts and busy traffic on S.W. Front Ave-* nue. Courtesy, Harper's Weekly

CHAPTER III
GROWING UP
AND SETTLING DOWN

At the time of its railroad revolution Portland was still a small community. With only 17,000 residents on the west side of the Willamette and a few hundred more scattered among the fir-covered ravines and knolls of the east side, Portland in 1880 was similar in size to Roseburg or Pendleton today. In an 1880 compendium titled *The Social Statistics of Cities,* which compared the development of 222 American cities, the Census Bureau reported that "the growth of Portland has been moderately steady." The tone of Portland life in that year appeared to federal officials to be that of a country town rather than a bustling city: "The population is American, with a large mixture of Europeans and Mongolians [Chinese]. Business is in the hands of men from the eastern and middle states, Great Britain, and Germany. Education is guided by Americans from New England and the northern states. The New England element has had a marked influence throughout."

Twenty years later, Portland had become a metropolis. Transcontinental railroad links facilitated immigration, boosted business, and helped to more than quintuple Portland's population to 90,000 in 1900. Portland in its first generation had been the isolated center for an "island" of settlement along the Willamette and Columbia. But during the 1880s and 1890s, the Northern Pacific and Union Pacific joined it to the rest of the nation. In the words of historian Malcolm Clark, Jr., the transcontinental connection by steel rails "cracked Oregon's insularity, though it did not shatter it."

Portland was a diversified city at the time that it made its transcontinental railroad connection. About 1,000 workers in small factories manufactured iron products and processed agricultural goods for customers in the Northwest and produced lumber, furniture, sash and doors, and other wood products for buyers up and down the West Coast. The city directories of the early 1880s listed about a hundred merchants under the categories of dry good wholesaler, liquor dealer, grain dealer, commission merchant, grocery wholesaler, and hardware dealer. The city's middle class included lawyers, bank tellers, clerks, and retailers. A larger working class supplied the muscle power for transportation and construction work.

Portland as a small town in 1880 had a "self-help" approach to public services. Residents bought water and coal gas for lighting from private companies. The Portland Street Railway Company operated a tiny street railroad with a mile and a half of track along First Street; five one-horse-powered cars hauled 600 passengers a day for ten cents each. The city paid the bills for a variety of unsatisfactory street pavements—stone blocks, chunks of wood set grain-end up, gravel, and planks, but

The docks provided lively scenes during loading and unloading of passengers and freight. Here, the boat is the Olympian, an Oregon Railway & Navigation Company sidewheeler built in the East in 1883. The boat ran to Ilwaco, Washington Territory, in 1886. (OHS)

adjacent property owners were required to sweep or scrape the pavements every Friday afternoon. Householders were responsible for hauling their garbage and street sweepings to the outskirts of the city. Protection from serious fires, such as the city had suffered in 1872 and 1873, was still in the hands of five volunteer engine companies and a hook and ladder company. A paid fire chief and two assistants provided professional supervision for 400 volunteers. The city owned a police station (with jail) and several firehouses, but the mayor, city treasurer, and city attorney had so little work to do that the city didn't even provide them with office space.

The informal approach to public services and government came to an end in the decade following the arrival of the transcontinental railroad. By the 1860s the city government had increased its responsibilities to include parks, street lighting, sewers, water, and public health. The police department had been expanded and the fire department was

converted to employ full-time professionals.

Among the most important new services were bridges across the Willamette built by both private and public enterprise to open up the east side of the river to residential development. The first was the Morrison Bridge, which was the largest span west of the Mississippi when completed by the Willamette Iron Bridge Company in April 1887. By contributing to east side development, it also marked a basic change in the shape of the city. A railroad bridge (Steel Bridge) followed in 1888; it opened to wagons and streetcars a year later. Private investors built the rickety wooden Madison Street Bridge in 1891 and sold it to the city a year later. The city erected the expensive Burnside Bridge in 1894. The first three bridges have been replaced twice and the Burnside Bridge is in its second incarnation.

Portlanders could reasonably expect to walk around a city of 17,000, but

they needed the help of mechanically powered streetcars in a city of 90,000. Between 1885 and 1895 the City Council granted dozens of franchises allowing private companies to build and operate street railways. Small steam engines on the first east-side line hauled passengers across the Morrison Bridge to the new neighborhoods of Sunnyside and Mount Tabor. Cable cars began to climb Portland Heights in 1890. The first electrified trolley ran across the Steel Bridge to Williams Avenue in 1889. By the mid-1890s, almost all the new lines and most of the old used electric power. The public transit lines covered more than a hundred miles, reaching to Willamette Heights, Portland Heights, and Fulton on the west side and to Oregon City, Lents, Montavilla, St. Johns, and the Vancouver ferry landing east of the river.

The booming city required better water than the privately owned Portland Water Company could pump out of the Willamette opposite Milwaukie. In

Left: Portland Traction Company, successor to the Cable Railway, operated an electric and cable street railway from the Union Depot to Portland Heights and the city park. Connections were made with Portland Railway Company and East Side Railway Company. Courtesy, Fred DeWolfe: Old Portland.

Left, below: In 1890 the Portland Directory predicted the cable and electrical railway systems would soon "do away entirely with the tedious and obsolete horse car." This 1890 photo shows the cable route on to Portland Heights, still relatively wooded and untouched. (OHS)

1885, the Oregon legislature authorized the city to issue bonds to buy out the water company and bring pure water from the mountains. A committee chaired by banker and investor Henry Failing selected the Bull Run River in 1886; Bull Run water reached the Mount Tabor and Washington Park reservoirs late in 1894 and flowed through Portland taps on January 1, 1895. The names on the Portland water committee—William Ladd, Henry Corbett, Cicero H. Lewis, Frank Dekum, Simon Rees, William K. Smith, Joseph Teal—

show the importance that major businessmen attached to good water. Combined with Portland's low density of population and its extensive sewer system, a reliable water supply helped to make Portland one of the healthiest places in the country in 1900. The death rate was far below that in most Eastern cities.

Bridges, streetcars, and Bull Run water were the keys to successful suburbanization east of the Willamette. In the 1870s and 1880s, East Portland and Albina were Portland's Jersey City and Hoboken, secondary industrial centers built around docks, sawmills, flour mills, and railroad yards. East Portland—stretching from the present Northeast Halsey to Southeast Holgate streets—had been platted in 1861 and incorporated in 1870. Albina was laid out in 1873 and incorporated in 1887; it was dominated by the Oregon Railroad and Navigation Company, whose riverfront shops employed hundreds of workers. One of those employees, D.M. McLaughlin, served as mayor from 1888 to 1891.

The east side boom arrived in 1887 with the opening of the Morrison Bridge. Speculators rushed to take advantage of improved transportation by laying out new middle-class subdivisions on higher land back from the rowdy east-side waterfront. Irvington dates from 1887; Sunnyside and Central Albina (Boise) from 1888; and Woodlawn, Kenilworth, Woodstock, and Tabor Heights from 1889. Portlanders continued to pin high hopes on real estate development in the early 1890s, years that saw the promotion of Ladd's Addition, Brooklyn, Richmond, Arbor Lodge, University Park, and Piedmont. Every developer issued special maps and colored brochures promising fine residential neighborhoods to the city's newcomers. The brochure titled *Piedmont, The Emerald, Portland's Ever-*

green Suburb, Devoted Exclusively to Dwellings—A Place of Homes was typical. Developer Edward Quackenbush assured potential customers that "no dwelling can be built at a cost of less than $2,000. Thus the surroundings are assured."

One result of the rapid economic and population growth brought by the railroad was the great consolidation of

The Skidmore Fountain was installed in the business district in 1888. In New York in 1887 sculptor Olin Warner posed with a plaster model of the maiden destined for the fountain. The figure was cast in bronze and shipped in 1888. (OHS)

Portland, East Portland, and Albina. After disappointing results in the 1890 census, which showed limited growth within the city limits, the Portland Chamber of Commerce began to push for the consolidation of all adjacent neighborhoods. East siders would benefit from the removal of bridge and ferry tolls, while businessmen would be able to impress outside investors with a high population total. Consolidation of Portland, Albina, and East Portland into a single city of Portland passed overwhelmingly in all three towns in a general referendum held in 1891. The area within Portland city limits jumped from seven square miles to twenty-six. Two

years later the city grew by another 50 percent in area by annexing chunks of the southwest hills, Sellwood, and subdivisions east of Twenty-Fourth Street. In 1880, when it had 3,000 residents, the east side had been a neglected fringe. Twenty years later, the 32,000 east siders were an essential part of the city.

The Census Bureau's brief summary of Portland's population mix in the 1880 census—American, with a large mixture of Europeans and Orientals—was actually a preview of the segmented city that would emerge by the turn of the century. The Willamette bridges and streetcar lines not only allowed local builders to put up thousands of new homes on previously inaccessible land, they also made it possible for the city's residents to segregate themselves by race, nationality, and income. The process created a neighborhood pattern somewhat like an elongated archery target. Downtown was the bullseye, surrounded by a ring of low-income neighborhoods of immigrants and unskilled workers. Further out was a second ring of middle- and upper-class neighborhoods for more established or successful families.

Portland was, in fact, an immigrant city by the end of the century. The 1880s ushered in a thirty-year surge of European immigration to the United States, with a new influx of immigrants from Italy, Greece, Hungary, Poland,

and Russia joining the established streams from Germany, Ireland, and Scandinavia. Portland never welcomed the volume of newcomers who landed in New York or who clambered off the trains in Chicago, but nevertheless, by 1900, 58 percent of its residents— 52,000 out of 90,000—had either been born outside the United States or were the children of immigrants.

By 1890 Portland's Chinatown was second in size only to San Francisco's. The Chinese had come to Oregon originally to construct the railroads, but as the railroad jobs dried up, more and more settled permanently in Portland. The city's Chinese population grew rapidly, from 1,700 in 1880, to 4,400 in 1890, to 7,800 in 1900. Their numbers

Mt. Hood rises above this 1890 panorama of Portland. Many new buildings reflected the city's prosperity after completion of railroad lines. Courtesy, National Archives

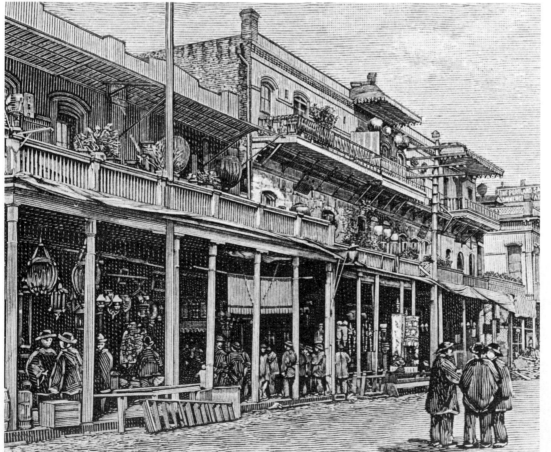

Above: *Chinatown has been a distinctive downtown area of Portland for a long time. Oriental garb was common, as shown in this 1900 scene. In earlier years, Chinatown was concentrated in the S.W. Second Avenue area. Now Chinese businesses are across W. Burnside Street, in the Northwest section. (OHS)*

Left: *Chinese formed a working class in Portland, and provided some of the best vegetables each season, a writer observed in the late 1880s. The Chinese quarter was a subject of interest for visitors, who were intrigued by the oriental customs. Courtesy, Harper's Weekly*

included refugees from less tolerant Seattle and Tacoma, which drove out their Chinese residents in 1885 and 1886. The center of Portland's Chinese neighborhood was Second and Alder. Most observers agreed that the district stretched from Ash or Pine to Salmon between the river and Third Street. Portland's standard brick and cast-iron buildings were transformed to an Oriental style with wrought-iron balconies, paper lanterns, and brightly colored signs for Chinese food stores. The Chinese operated more than a hundred businesses by the late 1880s, but most worked as laborers, dishwashers, cooks, and laundrymen. Hundreds commuted seasonally to farms, lumber camps, and

Columbia River salmon packing plants. By the end of the 1890s, about 1,200 newly arrived Japanese worked on railroad construction crews with Portland as home base; early in the new century they would begin to turn to farming in the Portland area.

Meanwhile the South Portland neighborhood of Italian and Jewish immigrants developed along the streetcar line that ran south from downtown on Third, jogged on Grant, and continued on First toward the furniture and wood processing factories of Fulton. Its small affordable houses and apartment buildings attracted the growing population of immigrants. Easy access to downtown made South Portland convenient for

newcomers with jobs as construction workers, peddlers, and salesmen. The neighborhood was still in its formative stages in 1900, but the outlines of a classic ethnic district were clear. The commercial core of kosher markets, bakeries, groceries, and drugstores was First and Front streets between Sherman and Arthur, an area virtually obliterated in the 1960s by urban renewal and I-405. The Italians had their benevolent societies and St. Michael's Church, established in 1901. Orthodox Jews worshipped in Shaarei Torah and later in Kesser Israel. Children from both groups attended Failing School. Women from Portland's long-established community of German Jews operated Neighborhood House, the "Industrial School and Kindergarten," located on First Street from 1904 to 1910 before moving to a new building at Second and Woods. Neighborhood House provided recreation, meeting rooms, sewing and manual arts training for children, and adult education for

Lodge buildings, churches, and social clubs helped provide a diversity of activity in and near the downtown. One of many gatherings was this children's party, at the Beth Israel synagogue in 1898. Some youngsters were probably children of immigrants who had recently come from Europe. (OHS)

Jewish and non-Jewish immigrants alike.

Only fragments survive in the present, but turn-of-the-century Portland also counted several other distinct immigrant neighborhoods. A small colony of Croatians clustered around northwest Nineteenth and Savier, in the Slabtown district close to jobs in sawmills, factories, and rail yards. The Roman Catholic Croatians replaced earlier Irish immigrants as parishioners for St. Patrick's church.

Many of Portland's 3,000 Scandinavian immigrants and their children lived in Albina, with the working men near the railroads below the bluff and the middle-class families on higher land around Williams and Union avenues. They supported a community center known as Scandinavian House on Northeast Seventh; mutual aid societies for Danes and Swedes; and Scandinavian, Swedish, and Danish Lutheran churches. The same area held a large

German population, while Polish immigrants had begun to settle a little to the north around Interstate and Failing, where St. Stanislaus Church would open in 1909. German-Russian immigrants—the descendants of Germans who had settled lands along the Volga in the 1700s—clustered a few blocks inland near the present Irving Park.

Underscoring the division between newly arrived immigrant and established Portlander was the social distinction between unattached men and family households. Through the 1880s and 1890s, there were in Portland three males to every two females. The Chinese, almost all of whom had come as single men, accounted for about half of the excess of 16,000 men at the end of the nineteenth century. The rest were European immigrants and native-born Americans.

It was easy to find men without families. All one had to do was to follow the loud music and the smell of stale beer

Part of downtown Portland developed a roistering atmosphere of which the more straitlaced residents disapproved. Saloons were the center of much of this activity. In 1892 this load of St. Louis Lager beer arrived at Louis Secchtem's Fountain Saloon on S.W. Washington Street and S.W. Second Avenue. (OHS)

to the riverfront blocks and downtown wards from Everett Street south to Jackson. The district included China-town, with its gambling halls, brothels, and opium parlors, and a growing skid road around Burnside Street. The onset of each rainy season brought several thousand seasonal farm, lumber, and railroad workers to winter in the city's rooming houses, cheap hotels, and the back rooms of saloons.

Portland's not unjustified reputation as a wide-open town was an important factor that pushed the respectable mid-dle class into the new suburbs east of the river and the elite toward higher ground on the west. The increasing seg-regation of single men in a downtown

Above: *For twenty-one years, since its incorpora-tion in 1870, East Portland was an independent com-munity. The Willamette River cut the town off from Portland. Among East Portland businesses was an agency of the Studebaker Brothers Company, on S.E. Morrison Street.* (OHS)

Left: *Sylvester Pennoyer supported the Democratic party with his* Oregon Her-ald. *In the late 1880s he served as Oregon governor and later spent two contro-versial years as Portland mayor. Pennoyer was a leader in the movement against Chinese laborers.* (OHS)

district that met their needs and took their money also provided a prime target for moral reformers. The ensuing battles for temperance and clean living represented efforts to impose the standards of the native-born middle class on immigrants and workers and to demonstrate that Victorian family values had triumphed over the raw frontier.

The Chinese were the most obvious target for a police chief or mayor who wanted to prove his moral fiber. An 1851 ordinance against gambling had gone virtually unenforced until William Watkinds took office as police chief in 1883. Ignoring the thousands of white gamblers sitting down every night to faro and poker in Portland saloons, he systematically raided the dozens of fan tan dens along Second Street and made nearly 500 arrests before the year was out. His patrolmen also brought in several dozen Chinese women on charges of prostitution, continuing the pattern of racially selective enforcement of the city's 1871 anti-prostitution law. Watkinds' immediate predecessor, James Lappeus, had been more concerned about Ordinance 2073 which prohibited the smoking, buying, or possession of opium; Lappeus arrested several dozen offenders in 1879 for keeping or visiting opium houses, explaining in his annual report:

Another evil, and a rapidly growing one, is the habit of opium smoking, which is ruining the health and destroying the minds of many of our young men and girls. There are a large number of these dens, kept principally by Chinese, where men and women . . . congregate and indulge in this vile and filthy habit, and sleep off their stupor. Some of the females who frequent these places are married and have families, and young girls of the most respectable class of soci-

The wholesale grocery business was the key to success for William S. Mason. He also served as mayor in the early 1890s and won another term as mayor in 1898, when he purged the police force. He died in office. (OHS)

ety. Could their names be published society would stand amazed. . . . Some more stringent and severe measures should be taken to break up these dens of infamy.

Although Lappeus thought that several hundred white Portlanders puffed the opium pipe, their most common downfall was whiskey. In the spring of 1883, City Council adopted a prohibitive annual license fee of $500 for each of the city's 162 barrooms and saloons. Both the temperance advocates and the liquor interests focused their attention on the coming 1883 council election, which would determine if the high license fee was sustained or repealed. The *Oregonian* and the Women's Christian Temperance Union thought that the election was a contest between the "immoral, vicious, and disorderly classes" and the "decent part of the community." Local politicians saw only another power play in which the temperance cause was a screen for maneuvering by political fac-

Left: *A variety of conveyances were clustered on S.W. Second Avenue north of S.W. Yamhill Street in this sketch from L. Samuel who included his* West Shore *magazine office at the left. Portland's businesses were still mainly situated near the waterfront.* Courtesy, *Portland and Vicinity*

Below: *Among vestiges that Portland retains of its past are some Victorian homes, such as this building on N.W. Hoyt Street used in later years by a rug dealer.* Courtesy, *Ted Van Arsdol*

tions. Leaders of both political parties quietly stacked the nominations with candidates who favored business as usual, and Portland awoke after the election to find operators of two saloons on its governing body.

A decade later, the Portland Ministerial Association tried an even more direct approach to fighting the liquor business. It researched and published the names of landlords of more than 200 drinking joints that operated illegal-ly or after hours. A large proportion of leading businessmen appeared on the list of property owners who profited from Demon Rum. Despite public embarrassment, there were enough members of the upper crust on the list that most owners decided to ride out the fuss and bother without evicting their disreputable tenants.

The general lack of enthusiasm for the temperance campaigns demonstrates one way in which Portland's "other

Left: *Construction of Union Station started in 1890 but financial problems delayed the opening until 1896. The depot, a cooperative venture of the Union Pacific, Southern Pacific, and Northern Pacific, was quite active until post-World War II, when freeways and airlines trimmed train business. (OHS)*

Below: *Portland of the 1870s and 1880s offered opportunities for wealth and prominence to some residents. One who rose to the top in journalism was Harvey W. Scott, Oregonian editor, called "a molder of opinion" on this statue by Gutzon Borglum at Mount Tabor Park.*

half" could defend its interests against residents of middle- and upper-class neighborhoods. Portland in the 1880s and 1890s was a city in which political party bosses mediated between working-class voters and the elite of the business community. Each of the city's wards, of which there were eight after the consolidation of 1891, elected two members to the city council. The councilmen themselves were most often businessmen or employees of large firms, yet political common sense dictated that they work to protect the interests of their constituents. The mayor had relatively little authority, and, after 1885, shared executive authority with a separate Board of Police Commissioners. The police commissioners formed a corrupt alliance with the political machine. Mayor William Mason complained in the early 1890s about his inability to force tough law enforcement: "We lack the power

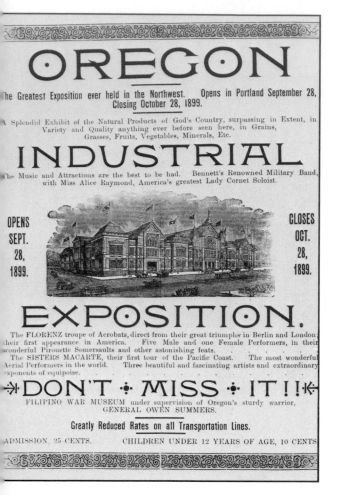

to enforce the laws. . . . Our police perambulate the streets day and night and we hear of no arrests for violations." Mason's fear that the police were "the protectors, the sharers in the spoils" of a corrupt system was certainly correct in the North End, where entrepreneur and future U.S. Senator Jonathan Bourne was the political boss who called the shots.

Although bosses claimed to look after working-class interests, labor unions offered a better long-run goal. Efforts to organize Portland's skilled workingmen dated to the 1870s, but one of the first major events in local union history was a mass meeting in 1880 in which an organizer for the Knights of Labor addressed a crowd of 4,000. The following years brought the organization of several craft unions such as Local 50 of the

Brotherhood of Carpenters and Joiners. When AFL President Samuel Gompers visited Portland in the late 1880s, the city's Federated Trades Assembly had fifteen unions representing 400 members. The early union movement came to a climax in 1890, when Portlanders participated in a national drive for the eight-hour day in the building trades. Carpenters, painters, plumbers, and trimmers participating in a general strike and lockout settled by agreeing to an eight-hour day with proportionately reduced wages. In the mid-1890s, as the United States plunged into its deepest depression of the century after the Panic of 1893, Portland unionists struggled, though with limited success, to hold onto the gains of the previous years.

In the depths of the same depression, hundreds of other Portlanders marched behind the banner of the "United States Industrial Army." "Coxey's Army," as it was called, was the plan of Ohioan Jacob Coxey to bring thousands of the unemployed from all over the United States to a grand rally in Washington, D.C., when they would petition the federal government for work relief. In April 1894, recruiters for Portland's "commonweal companies" set up tables on the sidewalks of the North End and

Left: *Portland's Industrial Exposition building, opened in 1889, was reportedly capable of holding 15,000 persons "without crowding." Entertainment and exhibits drew throngs. The 1899 exposition advertised a Filipino war museum, reflecting high interest in the Spanish-American conflict. (OHS)*

Below: *Longtime real estate developer William Killingsworth called Portland the future "New York of the Pacific." He was especially active in development of North Portland. A street is named for him in "The Peninsula," the section between the Willamette and Columbia rivers. (OHS)*

Left: *The Multnomah Athletic Club football team was togged out in assorted uniforms for a photo about 1898. Erskine Wood, later an attorney in Portland, is at far left. He was the son of C.E.S. Wood, soldier, lawyer, writer, and an early civil rights activist. Courtesy, Fred DeWolfe*

Below: *Henry Failing was among the most prominent merchant leaders in Portland. He was a banker and a business associate of his brother-in-law, Henry W. Corbett, another community leader. Failing served as mayor of Portland from 1864 to 1866 and again from 1873 to 1875. Courtesy, H.W. Scott's* History of Portland, Oregon

directed several hundred enlistees to a camp at the mouth of Sullivan's Gulch. Attacked by the press as "herds of vagrants" and lazy tramps, and denied food by the very proper Board of Charities, the army walked the dozen miles to Troutdale, where, on April 27, they seized an Oregon Railway and Navigation Company train. Their intention was to head east, picking up recruits along the way and depending for help on the sympathetic railroad workers. They got as far as Arlington (with a festive stop at The Dalles where they were cheered on by residents) before a detachment of cavalry from Walla Walla rescued the property of Portland's most powerful investors and arrested the train's hijackers. Federal judge C.B. Bellinger reprimanded and released the 439 prisoners. A crowd of sympathizers milled angrily around the Oregonian Building

for several hours but dispersed without convincing editor Harvey Scott that the unemployed needed jobs rather than contempt.

Portlanders from overseas had to turn to each other to build their communities in the boom years of the 1880s and 1890s. Churches, neighborhoods, and benevolent societies all helped these new Americans to make their place in the growing city. Residents at the bottom of the economic pyramid—often these same immigrants and their children—also organized through trade unions and ward politics to protect their interests and battle for a share of the benefits of growth. Portlanders at the top of the economic structure had no such problems. They ran the city, and they assumed that to do so was their privilege and responsibility. *The Oregonian's Handbook of the Pacific Northwest*, a regional guide published in 1894, drew a clear-cut line between "progressive, intelligent, and cultured" citizens and "the debasing influence of foreign paupers." Editor Harvey Scott, who was confident that he spoke for the "better" sort, was scornful of those who needed help in ascending to the heights of the "first-class" citizen. From the pages of the *Oregonian* he growled against public high schools, women's suffrage, and the

reform movement of the Populist Party. He thought that the Chinese were "not very desirable people" but worth tolerating because their services in housework, wood-cutting, laundries, and construction gangs allowed for work of a more "rewarding kind for the

American."

Portland's "Americans," particularly the fortunate few, were directly affected by the emergence of large corporations that marked a change in the national economy at the end of the nineteenth century. After 1880, the *Portland City Directory* found it impossible to continue to list every new building and every incorporation for the past year. The general-purpose merchant of Portland's pioneer decade was gradually replaced by firms that specialized in fruit or hardware or men's furnishings. There was one category of insurance broker in 1880 and a dozen types by 1900. Before the arrival of the Northern Pacific, the typical factory was a small shop where the owner knew all of his six or seven employees. Though Portland still had no giant factories on the scale of Pittsburgh or Chicago at the turn of the century, its lumber mills averaged 100 workers in 1900 and 150 by 1905; its furniture factories, sash and door makers, and packing houses averaged thirty to forty hands.

Factory owners could show their wares and discover new ideas at the Portland Mechanics Fair, held every September from 1880 through 1888 in the Pavilion on the future site of the City Auditorium. The success of the Mechanics Fair paved the way for the North Pacific Industrial Exposition. A great success until attendance dropped in the depression of 1893, the Industrial Exposition occupied a vast new structure covering two full blocks at Nineteenth and Washington and included a music hall with seating for 5,000. Boosters claimed it was the largest building on the Pacific Coast.

The arrival of big manufacturing and specialized commerce required new methods to maintain common goals within the business community. The Portland Chamber of Commerce was organized in 1890 and the Manufactur-

Left: *William S. Ladd, who opened Portland's first bank in 1859, was active in a variety of business and civic activities before his death in 1893. The Ladd & Tilton bank name was widely known, and Ladd left a large estate, partly in undeveloped land. Courtesy, H.W. Scott's* History of Portland, Oregon

Left, below: *Frank Dekum's name survived as part of the Dekum building on S.W. Third Avenue. This native of Germany came to Portland in 1853 and was involved in real estate, banking, and the Portland Mechanics Fair Association. He imported songbirds from Germany. Courtesy, H.W. Scott's* History of Portland, Oregon

er's Association in 1895. Flamboyant real estate developer William Killingsworth helped to create a new Board of Trade in 1899 to attract men of "push and progress" in both commerce and the professions. Social clubs were an equally important way in which the elite set themselves apart from Portland's middle classes. The Commercial Club, founded in 1893, devoted itself to entertainment, socializing, and business promotion. The Arlington Club incorporated in 1881 and occupied an elegant new building in 1892. It was the city's most exclusive refuge for white gentile businessmen with big bank accounts. As historian E. Kimbark MacColl points out in *The Shaping of a City,* "the large banks, the utilities, the railroads, and Oregon's United States Senators were especially well represented within the Arlington Club's membership. During the 1890s the club could normally count at least four or five of its members serving in a session of the Oregon State Legislature. The direct political influence of the club reached its peak around 1900 with two successive mayors who were members."

In an increasingly segmented city, the economic upper class was eager not only to control the important decisions but also to create a life apart from the ordinary folk. The *Portland Blue Book* of 1890, published out of San Francisco, and the home-grown *Portland "400" Directory: A Residence Address, Visiting, Club, Theater, and Shopping Guide*

of 1891 imitated Eastern social registers and helped the "right people" identify one another. Elegant private parties, chronicled in the diary of Judge Matthew Deady, replaced the less sophisticated socializing of the 1860s or early 1870s. Families with leisure could follow the new fad of vigorous outdoor recreation in the 1890s by joining the new Multnomah Amateur Athletic Club and Waverly Golf Club. There were picnics on Ross Island, day trips on Portland's rivers, and weeks or entire summers to spend at the new resorts of Seaside and Gearhart, Oregon, and Seaview, Washington, where large hotels and new summer cottages overlooked the cold Pacific at the end of railroad lines. The hardiest Portlanders joined the Alpine Club, which built the Cloud Cap Inn, a resort on Mt. Hood, or the Mazamas, whose inaugural climb took 200 hardy souls to the top of Mt. Hood.

There were social strata even within the upper crust. The old-line elite consisted of influential families whose founders had arrived in Oregon in the 1850s and 1860s. By the 1890s, men like

Left: *Fortunes and reputations were made with steamboats. One Portlander near the top in this field was Jacob Kamm, a large stockholder in Oregon Steam Navigation Company and Willamette Transportation Company. He was associated later with Vancouver Transportation Company and Ilwaco Railway and Navigation Company. Courtesy, H.W. Scott's* History of Portland, Oregon

Below: *The Jacob Kamm home, built in the early 1870s, is significant as one of the earliest Portland mansions surviving into recent years. This photo of the 1930s shows the building before it was moved to The Colony, a restoration project on N.W. 20th Avenue. Courtesy, Oregon State Library*

Henry Corbett, Matthew Deady, Frank Dekum, Joseph Dolph, Henry Failing, William S. Ladd, Cicero H. Lewis, John H. Mitchell, Henry L. Pittock, Simeon G. Reed, Ben Selling, Joseph Simon, and Philip Wasserman had been accustomed to leading the city for a generation. They were for the most part merchants, bankers, and investors who, by the century's last decades, held controlling interests in the area's railroads, manufacturing, and real estate. Many had held public office and the most of the rest were like John C. Ainsworth, "willing to pull wires, and mean to do it." Newer monied arrivals in the city often shared the same outward characteristics as their more established counterparts, but they lacked some of the

Left: *The Willamette River, separating the main part of Portland from East Portland, was a threat during runoff time. Floods of 1887 and 1894 brought muddy waters into the street. Courtesy, Portland District, U.S. Army Corps of Engineers*

Below: *Sightseers were advised to "pass on, don't stand here," at a narrow boardwalk used to cross a flooded street in 1894. Seawalls were constructed later to protect the city from periodic floods of the Willamette River. Courtesy, Portland District, U.S. Army Corps of Engineers*

intricate marital alliances that united older families into economic cartels, and could not expect the respectful attention accorded to a Ladd or Corbett.

Portlanders with money were careful to pick the right neighborhoods for their increasingly palatial houses. Northwest Third and Fourth streets and the southwest Park Blocks were the favored locations of the 1860s and 1870s. By the 1890s, most of Portland's business and civic leaders had moved to the western edge of town—especially Nob Hill or "Nineteenth Street" in the northwest district. Double-sized blocks gave the space necessary for "substantial comfort and tasteful display" according to Harvey Scott. Completion of an incline and cable car line from Jefferson Street to Portland Heights in 1890 foreshadowed the next migration of the elite to the highlands in the twentieth century.

The building boom in the years around 1890 gave Portland's influential families some magnificent churches worthy of a major city. The wooden spires of Calvary Presbyterian—now preserved and restored as the Old Church—were adequate for 1882, but leaders of the burgeoning city soon preferred to worship in grander buildings. The First Congregational, First Presbyterian, First Baptist, St. James Lutheran, Grace Methodist, and Temple Beth Israel congregations all occupied new stone or brick buildings in a district located west of the business center from the Park Blocks to Thirteenth Street.

Portland's cultural institutions were as much the responsibility and prerogative of its upper class as were its economic decisions. The Library Association of Portland operated the city's main library on a subscription basis; 625 members paid $5 a year in 1895, cut from $9 because of the depression. Contributions of $10,000 each from Henry Failing and Simeon Reed, added to generous bequests, allowed the li-

Left: *Lawyer P.A. Marquam served as a Multnomah County judge and state legislator, and was also involved in real estate. His Marquam Grand Opera House at Portland was called "one of the finest specimens of architecture in Oregon." Courtesy, H.W. Scott's* History of Portland, Oregon

Below: *The old West Side High School, opened in 1885, was known as Lincoln High School shortly before World War I. The building, on S.W. Morrison Street, was known as Girls Polytechnic School in its final years. It was razed shortly before the Great Depression.*

The same list of established families provided much of the support for private charity, responding to the growing problems of an increasingly complex metropolis, although still lagging behind the needs during the hard years of the mid-nineties. More often than not, they followed the leadership of Thomas Lamb Eliot, pastor of the First Unitarian Church. He was chiefly responsible for organization of the Boys and Girls Aid Society in 1885 and the citywide Board of Charities, which coordinated the city's volunteer charities, in 1889. Like the Children's Home, which dated to the 1870s, these projects were commendable but limited attempts to treat specific symptoms rather than the larger problem of economic inequality. More valuable in the long run were experimental night schools for working men and boys sponsored by the YMCA, and similar schools for working girls sponsored by the Portland Women's League. The classes were adopted by the school board in 1889 at the urging of superintendent Ella Sabin.

It was the people on top who formulated Portland's late-nineteenth-century image of livability with advantages "as a place to reside, as a place to engage in business, and as a place enjoying the requisite educational and social attributes necessary for the proper rearing of a family," in the words of a promotional pamphlet titled *Portland Oregon in 1900*. Portland meant good health statistics, pure water, clean streets, pleasant homes, and, by the early twentieth century, roses in abundance. It also meant a bustling harbor with ships jostling to take on cargoes of lumber and wheat—the favorite illustration for articles about the city. In the first decades of the twentieth century Portland would truly fulfill its promise as what Henry W. Corbett called "a modern city of great wealth, and of truly metropolitan importance."

brary to move its 20,000 volumes into a new building at Stark and Broadway in 1893. Eastern library expert R.R. Bowker called it the finest such building on the coast. The new Art Association opened a small gallery of reproductions in the Library Building in 1895. Ladd and Corbett dollars allowed the Association to graduate into a new building in 1905.

Left: *Transcontinental railroads brought more prominent entertainers to Portland, adding to the metropolitan flavor. Jeannie Winston, touring with her own company, was a favorite in light operas in the 1880s. She frequently appeared in male roles. (OHS)*

Left, below: *Portland of earlier years was "a sober-sided town," the Reverend Thomas Lamb Eliot recalled. Eliot, pastor of the Unitarian Church, was active in philanthropic and cultural work and supported prison reform, temperance, and women's suffrage. He came to Portland in 1867. (OHS)*

Above: *Turn-of-the-century delivery men from Meier & Frank pose before their horse-drawn vans at the Meier & Frank Delivery Depot on N.W. 14th Avenue and Everett Street. Courtesy, Meier & Frank Company*

Left: *Umbrellas are always a common sight on downtown streets. Rainy weather earned the name "webfooters" for Oregon residents, and postcards such as this one from 1906 by Murray Wade poked fun at the situation. Courtesy, Webfooters Postcard Club*

Flower-decorating crews have always paid meticulous attention to entries competing for Rose Festival awards. This float, circa 1915, claimed that "human rosebuds" were Oregon's crowning glory. Courtesy, Webfooters Postcard Club

CHAPTER IV
THE FAIR AND THE CITY

In the decades around the turn of the century Portlanders loved a parade. Before movies and television, parades were a major form of entertainment, grand spectacles that brought citizens together to share the excitement of city life. In 1890, the *Oregonian's* Harvey Scott noted that "scarcely a day passes but thick or thin files of men, accompanied by drum and brass band and banners, march to and fro." There were torchlight processions for political candidates. There were parades that included hundreds of cyclists during the bicycle craze of the 1890s, and parades featuring dozens of proud automobilists in the next decade. In June 1907 Portland staged the first annual Rose Festival with three days of pageantry. The grand parade included twenty illuminated floats built on flatcars carried on the trolley system.

One of the grandest parades of that era started at the corner of Sixth and Montgomery at 10 a.m. on June 1, 1905. Mounted police and a detachment of U.S. Cavalry led off, followed by marching bands, 2,000 National Guardsmen, and more police to bring up the rear. As the marchers trooped up Sixth, their ranks opened in front of the elegant Portland Hotel to make way for the carriages of visiting Congressmen, governors, and Vice President Charles Fairbanks. Their destination was northwest Portland and the inaugural ceremony for the Lewis and Clark Centennial Exposition, where the opening-day crowd of 40,000 could listen to nearly a dozen long speeches about the importance of Portland and its world's fair.

Visitors who drifted away from the oratory discovered 400 acres of fairgrounds planned around the shallow waters of Guild's Lake. The formal layout imitated the "White City" of Chicago's magnificent Columbian Exposition in 1893. The majority of the exposition's buildings overlooked the lake from the bluff on which the Montgomery Ward warehouse later stood. A wide staircase led downslope to the lake and "The Trail," the amusement arcade where the wonders of the world were available for a dime or a quarter. A "Bridge of Nations" connected the mainland to the United States government buildings which were situated on a peninsula in the middle of the lake. For no apparent reason, the major exhibition halls followed the "Spanish Renaissance" style with domes, cupolas, arched doorways, and red roofs. The federal building was built in a style that combined the architectural features of a railroad depot and a Mexican cathedral. The whitewashed stucco of the light frame buildings gleamed against the West Hills in the occasional Portland sun—like "diamonds set in a coronet of emeralds," according to one speaker.

From June 1 through October 15, nearly 1.6 million people paid for admission to the fair. Four hundred thousand of them were from beyond the Pacific Northwest. They could attend high-minded conferences on education, civic affairs, and the future of the United States in the Orient or partici-

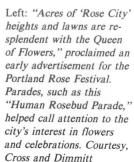

Left, below: *Floats and marching units enlivened the annual Rose Festival parades. In 1911 the cadets of Oregon Agricultural College at Corvallis were photographed in military array. Soldiers from Vancouver barracks and other martial units also paraded frequently in Portland.*

pate in national conventions of librarians, social workers, physicians, and railroad conductors. They could inspect the exhibits of sixteen states and twenty-one foreign nations. They could fritter their money on such carnival-like exhibits as "The Streets of Cairo," Professor Barnes' Educated Horse and Diving Elk, who plunged into a tank of water from a forty-foot ramp. They could listen to band concerts or gape at the Forestry Building, the "world's largest log cabin." Constructed entirely of undressed logs, the "cabin" stretched 105 feet by 209 feet. The visitor entered through a portico of natural tree trunks into a vast interior colonnaded with more trees. The largest foundation logs weighed in at thirty-two tons and measured fifty-four feet long and five across.

The city's business leadership gave wholehearted support to the planning and promotion of the Lewis and Clark

CHANTICLEER CROWS FOR OREGON

Exposition because its purpose was a bigger and better Portland. It was an age when every ambitious city aspired to put on a national or international exposition. The list from recent decades already included Chicago, Omaha, Buffalo, St. Louis, Atlanta, and Nashville; it would soon add Norfolk, Seattle, San Francisco, and San Diego. At the least, a well-planned and successful event would show Easterners that Portland was a mature and "finished" city rather than a frontier town. At most it could give Portland an edge in the ongoing competition with upstart Seattle and confirmed the city as a commercial center for the Pacific. When Oregonians of today speak about the importance of trade with the Pacific Rim, they are reiterating ideas that were common eighty years ago. The official title of the event was the "Lewis and Clark Centennial Exposition and Oriental Fair." The

SEE OREGON ROSES BLOOM

PORTLAND ROSE SHOW AND FIESTA

Carnival Days:
June 19-20-21-22, '07

Wednesday, June 19th
Oregon Pioneers' Day

Thursday, June 20th
Competitive Exhibit of Oregon's Rare Rose Blooms at Forestry Building. Floral Parade of 2000 school children, trained in Kaleidoscopic marching movements, by Prof. Krohn.

Friday, June 21st—FIESTA DAY
Monster parade of Floral Decorated Automobiles, Competitive Floats, Equestrian Clubs, Military and Bands, Trophy and Cash Prize Awards. Convening of Oregon Development League.

Saturday, June 22
Continuation, Oregon Development League Convention. No set public program announced for Wednesday and Saturday of Carnival Week. Special Rose Matinees at Theatres and visitors will enjoy those days going about gaily decorated Portland when acres of the "Rose City" heights and lawns are resplendent with the Queen of Flowers.
Building decorations and illuminations during the Carnival Days will follow the color scheme of Rose Pink and Leaf Green.

Above: *Organizations and communities have vied with each other to produce the most colorful and attractive floats in annual Portland parades since 1907.*

Left: *A tradition was established by the Rose Show and Fiesta in 1907. Carrie Lee Chamberlain, daughter of Governor George E. Chamberlain, reigned as Queen Flora. Parades of children, floats, and decorated cars were highlights of the first rose festivals.*

Crowds surged across the Willamette River, along with packed streetcars, headed for exposition fun in 1905. The streetcars which brought fairgoers had also been instrumental in helping to open up new outlying residential neighborhoods. Courtesy, Fred DeWolfe

motto over the entrance gate was "Westward the Course of Empire Takes Its Way." The biggest foreign exhibit came from Japan. As Exposition president Henry Goode explained, the first large international fair on the West Coast would "demonstrate to the commercial world . . . the actual inception of the era of new trade relations with the teeming millions of Asiatic countries." Even Portland's prestigious *Pacific Monthly* took time out from publishing stories by Jack London and essays by John Muir to tell readers about Portland's role in "The Coming Supremacy of the Pacific." A visiting journalist agreed that "the whole fair is a successful effort to express . . . the natural richness of the country and its relative nearness to Asia."

Civic boosters had plenty to crow about. The Exposition, in the words of *Harper's Weekly,* "marked the close of an old epoch and the beginning of a new one for Portland." The Exposition had helped launch a boom in both business and population. Skyrocketing prices in downtown real estate made speculators rich and millionaires richer. The annual value of new construction quintupled between 1905 and 1910. Portland's population passed 200,000 by

1910 and may have reached 225,000 by 1913 when the boom finally ended.

A primary reason for expansion was Portland's increasingly significant role as a trade center and port. As early as 1891, the state legislature had created the Port of Portland to maintain and improve harbor facilities. Given the city's situation as a river port, the agency's most important service was to maintain the channel in the Willamette. It also operated a dry dock and improved towing and pilotage services. Its work was supplemented by the Army Corps of Engineers, which began to improve the dangerous mouth of the Columbia in 1884. Between 1903 and 1917, the Corps deepened the bar channel to thirty-seven feet and maintained a minimum depth of twenty-six feet upriver.

Local manufacturing expanded in the same years, especially in lumber, wood products, and furniture, but the biggest growth was in trade and transportation. James J. Hill, the railroad magnate who had built the Great Northern Railroad and made the fortunes of Puget Sound cities, started work on a North Bank railroad (the Spokane, Portland, and Seattle), from Pasco to Portland in 1906. Completion of the road in 1908

gave the Northern Pacific and Great Northern independent access to Portland.

Within a few years Hill was locked into one of the last great railroad-building contests, in which the adversaries vied to tap the lumber and cattle country of central Oregon. "James J. Hill spends millions to tap interior" said one headline in the *Oregonian* describing the line he built up the Deschutes River. "Harriman Road has 2600 men at work" trumpeted another article in the same issue. "Harriman" was E.H. Harriman, who controlled both the Union Pacific and Southern Pacific. After open warfare in the Deschutes Can-

yon, the two tycoons struck a deal and the rails reached Bend in 1911.

Now that the city had a link to the interior, Portland bankers financed the developing cattle, wool, and grain businesses of the Inland Empire. Portland wholesalers supplied the farmers and ranchers with tools and tobacco. Portland longshoremen loaded the ships that made the city one of the nation's leading ports for the exportation of lumber and wheat. Insurance agents, railroad hands, draymen, carpenters, lawyers, retail clerks—nearly everyone benefited from the growth of Portland's commercial empire.

Voters took steps to assure that

A deluxe bandstand, topped by flags, was erected for the Lewis and Clark Exposition in 1905. In the background is Guild Lake. The exposition celebrated the 100th anniversary of the arrival of the Lewis and Clark expedition in the Portland area. (OHS)

growth in 1910, when they approved a charter amendment creating a Commission of Public Docks. Portland's waterfront in the early twentieth century was in the tight grip of the railroads, which had a limited interest in promoting maritime trade. Every functioning dock—downtown, northwest, and east side—was privately owned. Most had been built for the coastwise trade to California and were inadequate to serve transoceanic shipping. Under the direction of Portland's business establishment, the Docks Commission opened Municipal Dock No. 1 on North Front Street in 1914. A major motivation for the annexation of the independent city of St. Johns in 1915 was to enable the Docks Commission to fund the improvement of the St. Johns city dock. Still to come in the 1920s was the Port of Portland's massive dredging project that shifted the Willamette channel from the east side of Swan Island to the west.

The boom years also opened regular

employment to thousands of Portland women, who made up only 15 percent of the city's wage earners in 1900 but 24 percent by 1920. Women dominated half a dozen job categories, ranging from servant to dressmaker to boarding-house keeper. By 1910 more than 2,000 women worked in the lower-paying professions as nurses, music teachers, musicians, and schoolteachers, and 6,000 more worked in white-collar jobs as "typewriters," stenographers, salespeople, telephone operators, and clerks.

In the early years of the century, thousands of other Portland women earned their livelihoods, in full or in part, from prostitution. In 1893, the Portland Ministerial Association found prostitution concentrated in the parlor houses and saloons of the North End and waterfront. Rich and poor alike, Portland's men could indulge in drink, gambling, and illicit sex as a single vice because, according to a report by the Ministerial Association, "saloons and

Above: The T.J. Potter connects with a train at Megler, Washington, near the coast.

Facing page, top: Railroads were a major factor in the city's growth, but some were not as successful as others. The Portland, Vancouver and Yakima Railroad, seen here about 1899, was intended to cross the Cascades. However, the railroad only reached the Cascade foothills, near Chelatchie, Washington. Courtesy, The Columbian

Facing page, bottom, far left: James J. Hill made his reputation constructing the Great Northern Railroad across the country.

Facing page, bottom, left: E.H. Harriman, shown here in 1905, was a powerful figure in railroad circles in Portland, in Oregon generally, and in other parts of the West. (OHS)

houses of ill-fame were generally combined in the same building." In 1907 and 1908, new ordinances barring women from saloons and stringent law enforcement by a reform administration forced many prostitutes out of the houses and into the roles of streetwalker and call girl. Still, the Vice Commission in 1912 found more than 400 downtown hotels, apartment buildings, and lodging houses that condoned or encouraged use by an estimated 3,000 "sporting women."

Middle-class and working-class families who wanted to keep themselves carefully separated from the seamy neighborhoods around the business district could thank the expansion of the electrified transit system that made it easy to reach outlying neighborhoods. Back room deals and Wall Street buyouts brought more than a dozen separate companies into a single streetcar monopoly in 1906. The Portland Railway Light and Power Company (PRL&P) operated 161 miles of railway and six electric power plants and carried sixteen million passengers by 1910. In that year a thousand streetcars a day rattled and clanked across the Willamette bridges, creating huge traf-

fic jams on Southwest Morrison and Washington. The volume of streetcar traffic quadrupled in the first decade of the century and Portlanders hopped on trolleys twice as often as they had a few years earlier.

The Portland streetcar system, which ran largely within the city limits, was complemented by dozens of electric interurban railroads that stimulated the growth of a suburban ring between five and fifteen miles from the center of town. At the height of the interurban system in 1915, the suburban division of PRL&P ran to Troutdale, Gresham,

Facing page, top: *This group of women turned out for a physical culture class in 1906 at Gladstone, a short distance south of Portland. The activity was part of a chautauqua. Traveling chautauquas presented popular lectures and entertainment across the nation in the early 1900s. (OHS)*

Facing page, bottom: *Beatrice Morrow Cannady, a graduate of Northwestern College of Law in 1922, was a teacher, a newspaperwoman, and the first black woman to practice law in Oregon. She established a number of chapters of the National Association for the Advancement of Colored People. (OHS)*

Left, top: *Lola Baldwin was said to be the first policewoman appointed under the U.S. Civil Service in 1905. She headed the Women's Protection Division of the Portland Police Bureau, and helped establish the Multnomah County Juvenile Court, and the Oregon Industrial School for Girls, later Hillcrest School for Girls. (OHS)*

Left, bottom: *Before historic preservation became popular, many Portland landmarks were removed without thought of the future. One of the more distinctive, now vanished, businesses of the pre-World War I period was the Lotus Buffet and Billiard Parlor on S.W. Sixth Avenue, with its fancy facade. (OHS)*

Streetcars were lined up near S.W. Second Avenue and S.W. Morrison Street about 1905 for what appeared to be an excursion. The man with the sign advertised a Columbia River steamboat trip to Cascade Locks. Some trolley excursion trips in early days were scheduled to amusement parks. Courtesy, Alex Blendl

Boring, Estacada, and Oregon City. Oregon Electric, controlled by James Hill's railroad empire, ran one line to Beaverton, Hillsboro, and Forest Grove and a second through Tualatin and Wilsonville to Salem and Eugene. The Southern Pacific Red Electrics ran to Garden Home, Beaverton, and Hillsboro before swinging south to McMinnville and Corvallis.

Streetcar and interurban companies generated their own traffic by building parks and amusement centers alongside the lines. In the early 1900s, before the typical family owned their Model-T, summer weekends and holidays meant packing a picnic basket and fishing gear for an interurban excursion to Canemah Park above Willamette Falls, Estacada Recreation Park on the Clackamas River, or Dodge Park on the line to the Bull Run power plant. Closer to town were the Oaks Amusement Park, featuring concerts, vaudeville acts, skating rink, rides, and food; and Council Crest Park, whose roller coaster gave the best views in the city to riders who were brave enough to open their eyes.

Prosperity plus new streetcar lines provided the impetus for a residential real estate boom that surpassed even the subdivision mania of the late 1880s and early 1890s. The list of new developments between 1904 and 1910 includes

These three young women were garbed in the popular fashion of 1913 on an outing at Council Crest park, where a scenic railway was a prominent attraction. Courtesy, Webfooters Postcard Club

dozens of names familiar to Portlanders. The 1920s would see the rapid development of Council Crest, Burlingame, Arlington Heights, Willamette Heights, and other new plats in the West Hills. With relatively level land suitable for trolleys, the east side continued to monopolize residential growth in old neighborhoods and in new entries such as Overlook, Montavilla, Rose City Park, Gregory Heights, Kenton, Beaumont, and Westmoreland. The most exclusive new developments were Eastmoreland, Alameda Park, and Laurelhurst. Restrictions written into individual deeds protected residents from the intrusion of apartment buildings and nonwhites.

The Exposition boom made Portland into an "east-side" city. For a decade, virtually all the new housing was built on the east side, and the population balance between the two parts of the city tipped toward the east as early as 1906. In 1916 the telephone company estimated that there were two east-siders for every west-sider. In addition to St. Johns, other east-side neighborhoods including Mount Tabor, Montavilla, Rose City Park, Woodstock, Eastmoreland, and Mount Scott chose annexation to the city to assure good water and streetcar service.

Private developers made money from selling lots and by providing streetcar service to and from the new residents' homes. It was these new property owners, however, who footed the bill for the expanded public services needed because of rapid development. A second water pipeline from Bull Run to a second storage reservoir at Mount Tabor cost taxpayers $1,720,000 in 1911. The bill for streets and sewers came to $28,000,000 from 1905 through 1914, compared to $8,000,000 for the previous *four* decades. The development of new neighborhoods also brought the need to link their residents with downtown jobs. The replacement of three old bridges and the construction of the new Broadway Bridge in 1913 cost $4,500,000.

The Board of Park Commissioners was established in 1900, when the city decided it needed systematic management of Washington Park, Macleay Park, and smaller properties. Under the leadership of Thomas Lamb Eliot, a Unitarian minister and social reformer who was as much an environmentalist as he was a crusader, the board split the cost of hiring landscape architect John Olmsted with the Exposition Company. For a total of $10,000, Portland bought the design for the Exposition grounds and its first comprehensive park plan from the nation's premier firm of landscape planners. John Olmsted followed in the footsteps of his stepfather, Frederick Law Olmsted, who had designed New York's Central Park, and he continued the family landscape architecture and planning business. His ideas for Portland included small playgrounds and neighborhood parks as well as the improvement of large rural and suburban tracts and the development of parkways. He wanted the city to turn the wetlands along the Columbia, and at Ross Island, Guild's Lake, and Swan Island into expansive park reserves. A loop of smaller parks and parkways would rim the west hills and connect the bluffs and ridges of the east side.

Portlanders thought that Olmsted's ideas were fine but feared that the price would be too steep. A one-million-dollar bond issue was responsible for the construction of three miles of Terwilliger Boulevard, and secured public ownership of Laurelhurst, Sellwood, Mount Tabor, and Peninsula parks before the

money ran out in 1910. But voters turned thumbs down on new park spending in the 1910s. Most of the riverfront land that Olmsted had allocated for parks went to industry and airports over the following decades. Parkways seemed of less importance than roads as the automobile took over as the primary mode of transportation. The vast expanse of Forest Park is the result of public foreclosure of tax delinquent property during the Depression of the 1930s, not of systematic planning by the preceding generation.

As work lagged on the park system, a meeting of planning enthusiasts in the fall of 1909 led to the formation of a group called the Civic Improvement League, which quickly raised $20,000 from private donors to hire an outside expert to formulate a comprehensive plan for making Portland an "ideal city." The League's major contributors and executive committee comprised a "who's who" of successful Portlanders. The planner who got the job was Edward Bennett, a British-born architect who had assisted the famous Daniel Burnham in the preparation of landmark plans for Chicago and San Francisco. He received $500 a month and

Passengers for the Oregon Electric cars could slip into the Salem Road Cafe for food or a glass of beer. The station was at S.W. First Avenue and S.W. Jefferson Street, and the year was about 1916. (OHS)

Above: *Tourists were ready for a look at the sights of Portland in the open-air vehicles* Willamette *and* Multnomah. *In the years when cars were becoming common, Portland was more compact than today and could be viewed easily during a short tour.* (OHS)

Left: *Oaks Amusement Park on the Willamette River opened just before the Lewis and Clark Exposition. Concerts were frequent at the Oaks, and shortly before World War I the Oaks Park Band and Metropolitan Quartet were entertaining the crowds.*

Left: *Council Crest over-looks much of Portland from a height of almost 1,100 feet. In earlier years it was at the end of a trolley ride, a popular trip for weekend crowds. Funseekers posed on a rickety fake biplane at Council Crest.*

Below: *Exotic plants graced the courtyard of the Portland Hotel. This scene dates to shortly before World War I, a heyday for the hotel business. Two other major hotels, the Benson and the Multnomah, were completed about this time. Courtesy, University of Oregon Library*

expenses in exchange for his expertise. Bennett presented his preliminary sketches to the Civic Improvement League in February 1911 and had the final plan completed by the end of the summer.

The plan worked outward from the center of the city. Anticipating an eventual metropolitan population of two million, Bennett called for the construction of three civic centers to anchor the business district—government offices grouped around the City Hall for "nobility of appearance"; a transportation center including post office and new railway station; and a cultural center with auditorium and museum below Washington Park. The plan suggested radial highways, parks, and parkways to serve the east side. New rail yards and docks would be built downstream, with the upper Willamette reclaimed for parks and pleasure boats in the style of Paris or Budapest.

Business and civic associations were enthusiastic about the plan. Mayor Albion G. Rushlight proclaimed February 29, 1912 as Greater Portland Day. Canvassers fanned out through the city at precisely 10:30 a.m. to kick off a mem-

bership campaign that eventually sold 10,000 Greater Portland Plan buttons at one dollar each. The campaign concluded with an evening parade on October 30 led by loud music and horn-tooting automobiles. The final step was to secure formal recognition of the plan by the voters, without asking them to allocate the necessary millions immediately. The vote on November 2, 1912, was two to one to approve Bennett's conception as Portland's official plan, to be followed as closely as possible so long as it proved reasonable and practical.

Within weeks, Bennett's plan took a back seat in local politics to the campaign for a commission form of city government. The narrow vote amending the city charter climaxed a decade of effort at political reform, for the clean-scrubbed face that Portland put on for tourists and businessmen at the Lewis

and Clark Exposition masked back-room politics that were as corrupt as ever. Historian Gordon Dodds, in his *Oregon: A Bicentennial History,* has described the alliance of "business interests, gamblers, and thugs" that ruled the city in the interests of licit and illicit commerce behind the figurehead mayor George H. Williams, whose term lasted from 1902 to 1905. In an era of political bossism, Portland's version of the party boss was W.F. "Jack" Matthews, who pulled the strings in the city and state Republican parties while occupying a series of patronage jobs and generally trying to keep his picture out of the papers. As muckraking journalist Burton Hendrick would write in *McClure's Magazine* in 1911, "the kind of government with which the Republican machine was identified was concretely illustrated in the municipal

Drinking water was provided for thirsty horses in front of the Commonwealth Building, on S.W. Sixth Avenue between S.W. Ankeny and W. Burnside streets. The building, dating from 1892, was typical of many ambitious, sometimes ornate, structures started before the 1890s depression. Courtesy, Fred DeWolfe

administration of Portland. Even on the Pacific Coast, Portland enjoyed a peculiar fame as a wide-open town . . . . the city had become a popular headquarters for all the vicious characters in the Pacific Northwest."

Then in 1904 and 1905, headline-making indictments and trials of leading politicians for involvement in schemes to obtain fraudulent title to northwest timberlands shattered the Oregon machine. President Theodore Roosevelt removed Jack Matthews from his position as U.S. Marshal, thus creating a vacuum in local politics. The mayor's office was up for grabs. The reformer who defeated Williams in 1905 was Dr. Harry Lane. A Democrat, Lane ran with the

support of progressive businessmen, the new *Oregon Journal,* and the respectable middle class. Grandson of Joseph Lane, Oregon's first territorial governor, Doc Lane was an outdoorsman of the Teddy Roosevelt mold who enjoyed making surprise visits to construction sites to find out for himself if the city was getting full value for its dollar. He was honest beyond question. When he later served in the U.S. Senate, colleagues called him "the human question mark" for his tendency to question federal spending. Lane vetoed scores of ordinances during his four years in office, but a city council that listened closely to liquor dealers and railroad executives usually overrode the vetoes on 13-2 votes. Nonetheless, Lane's record included successful cost-cutting on city contracts and an effective crackdown on saloons and bordellos. Yet he lost most of his battles to preserve the public interest against the "big boys"—Portland Railway Light and Power; the Spokane, Portland, and Seattle Railroad; the Union Pacific; and the Southern Pacific. Lane's strongest support in 1905 and in his 1907 re-election campaign came from the middle-class homeowners of the east side, who worried about the political alliance between the moguls of the Heights and the economically marginal residents of the North End.

When Tammany Hall ward boss George Washington Plunkitt told a New York reporter that "reformers are only mornin' glories," he was talking about the resiliency of political machines and the general inability of middle-class reformers to parlay single electoral victories into permanent changes. He might well have been talking about Portland

in 1909 and 1910 under the leadership of Mayor Joseph Simon. Coming to office at the end of a thirty-five year career that had taken him as far as the U.S. Senate, Simon was the smoothest of Portland's professional politicians. In public he supported such respectable causes as park acquisition and the Bennett plan, while behind the scenes he guided a well-oiled political machine.

The impetus for permanent change finally came from two objective reports. In the first, the 1912 Vice Commission appointed by new mayor Albion G. Rushlight compiled detailed documentation on the extent of prostitution, the ubiquity of venereal disease, and the complacent attitude of the police and courts. The report certainly surprised no one who had ever walked around downtown Portland with open eyes, but the Vice Commission's building-by-building inventory and its candid interviews with scores of prostitutes were difficult to ignore. So was the conclusion that law enforcement amounted to informal licensing, when fines for prostitution and for maintaining a bawdy house averaged less than a good day's take.

For many businessmen and bankers, vice may have been embarrassing but government inefficiency was intolerable—not merely an insult to public morals but an injury to every taxpayer. The second report that jolted Portland's establishment into action came in April 1913, when the New York Bureau of Municipal Research reported on an investigation of Portland's city government. Editor C.S. Jackson used his *Oregon Journal* to publicize its findings by detailing the operational problems of ten city departments. Only the water

bureau got good marks. According to the report, the police department was disorganized; city accounting and budgeting departments were in shambles; health inspections were a sham; and public works a scandal.

The impact of these reports prompted the adoption of the commission form of government, as recently developed in Galveston, Texas. The proposed charter provided for nonpartisan elections, the abolishment of the ward system in favor of citywide elections, and the replacement of the mayor and city council with a mayor and four commissioners. Meeting together, the five would serve as the city's legislative body. Acting separately, each one would administer a city department and carry out the ordinances adopted as a group. The goal was to bring Portland more businesslike and less expensive government by eliminating political horsetrading and ensuring coordination among departments. In May 1913, Portland approved the charter—which has served since with minor changes—by 722 votes. Liberal Republicans, planning enthusiasts, Roosevelt Progressives, and social reformers backed the change. Old guard Republi-

cans, who were satisfied with their control of the local political machine, dug in their heels to resist the new charter. At the other end of the political spectrum, the local labor newspaper, the *Labor Press,* thought that workingmen

should wait for more significant changes. The charter represented middle-class and working-class reform, with the margin of victory coming from the east side.

Commission government meant government for homeowners, small businessmen, professionals, skilled workers, and the other members of Portland's great middle class. It also helped to set the city's tone for the next two generations. In the first years of the twentieth century, Portland had been a rambunctious town caught up in the excitement of headlong growth. There were new opportunities to try, money to be made, and new communities to build. By the 1920s and 1930s, the city would slow down and grow conservative, concerned to maintain its obvious attractions rather than risk changes. The city would continue to change, but more slowly and more cautiously, with an eye to stable neighborhoods and low taxes.

Above: *Buildings constructed on pilings extended out over the river near Portland's downtown. This view, looking toward the northwest in about 1914, shows much of the downtown, with the* Journal *tower in the distance at left. A seawall was constructed later along the waterfront.* (OHS)

Left: *C.S. Jackson took over the faltering* Journal *in 1902 and built it into a major afternoon paper, challenging the long-entrenched* Oregonian. *He previously had published* The East Oregonian *at Pendleton. At the time,* The Oregonian *was also publishing an afternoon daily, the* Telegram. (OHS)

BUILDING A CITY OF HOMES

Every newspaper and chamber of commerce likes to claim that its community is a "city of homes." The claim may be only wishful thinking in some communities, but it is fully justified in Portland. For the last three generations, the "Rose City" has had a higher percentage of homeownership than most other American cities.

The shift to homeownership in Portland dates back to the real estate boom of 1905-1912 that followed the Lewis and Clark Exposition. A few statistics tell the story: Portland in 1900 ranked 26th among large American cities in the percentage of households that owned their own homes. Just ten years later, Portland ranked fifth in the nation; 46 percent owned homes compared to 32 percent for all other large cities.

Portland has maintained its edge ever since. Most recently, nearly two-thirds of the housing units in the Portland area have been owner occupied. The comparative figure for all metropolitan areas in the United States is approximately three-fifths.

High homeownership in Portland has resulted in a population that is not only stable but conservative, exhibiting a cautious approach to public issues. A long series of journalists have found Portland's temperament "prudent and placid," to quote Freeman Tilden's words in 1931, and have remarked on its beautiful homes and conservative leaders. Local historians Tom Vaughan and Terry O'Donnell similarly have noted Portland's measured pace of life and careful approach to growth. Very recently, a team of reporters from the Chicago *Tribune* found

Portland to have a "small-scale, low-key ambiance," based on its physical beauty, tranquility, and a lack of deep social divisions.

Portland's high percentage of home ownership has also affected its physical appearance. For a century, the city has been characterized by the free-standing single-family home. Historically, residents have been opposed to apartment construction in both the city and suburbs, viewing attached or row housing as unsuitable for Portland. Thus, Portlanders have built a low-rise metropolis where residents can enjoy the advantages of both a large city and low-density neighborhoods.

It is actually possible to read the history of Portland's growth in its changing types of single-family homes. Centered in the downtown core are three "growth rings," each made up of neighborhoods built at roughly the same time and representing thirty to forty years of Portland home building. Today, all three of these rings provide sound housing and viable neighborhoods to meet the needs of area residents.

The inner ring includes the remnants of Victorian Portland, that portion of the city built before 1905. The majority of the nineteenth-century houses have been lost to time, to urban renewal, and to development. Those that remain include spacious and handsome Queen-Anne-style houses as well as smaller frame cottages with elaborate millwork on their porches and gable ends. Most of these homes can be found in a crescent-shaped area of close-in neighborhoods on the west side, including Northwest,

Goose Hollow, King's Hill, and Lair Hill. A few others are scattered in Albina and the inner southeast side, which were the centers of separate suburbs until 1891.

What survives of Victorian Portland has been preserved with the help of local government. Neighborhood plans and rezoning in Northwest, Buckman, and Corbett-Terwilliger-Lair Hill have fended off some of the pressures of land conversion and demolition. Designation of individual landmarks and creation of the Lair Hill conservation district by the Landmarks Commission and City Council have also helped.

Portlanders built a "middle ring" of housing between 1905 and 1940. This era saw the development of fine neighborhoods that spread along the crest of the West Hills. Owners of new houses in Westover, Arlington Heights, Portland Heights, and Council Crest could overlook the older Victorian city with the assurance that they had achieved economic success. Many of these homes were built in an emerging regional style that ignored "period" references in favor of natural wood and cedar shingles blending architectural design with the natural setting.

The climax of this second era was emergence of a distinct style of residential architecture defined by the work of John Yeon and Pietro Belluschi during the 1930s and 1940s. Yeon's Watzek House was based on Oregon vernacular forms, while Belluschi's Joss House spotlighted local materials with exposed trusses, unfinished cedar paneling, and spruce siding. According to historian George McMath, Belluschi's Jennings-Sutor House of 1938 had all the characteristics of contemporary design with its "concern for the

setting and integration of landscaping, the open functional plan, the broad sheltering pitched roof, and the use of naturally finished native woods." By the time he moved east to head MIT's School of Architecture in 1951, Belluschi had helped to create an elegant but informal approach to housing that especially suited the needs of Portland and the Northwest.

On the east side, residential development in the first decades of the twentieth century followed the streetcar lines. Portlanders moved into dozens of new neighborhoods and subdivisions that stretched as far as six miles from downtown. The new communities ranged from Alameda to Woodstock and Woodlawn, from Sellwood to Sunnyside, Sabin and St. Johns. These areas were within a half-hour trolley ride of downtown in 1930; today, they are still only half an hour from downtown via Tri-Met. These communities are also marked by the survival of neighborhood shopping districts along the old trolley routes.

The home typical of these streetcar neighborhoods is the Portland bungalow. Only a decade ago, this Northwestern version of a California housing style seemed old-fashioned. Now we have rediscovered the appeal of wide porches, overhanging roofs, exposed rafter ends, and unboxed eaves. Today's real-estate ads show that this "Old Portland" style is popular once again. We have also discovered that the bungalow's open floor plan is as livable in the 1980s as it was seventy-five years ago. The Laurelhurst neighborhood, developed in the 1910s and 1920s, provides a particularly rich sampling of bungalow styles.

Public assistance has played an important role in maintaining the attractiveness of these middle-aged neighborhoods. Housing rehabilitation programs coordinated by the Portland Development Commission have made low-interest loans available for modernizing and improving more than 7,000 houses. Since 1974, Portland has used a higher percentage of its federal Housing and Community Development money for housing rehabilitation than almost any other city in the country. In a neighborhood like Irvington in Northeast Portland, the long-term impact of these efforts has been dramatic. At the same time, the city's Office of Neighborhood Associations has been available to assist community groups in improving city services and upgrading their environment.

Portland's outer ring consists of one-story neighborhoods built after 1945 and oriented to the automobile. On the east side of the Willamette, these suburbs run roughly east from 92nd Street, which marked the limit of streetcar and bus service before 1940, and south from the Multnomah-Clackamas county line. West of the river, new housing spilled down the far slope of the West Hills onto the rolling farmland of the Tualatin Valley. Annexations in Southwest Portland since 1950 have brought typical "suburban"

A garden grows near E. Belmont Street and S.E. 54th Avenue. (OHS)

areas within city limits. The greatest focus for growth since 1960, however, has been Washington County.

Growth of the one-story ring has been dependent on aid from the federal government. The loan insurance and guarantee programs of the Federal Housing Administration and Veterans Administration primed the huge building boom that added more than 300,000 housing units in the metropolitan area between 1950 and 1980. Federal grants for parks, planning, and especially sewers have made it economically feasible to build the new neighborhoods that thousands of Portlanders have preferred. Without this aid, growth in Washington and Multnomah counties would have been seriously slowed after 1970.

The "city of homes" has been the product of generations of private action and investment, with a healthy assist in recent decades from local and national government programs that have helped to preserve the oldest houses, to modernize middle-aged houses, and to finance the purchase of new houses.

A new-fangled traffic sign was the focus for this scene downtown. Mayor H. Russell Albee, mayor from 1913 to 1917, surveyed the situation at the left. Cars were increasing considerably on the main streets. (OHS)

CHAPTER V
MODERN TIMES

The problems and opportunities of modern times arrived in Portland with assistance from the Great War in Europe, which turned the city's tiny shipbuilding business into a major industry. The success of Germany's U-boat campaign in 1916 and 1917 spurred Allied orders with Portland shipbuilders to replace the lost merchant vessels. After the United States entered the war in April 1917, the U.S. Emergency Fleet Corporation made itself the sole customer for scores of Portland-built steel-hulled and wooden-hulled ships. Shipyard employment climbed to 28,000 at the end of 1918. Foundries, machine shops, and sawmills that supplied materials for the shipbuilders accounted for another 5,000 jobs. Rents rose; newcomers, attracted by wartime jobs, crowded the streets; and workers on three shifts kept the city open twenty-four hours a day.

Like most other Americans, Portlanders saw the war effort not only as a chance for a better job but also as a patriotic crusade from which there could be no dissent. Suspicions against immigrants, particularly Germans, ran high. German-born residents were required to carry a registration card to work near the waterfront. The Brooklyn neighborhood showed its loyalty by renaming streets, with Frankfurt Street becoming Lafayette and Bismarck becoming Bush, but City Council members ignored the Linnton workers, who wanted Germantown Road renamed Libertytown Road.

The loudest voice for 100-percent "Americanism" belonged to George Baker, who began his sixteen-year career as mayor in 1917, a few weeks after Congress declared war. His campaign promise that "smokestacks will be as numerous as the trees in the Forest" continued the tradition of business boosterism. A last-minute revelation that his labor-backed opponent had once applied for membership in the Socialist Party successfully played to a growing wartime hysteria. Baker led Liberty Bond rallies and held breakfasts at the Civic Auditorium for each contingent of Oregonians bound for the trenches in France. Throughout the war years eighty police officers dealt with "outside activities" such as registering aliens, raiding radical organizations, patrolling railroads and docks to ward off sabotage. Baker also enlisted the police on the side of management and "Americanism" in any labor dispute.

Baker was the most colorful politician in Portland's rather bland political history. He stood over six feet tall, weighed in at more than 200 pounds, and easily earned the nomination of the *Oregon Voter* magazine as "the champion loud noise of the Pacific Northwest." Born in The Dalles in 1868, he quit school at the age of nine to shine shoes and sell newspapers on the streets of San Francisco. He came to Portland in 1889 and worked his way up from the bottom in the theater business. By the first decade of the new century, he owned downtown theaters, managed his own stock company, and joined almost every club and organization in town. He served on City Council from 1898 to 1900 and again from 1907 to 1913, representing the downtown voters and vice

kings of Ward Four.

Portland's record of intolerance showed no improvement after the Armistice. Fears of international Bolshevism and domestic radicalism intensified in 1919 and 1920. These years also brought severe inflation and high unemployment as the shipyards shut down and veterans returned home. A general strike in Seattle early in 1919 and a November shootout in Centralia, Washington, between members of the American Legion and the radical Industrial Workers of the World (Wobblies) made the Portland establishment more than nervous. Mayor Baker's response was to raid the city's IWW offices and to prohibit banners announcing strikes or workers' meetings from the streets of Portland.

Two years later, seamen in the Pacific Northwest went out on strike against a 25-percent pay cut imposed by the U.S. Shipping Board. Violence came to the Portland waterfront on June 20 when police officers appeared on the docks in plain clothes and confronted pickets. The confused melee of gunfire that ensued ended with striker Nestor Varrio dead and his union hauled into court to fight a conspiracy charge. Confrontation on the waterfront occurred again in the fall of 1922, when 1,000 longshoremen and members of the Marine Transport Workers (affiliated with the IWW) walked off the job. George Baker put the weight of city government firmly on the side of the Water-

Small businesses were plentiful downtown. Among these were confectioneries—eighteen in just five blocks of Washington Street in 1921, as listed by the city directory. One was the Foss Confectionery, above, at 753 S.W. Washington Street, offering Fatima cigarettes, Dromedary dates, and other items. (OHS)

front Employers Association. City Council appropriated $10,000 to fight the "radical revolution." A hundred special police officers descended on the picket lines, arrested all known Wobblies as vagrants, and searched trains entering and leaving Union Station. On the same day that the strike was settled to the satisfaction of the employers, the mayor took credit for averting a revolution.

By the time of the dock strikes, Portland had also heard the appeal of the "Invisible Empire" of the Ku Klux

Above: *G.M. Standifer Construction Company, with yards at North Portland, shown here in 1918, and Vancouver, was just one of a number of firms active in World War I shipbuilding. This was a forerunner of an even bigger ship construction effort in the early 1940s in the Portland-Vancouver area. (OHS)*

Left: *Increased wartime economic vitality was reflected by plants such as the Grant Smith-Porter Ship Company at St. Johns. After the Armistice in 1918, waterfronts were glutted with ships, and contract cutbacks were rapid. (OHS)*

Klan. As it spread across the South, Middle West, and West in the early 1920s, the Klan appealed to Americans who were disturbed by the rapid pace of social change. The Klan's two million members—factory workers, dentists, storeowners, clerks, and craftsmen—were united by their fear that the familiar America was disappearing. The growth of the Klan was in part a reaction against the disturbing times of high prices, scarce jobs, and labor agitation. Klansmen blamed "outsiders" and "aliens"—particularly blacks, Jews, and Roman Catholic immigrants—for these social ills, and these groups bore the brunt of the Klan's attacks.

The Klan came to Portland in the summer of 1921, finding fertile soil in a largely Protestant community that had just experienced five years of turmoil. Kleagle Luther Powell was the chief organizer. The Exalted Cyclops was Fred Gifford, an electrician who had left his union for a job with Northwest Electric Company. It is unclear whether George Baker joined the Klan, but he certainly welcomed their support. Compared to other parts of the country, Portland's Kluxers largely refrained from vigilante

violence, and concentrated instead on the voting booth. In May 1922, Klan-backed candidates won two of three seats on the Multnomah County Commission and twelve of the county's thirteen seats in the state legislature. Portland supplied the victory margin in November for a statewide compulsory public school initiative, which was intended to make all private schools illegal, but the law was struck down by the U.S. Supreme Court before it went into

Above: Many ships produced in the Portland-Vancouver area during World War I were a boon for private shipping later when they were sold by the government. One typical ship was the West Kyska, *a steel freighter built in 1918 by Willamette Iron & Steel Works. Courtesy, Oregon State Library*

Below: Women with large hats predominated in this milling crowd at the Baker Theater shortly after the turn of the century. George Baker, who operated the business, started the Baker Stock Company, which presented many plays before movies and radio diminished the audience for live theater. (OHS)

effect. As in other cities and states, interest in the Klan declined when the novelty of their costumes and rhetoric wore off, and particularly when people discovered that Klan-backed politicians could be just as venal as the men they replaced.

By 1923 most Portlanders were more interested in enjoying their new automobiles and the products of postwar production than in rooting out Reds or fighting the imaginary threat of minorities. When the United States entered World War I, there was one automobile in Multnomah County for every thirteen residents. By 1925 the ratio increased to one automobile for five residents; and one for every 3.7 residents by 1929.

Automobiles were becoming a big business in Portland. At the end of the 1920s there were eighty dealers in the first "automobile rows" along North Broadway, between Tenth and Twenty-First west of downtown, and on the near east side. Portland residents spent as much on automobiles as they did on food and 8,000 depended directly on automobiles for their jobs according to the 1930 census.

As early as 1913, a hundred business and professional men formed a kind of posse of automobilists known as the "Flying Squadron," roaming town in their own cars to enforce ten- and fifteen-mile per-hour speed limits and generally trying to maintain order in the streets. The first comprehensive city code for motorists and pedestrians came in 1914. The police department set up an auto theft bureau in 1920 and a "speed squad" in 1922. Congestion downtown became a special headache as thousands of cars clogged narrow streets, fought streetcars for the right of way, and parked wherever they pleased. The twenties brought the first no-parking zones and the first automatic signals, though as late as 1931 only a quarter of downtown intersections had the two-color lights that announced their change from green to red with a clanging bell.

"Autoists" demanded wide, hard-surfaced roads and new bridges. The Interstate Bridge across the Columbia opened in 1917, connecting Portland to

VOTES FOR WORKERS

Far left: *Some groups agitated for improved working conditions before World War I, as illustrated by this 1914 poster of a woman worker. Some of these groups ran into a super-patriot backlash during the war, while improved economic conditions also frustrated attempts at reform.* (OHS)

Left: *Dr. Marie Equi, physician, pacifist, and birth control advocate, served ten months in San Quentin prison for her anti-military activities at Portland in World War I. In 1913 she suffered a fractured back when she was run down by mounted strikebreakers while she supported women strikers. Critics called her "the Bolshevik Queen."* (OHS)

Below: *The waterfront presented a picturesque, if somewhat rickety, appearance in 1919 as steamboats and other craft moved in and out of docks. About a decade later, wharves and riverside buildings between N.W. Glisan and S.W. Jefferson streets were removed to make way for a seawall. Courtesy, Alex Blendl*

Vancouver over an improved Patton Street, appropriately renamed Interstate Avenue. By 1924, motorists could follow the paved Pacific Highway from downtown Portland across the Broadway and Interstate bridges all the way to Tacoma and Seattle. The city spent millions widening east and west Burnside, Sandy Boulevard, Union Avenue, 82nd, and other arterial streets. Multnomah County put millions more into reconstructing the flimsy Burnside Bridge and building the Ross Island Bridge. While the new bridges served real needs, the Sellwood Bridge, built in 1925, and St. Johns Bridge, built in 1931, were harder to justify to taxpayers in terms of traffic; but they did help to tie the two historically isolated neighborhoods, for which they were named, more closely to the rest of the city.

Left: *The battleship Oregon, no longer considered necessary for the peacetime Navy of the 1920s, found a new home on the Willamette River. The ship was a reminder of Spanish-American War days, when the United States expanded its interests in the Caribbean and Pacific. Courtesy, Alex Blendl*

Below: *With its new seawall, the western side of the Willamette River presented a neat, uniform appearance by 1929. Warehouses and other buildings of East Portland are in the foreground. The Weatherly building, first skyscraper on the east side, was completed shortly after this photo was taken. Courtesy, The Neighborhoods Office, City of Portland*

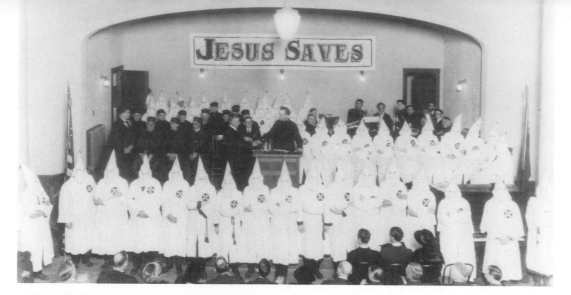

Left, top: *The Ku Klux Klan showed considerable political strength in Portland and elsewhere in Oregon in 1922. However, interest in the group soon ebbed. Nationwide, the KKK claimed five million members in the early 1920s. It opposed blacks, Jews, and other "un-American" people. (OHS)*

Left: *A Shrine group, one of many fraternal organizations in Portland, lined up in picturesque attire at the Masonic Temple. Several of the largest still-surviving downtown buildings were constructed by fraternal and social groups, including the Masonic Temple on the Park Blocks. (OHS)*

Below: *Cowboys were the inspiration for this patrol of Mooseheart Legion of the World, which won a fraternal orders drill contest at the Stock Yards at North Portland in 1929. Some of the city's social and fraternal groups demonstrated their skills in parades and drills. (OHS)*

Left: *Motorcycles were enlisted early in the auto age to chase speeding cars. City officials wrestled with speed limits, drunken driving, and other issues that had not been problems in the horse-and-buggy era.* (OHS)

Below: *Two parades, one from the east side, the other from the west, converged on the new Burnside Bridge at its opening day on May 28, 1926.* (OHS)

Automobiles and paved streets made it feasible to develop areas that had been inconvenient for streetcar riders. A building boom in the 1920s brought Portland 25,000 new houses. There was rapid development of sections of the West Hills where automobiles were almost a necessity for access. Builders and buyers also filled in vacant lots in east-side neighborhoods such as Eastmoreland, Mount Tabor, Grant Park, and Concordia, all of which were located three to six miles from the center of town. New high schools—Franklin, Roosevelt, and Grant—served the growing neighborhoods and provided a focus for community identity.

Prosperity during World War I and again in the early 1920s because of a thriving timber industry made it easier for immigrants or their children to move from core neighborhoods to new middle-class housing. Historian William Toll, for example, has traced the movement of successful Jewish shopkeepers and professionals from South Portland and older sections of Northwest Portland to Laurelhurst, Irvington, and Westover Terrace. Many German and Scandinavian families moved to newer and nicer housing within the northeast sector of the city in the post-World War I era.

These ethnic migrations opened older parts of Albina to a gradually growing black population. Before World War I, the majority of Portland's 1,000 blacks lived between Burnside, Glisan, Northwest Fifth, and Northwest Twelfth because of the area's convenience to hotel and railroad jobs. By the end of the thirties, the census counted 2,000 black residents. Only 130 were left in Northwest. More than half lived in Albina, where inexpensive older housing allowed widespread homeownership among stable working-class families and a smattering of businessmen and professionals.

Other blacks were scattered throughout the east side. Discrimination was a matter of knee-jerk prejudice. Realtors urged each other to confine home sales to Albina, and unions ranging from hotel workers to the longshoremen barred black members. The major hospitals admitted blacks as patients but refused to accept their applications as nurses.

New neighborhoods and more automobiles also meant the expansion of commercial strips along major streets. Eighty-second Avenue changed from a country road to a string of stores and gas stations between 1920 and 1940. The new Barbur Boulevard, built on an unused Southern Pacific railroad right-of-way in the early 1930s, avoided the same fate through protective zoning. Sandy Boulevard became the shrieking symbol of an automobile city. Architect Al Staehli has described it as "a linear Disneyland of buildings which were also the symbols of their function. Stucco shoes for shoe shops, gas pumps tucked under mushroom canopies, giant milk bottles crowding a dairy, jug taverns, and the grinning black-face entrance of the Coon Chicken Inn [now mercifully vanished] provided a series of visual exclamation points."

After 1924 zoning took on the larger function of protecting residential neighborhoods against the intrusion of businesses, apartment houses, and gas stations. George Baker and his establishment allies first proposed land-use zoning in 1919 and 1920 as a response to the wartime boom and its uncontrolled growth. Voters in 1920 narrowly rejected the plan, with most working-class neighborhoods opposed, and upper-middle class areas in favor. Banker John C. Ainsworth had argued that zoning would "harmonize the property interest of owners and the health, safety and convenience of the public," but many small property holders were suspicious of any restriction on development rights.

A second try succeeded in 1924. The simple code written jointly by the Planning Commission and Realty Board divided the city into four zones—one was limited to single-family houses; another allowed apartments; a third allowed businesses; and a final industrial zone allowed virtually anything else.

With the help of the automobile Portland carried on its intense love affair with the outdoors. One of the community's most enduring accomplishments was the Columbia River Highway, opened between Troutdale and Hood River in 1915 and completed to The Dalles in 1922. Engineer Sam Lancaster designed a road that complemented and

Top: *St. Johns Bridge rises 213 feet above the Willamette and has a main span of 1,207 feet. Construction started in 1929, and the $4-million bridge was dedicated in June 1931 as part of the Portland Rose Festival. Dr. D.B. Steinman of New York designed the span. (OHS)*

Above: *This pleased cab driver opened his door circa 1930 for contralto Ernestine Schumann-Heink, known for her operatic performances, touring recitals, and radio broadcasts. (OHS)*

blended with the spectacular landscape of the Columbia Gorge, achieving his aim "to find the beauty spots, or those points where the most beautiful things along the line might be seen to the best advantage, and if possible to locate the road in such a way as to reach them." The highway was built jointly by Multnomah County and the state, with essential help from millionaire lumbermen Simon Benson and John Yeon. The *Portland City Directory* called the high-

way "America's newest and greatest pathway for the recreationist." Hotels, auto camps, and restaurants sprang up in the Gorge towns, and the U.S. Forest Service opened a campground at Eagle Creek and set aside its first "Recreation Reserve" of 14,000 acres. Completion of a paved road to Tillamook and Seaside and a highway loop around Mount Hood in the 1920s brought the outdoors even closer to mobile Portlanders.

Portland slid inexorably from good times to bad after 1929. The city as a whole escaped the worst ravages that the Great Depression brought to Eastern industrial cities and Southwestern farmers, but local business grew worse and worse over four very long years. The Depression cut the city's exports and banking activity by more than half. The value of new construction in 1933 and again in 1934 was scarcely over two million dollars—6 percent of the 1925 record. Business failures peaked in 1932, but the worst was still to come for retailers. Thousands of families dug up their backyards for vegetable gardens and canceled their telephone service to save a few dollars a month. Theater owners went broke for lack of

customers despite drawings and give-aways. Two of every three small businesses were behind on their property taxes by 1933.

When Franklin D. Roosevelt took office, the Portland Public Employment Bureau listed 24,000 unemployed householders. Welfare payments, though inadequate, helped to support 9,100 families. From May 1932 through the end of the year, the City of Portland sold $845,000 in bonds to fund work relief projects. Eighteen thousand men signed up for jobs and 4,000 actually went to work on park and street improvements. In March 1933, when the money ran out, the city continued the program by paying the workers with scrip—formal IOU's which 2,500 merchants agreed to accept as cash, with the promise that the city would later redeem the scrip at full value.

Beyond the public jobs programs, the 1930s were a time when communities helped themselves out of necessity. The Catholic Women's League found temporary jobs for 500 women and girls in 1932 and gave short-term assistance to 500 others. The members of the Council of Jewish Women opened a bake shop to give supplemental employment to poorer residents of South Portland. The city's most prestigious families rallied around the Portland Symphony Society with contributions and memberships to keep the symphony playing in the 1931-

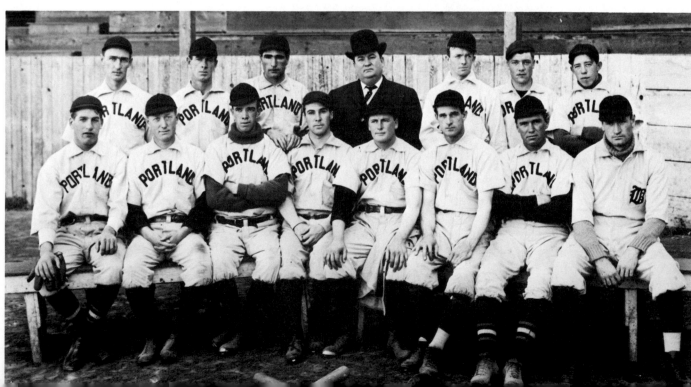

Rilcy joining Carson ar
position. The liberal Ra
joined in the minority b
mond Bean, who would
Council from 1933 to 1
from 1948 to 1966.

Not just the City Co
tire community was div
Longshore strike of 19
most bitter labor-mana
Portland's history. Sinc
1922, in which the wor
land's docks had been
employers. In the fall c
sponse to deteriorating
tions and wage cuts, th
Longshoremen's Assoc
ganized a single local
cific Coast. A coastwid
on May 9, 1934, and c

1932 season.

The citywide Council of Social Agencies organized ten neighborhood councils in 1934 to coordinate services for children and fight juvenile delinquency. By the late 1930s many of the councils had expanded their concern to the larger issue of neighborhood livability and to problems such as housing, health, and city services. These groups were the predecessors for Portland's neighborhood associations that have developed in the last twenty years.

Portlanders who went unassisted by public and private relief agencies often ended up in one of the city's "Hoovervilles"—shantytowns for the homeless. The biggest of these stretched along the slopes of Sullivan's Gulch from the Union and Grand avenue overpasses to 21st Street. Hundreds of men lived in self-built shacks made with scrounged lumber, scraps from construction sites, and liberated tarpaper. Much like a frontier mining camp, the settlement had its own rules and its own informal leadership. There were other squatter settlements at Ross Island and on the filled site of Guild's Lake.

The Depression polarized Portland politics. A wide spectrum of views and bitter arguments replaced the unventuresome "hail-fellow-well-met" City Council of the 1920s. On one extreme was the Red-baiting councilman J.E. Bennett, described even by the conservative *Oregon Voter* as contentious and obnoxious. At the other extreme was Councilman Ralph Clyde, a strong and persistent advocate for municipal ownership of electric utilities. Joseph Carson, mayor from 1933 to 1940, was a states' rights Democrat who worked hard to keep the New Deal out of Portland. He was a special friend of the private utilities and an enemy of organized labor. Proposals for new government programs such as public housing often lost three votes to two, with future mayor Earl

Left: *Simon Benson purchased and donated land that included Multnomah Falls and Wahkeena Falls as part of the Columbia River highway project. Benson was not only a wealthy lumberman, hotel builder (The Benson and Columbia Gorge Hotel), and temperance advocate, but he also donated Benson Polytechnic School to Portland. (OHS)*

Below: *Open-air touring cars carried passengers past scenic landmarks such as Shepherd's Dell on the Columbia River Highway. Courtesy, Cross and Dimmitt*

provided paychecks for 5,000 workers and held out the possibility of transforming Portland into what FDR described as "a vast city of whirling machinery."

New Deal liberals in Oregon hoped for an independent Columbia Valley Authority that would distribute the new power at equal rates throughout the Northeast. But the Portland Chamber of Commerce, Mayor Carson, and a procession of businessmen argued that Bonneville's electricity should be available at lower rates within a fifty-mile radius of the turbines. A Congressional compromise created the Bonneville Power Administration to market electricity

Left: One of the Northwest's largest art projects was completed in the Depression. The Reverend Bernard F. Geiser, a priestartist, worked on murals at St. Mark's Episcopal Church for seven years, starting in 1931. Courtesy, Oregon Journal, (OHS)

Below: Despite poor economic times, the Rose Festival continued, helping unite and entertain the community. Decorated floats pass the Oregon Journal Building in 1931. (OHS)

nately, the only injury was to the reputation of Portland. This incident, plus the threat of holding up Bonneville, gave Wagner leverage to force employers to agree to arbitration. Portland's establishment worked out the painful details in a secret meeting at the Arlington Club, tacitly recognizing the union by agreeing to submit the dispute to arbitration. The victorious longshoremen went back to work on July 31.

As Portland's business community well knew, the best chance for a new Portland during the troubled years of the Depression was the development of cheap hydroelectric power. From Franklin D. Roosevelt's visit to dedicate the site in August 1934 to official completion in September 1937, Portlanders on weekend excursions could watch the great bulk of Bonneville Dam rise across the channel of the Columbia forty miles east of the city. Construction

from Grand Coulee Dam as well as Bonneville over a grid connecting Portland, Spokane, and Seattle-Tacoma.

The key decisions involving Bonneville came in 1940. First, voters in the May primary turned down the creation of a public utility district which would have been empowered to buy out Northwest Electric (now PP&L) and Portland Electric Power (now PGE). As a result, private utilities remained the intermediaries that brought hydro power from BPA and retailed it to consumers. Second, the Bonneville Power Administration offered to sell cheap energy directly to major industries to encourage economic development. In January Alcoa Aluminum signed the first direct contract for its new aluminum reduction plant in Vancouver. By the following year, Bonneville electricity was also powering federally owned aluminum operations at Troutdale and at Longview, Washington. Within a decade, the dam

had made electro-chemical and electro-metallurgical industries the leading manufacturing sector in the greater Portland region.

The practicalities of power policy (and politics) defined one direction for a post-Depression Oregon. Portlanders who wanted other choices could listen to Lewis Mumford, the nation's leading writer on urban planning who visited in the summer of 1938. In a speech to the City Club and in a pamphlet called *Regional Planning in the Northwest,* Mumford called for active yet careful regional planning. He advised Portland to stabilize its population to allow time

Above: *Mayor Joseph Carson conferred with Fiorello LaGuardia, New York City's reform mayor, during a LaGuardia visit in 1940. (OHS)*

Above, left: *The mayor's job includes many ceremonial duties, along with weightier chores. Portland mayor Earl Riley was chosen to place crowns on two winners at the Redhead Roundup at Delake, a coastal community. Delake was later absorbed into Lincoln City. (OHS)*

Above: *A public market was a long-time downtown feature at S.W. Fifth Avenue and S.W. Yamhill Street. About 1930 William C. Hoffman's floral stand provided a colorful display at the market. In 1984 a new Yamhill Market was completed two blocks east. (OHS)*

Left: *President Franklin D. Roosevelt, with Mrs. Roosevelt and Governor Charles E. Martin of Oregon, visited Bonneville Dam for its dedication on September 28, 1937. Roosevelt pushed a button to start the first power unit. On the same day, he also dedicated Timberline Lodge. Courtesy, Oregon Journal*

Left: *The partially completed Bonneville Dam loomed impressively at the rugged Cascades of the Columbia in 1936. Since the arrival of the first settlers travelers had been forced to bypass these rough waters. Completion of the dam resulted in the flooding of the Cascades. (OHS)*

Below: *Motor vehicles proved useful in a variety of ways. Multnomah County Library began using trucks to bring books to patrons. J.J. Phillips was the driver of this truck, and page Esther Hawkes was seated at the table in this 1932 scene. (OHS)*

to clean up thousands of unfit houses, overcrowded apartments, and slum hotels. He also suggested decentralizing new industry into satellite towns whose carefully chosen locations and reliance on electricity would protect the natural environment.

Mumford set his suggestions within an even broader challenge to Portland's abiding conservatism:

I have seen nothing so tempting as a home for man as this Oregon country . . . and I am going to ask you a question which you may not like. Are you good enough to have this country in your possession? Have you got enough intelligence, imagination, and cooperation among you to make best use of these opportunities? . . . In providing for new developments you have an opportunity here to do a job of city planning like nowhere else in the world.

In fact, it took another thirty years of boom, bust, and business as usual before Portland and Oregon came to agreement on an agenda for the future. Not until the administration of Governor Tom McCall in the early 1970s would the sort of regional planning that Mumford called for attract the necessary combination of political leadership and popular support.

Wartime shortages of gas and tires forced many shipyard workers to ride the bus. This shift-change scene is at Oregon Shipbuilding Corporation near the mouth of the Willamette River about 1943. (OHS)

CHAPTER VI
THE WAR AND AFTER

World War II brought more excitement to Portland than anything since the great Exposition. In the language of city officials who worried about problems of the home front, the Portland metropolis was a "congested war production area." But in terms of the pace of daily life, it was a boom town—another Leadville or Dawson City with defense contracts in place of gold and silver mines.

Portland's new boom came from a single industry— shipbuilding. The first federal orders for new ships went to the Commercial Iron Company, the Albina Shipyard, and Albina Iron and Steel in 1940 and 1941. Industrialist Henry Kaiser of California, fresh from the construction of Boulder and Grand Coulee dams, also opened the huge Oregon Shipbuilding Company north of St. Johns in 1941. His Swan Island and Vancouver yards went into production two months after Pearl Harbor.

At the peak of wartime production in 1943 and 1944, metropolitan Portland counted 140,000 defense workers. Federal contracts totaled $2.4 billion for more than 1,000 oceangoing ships. The record-breaker for construction time was a Liberty ship launched on September 23, 1942, less than eleven days after workers laid down its keel.

The boom brought thousands of new faces to Portland. The Kaiser yards placed help-wanted ads in eleven states. The response almost emptied the rest of Oregon, and drew the unemployed from small towns in Idaho and Montana. Workers were brought in by chartered trains from the East Coast. Portland's population grew from 501,000 to 661,000 between 1940 and 1944. One could safely assume, in the war years, that every third person standing in line for the bus or a double feature was a newcomer to the city.

This phenomenal growth brought unprecedented problems for local governments. The job explosion on the north side of the city strained public transportation in an era of gasoline and tire rationing. Two hundred new buses, 150 trucks, and ferry service across the Willamette to Swan Island were scarcely enough to keep up with the demand. The tens of thousands of shipyard workers, many of whom were unmarried or without their families, also had money for liquor, gambling, and prostitution. While the circulation of books from the public library dropped, the pari-mutuel handle at the dog tracks skyrocketed. A clean-up drive in 1942 swept out the red light district north of Burnside. Gamblers, however, simply moved their shops to the side streets. Protection of public safety was especially difficult since the military services took about half of the city's police officers and firefighters.

With a seemingly endless demand for workers, the Portland and Vancouver shipyards provided high-paying jobs for tens of thousands of Portland women. By the end of 1943, the 20,500 women employed at the Kaiser yards made up nearly a quarter of their total work force. One out of three of these women filled the sorts of office jobs that were already open to women, but hundreds of others who had recently graduated from training classes at Benson High filled

jobs as electricians, painters, machinists, and pipefitters. More than 5,000 earned what was then an impressive $1.20 per hour as welders. Welder Ree Adkins later remembered that "in all this kind of work, the women and men were paid the same ... there didn't seem to be a speck of jealousy. The men did the same things that we did." Other women at Swan Island, Kaiser-Vancouver, Commercial Ironworks, Willamette Iron and Steel, and smaller firms were tool checkers, ship fitters, warehouse clerks, and shipwright helpers. Newly employed mothers relied on an instantly devised childcare system made possible by federal subsidies to the schools, to nonprofit agencies, and to employers. Kaiser's special Women's Services Department operated childcare centers on round-the-clock shifts synchronized with those of the shipyards and provided

"*Here comes Mom with her home work!*"

Special publications were issued for shipyard workers in World Wars I and II, telling of production activity and promoting good work habits. The best known in the Portland area in the 1940s was the Bos'n's Whistle, *a Kaiser publication, which printed this cartoon. Courtesy, Bos'n's Whistle*

take-out meals that could be ordered ahead of time and picked up by busy wives on their way home.

The influx of new residents affected the availability of housing as early as the spring of 1941. Newcomers fought for shelter in a city where only one out of every two hundred houses and apartments was for rent. Rented rooms and decent family apartments were at a premium.

By the time the United States entered the war, few observers thought Portland would be able to cope with its growth. Long-time residents regarded their new neighbors with mixed emotions—puzzlement, hostility, and often jealousy of their relatively high wages. "The people of Portland make it clear that an Arkie or Okie is the most undesirable person on earth," complained one refugee from the dust bowl. A writer for *Fortune* magazine summed it up: "Portland neither likes nor knows how to accommodate its Virginia City atmosphere."

Portland's actual record included a mixture of accomplishments and missed opportunities. On the positive side, it met the immediate emergency and managed to house 150,000 extra people. But at the same time, the city emerged from the war with a legacy of problems, and its leaders often took the easy route and treated only the short-range symptoms.

Portland's response to the housing emergency represented both aspects of its wartime experience. As industry began to mobilize during 1941, the City Planning Commission tried to meet housing needs with Columbia Villa, Portland's first public housing project, which offered newcomers 400 apartments near the shipyards on north Woolsey Avenue. Although its low-rise design and wide lawns pleased architects, the elaborate process of selecting among competing sites seemed excessively cumbersome.

The focus shifted from permanent to temporary housing when the City Council created the Housing Authority of Portland as an emergency measure.

Days after the attack on Pearl Harbor, the council picked a realtor, a banker, an apartment owner, and a union leader to serve on the new agency. Their goal was not to use public housing to shape a more efficient or pleasant city, but to build the minimum number of necessary units, which could be torn down after the war.

The housing crisis peaked in the summer of 1942, when federal officials projected the need for 30,000 additional rooms and apartments. Edgar Kaiser, managing his father's enterprises in Portland, took direct action. At a closed-door meeting in August, he signed a contract with the United States Maritime Commission for an immense 6,000-unit housing development (soon increased to 10,000 units). To the astonishment of city officials, Kaiser broke ground soon after Labor Day. Nearly 5,000 construction workers descended on one square mile of Columbia River floodplain outside the Portland city limits—the present site of Delta Park—to begin construction of 700 identical buildings. Less than six months later, on December 12, 1942, the first tenants moved into the instant city of Vanport.

Vanport paid a price for its hasty development. Though the "miracle city" had been built from a single blueprint, Housing Authority director Harry Freeman vehemently denied that it was a "planned city." Recognizing the antipathy of Portland's business leaders to anything that reminded them of government planning through New Deal programs, Freeman insisted that Vanport "grew on paper and on the ground as many other American cities have grown." With a population that exceeded 40,000 by 1944, Vanport was the nation's largest housing project and was billed as the second largest "city" in Oregon. No amount of promotion, however, could conceal the reality of its dull

gray buildings awash in a sea of winter mud.

It was the responsibility of the Housing Authority to maintain public safety in Vanport and to provide the minimum of social services such as schools and recreation. The former city manager of Oregon City took on the job of community manager. Although members of the social work staff tried to build community cohesion through tenant councils, the Authority ignored them more often than not. It was equally cautious about a proposal for a community newspaper. The result of this general disinterest was that nothing in either the development's community life or its crackerbox design could convince residents that Vanport was anything more than a huge tourist camp.

Vanport also contributed toward establishing racial segregation as a fact of Portland life. The city's black population had increased from 2,100 to 15,000 during the war and presented Portlanders with a new challenge that they largely failed to meet. During 1943, when the black migration had reached significant proportions, the weekly *People's Observer* chronicled racial incidents on the city buses, harassment by the police, and conflict with the segregated Boilermakers Union. Plans to set up a segregated USO in Northeast Portland were an additional slap in the face to many blacks.

Housing lay at the heart of the racial tensions. In 1942, white workers complained about sharing shipyard dormitories with blacks. For both single black men and black families, little private housing was available outside the Albina neighborhood in near northeast Portland. Neighborhood groups raised loud protests at every rumor of new black residents moving into their areas. Former City Commissioner J.E. Bennett even went so far as to suggest that Kaiser stop hiring black workers. Mayor

Earl Riley agreed in private that the racial migration threatened Portland's "regular way of life."

During the course of the war, the black population of Albina rose from 2,000 to 3,000, but most of the newcomers found homes in Portland and Vancouver defense housing projects where they were effectively segregated from the majority of Portlanders. The Housing Authority blandly denied a policy of discrimination, but it carefully steered the thousands of blacks at the Vanport and Guild's Lake projects into certain sections and buildings. Vanport blacks sent their children to integrated schools but there was a segregated hospital. The Multnomah County sheriff's office triggered a series of nasty confrontations when it tried to enforce segregated use of recreation centers.

By V-J Day, Vanport housed a largely segregated population of 6,000 blacks in addition to thousands of white veterans and their families, who occupied temporary quarters while the civilian housing market hurried to meet their needs. Until the Columbia River flood of May 30, 1948, which wiped out the "instant city" and forced its black residents to crowd into Albina, Vanport provided Portland a convenient district where blacks could be isolated from the rest of the city.

Vanport's postwar record had been mixed. Many established Portlanders shuddered at its undeserved reputation for crime and were quietly relieved when the brown floodwaters tore its buildings from their foundations and swirled them into a logjam of broken memories. But for many demobilized veterans, the college-level courses offered at the Vanport Extension Center by the Oregon State Board of Higher Education opened the door of new opportunity. When the classes were relocated to the old Lincoln High School building in downtown Portland in 1952, after a stopover at the old Oregon Shipyards, the city was well on its way to gaining its own public university. The legislature recognized it as Portland State College in 1955.

Portlanders greeted the end of the war with an immense sigh of relief. The

Albina, once a separate community, became home for many of the blacks moving into Portland. Businesses serving the residents occupied old Victorian buildings along N. Williams Avenue, shown above at N.E. Russell Street in 1962. (OHS)

Left: *Shipyard jobs were terminated soon after the end of hostilities, but many employees who had come from other states decided to stay. A large number of blacks found homes in North Portland. Young North Portlanders are shown here in 1949 at a neighborhood dance. Courtesy,* Oregon Journal, *(OHS)*

Below: *Stunned residents were able to move some vehicles to safety after the Columbia River inundated Vanport, but many were swept away by the rising waters. At the right is the N. Denver Avenue ramp, part of a dike system that was supposed to have protected the community. (OHS)*

Oregonian noted in 1945 that a few younger entrepreneurs were working diligently at industrial development, but that older and established businessmen were shrugging off their aggressive promotional efforts with the argument that Portland and its hinterland lacked the customers to attract manufacturing. Writing two years later in the *Saturday Evening Post,* journalist Richard Neuberger argued that "most Portlanders, if polled by Doctor Gallup, would probably say they want their city to go on being the sort of place it has always been. This means a slow and easygoing trading center, with lumber its principal shipment and scenery the great nonexportable resource." Having experienced the fever of the shipbuilding boom, residents were grateful that the economic and social temperature of their city was dropping back down to normal. Neuberger—a liberal Democrat later to be

elected to the United States Senate—
made the observation that everything in
Portland was slowing down, from the
speed of its traffic to its search for new
industries to replace wartime shipbuilding.

In the first decade after the war,
Portland voters consistently turned
down spending measures that would
have improved the quality of life. Voters
did approve $24 million in bonds in
May 1944, to fund highway, sewer,
dock, and school projects called for by
city planner Robert Moses in a special
report titled *Portland Improvement.* But
they later followed by rejecting tax increases or bond measures for a civic
center, a war memorial, sewer improvements, urban redevelopment, and general city expenditures. Voters also turned

down a forty-hour work week and pay
increases for city employees. They rejected an ordinance to make racial discrimination a misdemeanor; a proposal
to establish low-income housing in 1950;
and bond issues for the zoo and symphony in 1952. Portlanders carefully

filled their school board positions with realtors who could be trusted to keep property taxes low. A climax of sorts came to this conservative era in the spring of 1958, when Portlanders handed a stinging defeat to proposals for public transit funding and for a ten-year capital improvements program.

The city did flirt briefly with political change in 1948. Even during his wartime vice crackdown, Mayor Earl Riley had complained that it made more sense to regulate illegitimate businesses than to try to legislate human nature. It became apparent to concerned citizens soon after the war that many law enforcement officials were living well beyond their salaries. Riley's new police chief was Lee Jenkins, an old friend who had served sixteen years in the same position for George Baker and who was unlikely to reform the department. In January 1948, the nationally respected criminal justice expert August Vollmer, whom Riley had hired as consultant under pressure, found the Portland police to be demoralized and mismanaged. A month later, the City

Above: *Writer Richard Neuberger and his wife Maurine from Portland were the first husband-wife team in the Oregon State Legislature. (OHS)*

Left: *Locomotives headed for the Soviet Union under the Lend-Lease program were photographed at the Guild Lake yards about 1945. (OHS)*

Facing page, top: *Farmers, peddlers, and wholesale and retail buyers gathered at the Eastside Farmers' Market in 1949. Courtesy, James Rayner, (OHS)*

Facing page, bottom: *Lambert Gardens survived for a while into the postwar era. (OHS)*

Club counted eleven brothels and ten gambling dens that operated openly in the old red-light district north of Burnside.

Finance Commissioner Dorothy McCullough Lee stepped forward to challenge Riley in the May 1948 primary election when it looked as if the downtown establishment was willing to go along with business as usual. After her victory and inauguration as mayor in 1949, Lee reinvigorated the vice squad and took on the issue of basic reform in Portland's governmental structure. Asserting that rapid growth required a more efficient municipal administration, she appointed businessmen and civic leaders to a Committee on Municipal Reorganization. However, the city council balked at placing a city manager charter, recommended by the

mayor's committee, on the ballot, as individual commissioners defended their independent domains. Lacking the support of the daily papers, which argued that Portland enjoyed quite adequate, if somewhat unwieldly government, the city manager advocates failed to gather enough signatures for their petitions to place the proposal on the ballot.

After Portlanders refused Dorothy Lee a second term in 1952, city politics moved on two levels for the next decade and a half. Day-to-day decisions were dominated by three men who became local institutions. Public Works Commissioner William Bowes (1939-1969) modeled himself on Robert Moses and snorted at what he considered the disastrous notions of Lee and other reformers. Finance Commissioner Ormond Bean (1948-1966) was a curious combination of liberal and pragmatist who liked to bombard other members of City Council with pedantic memos. Mayor Terry Schrunk (1956-1971) walked the line between fiscal caution and the implementation of city projects. Whether his leadership seemed temperate or plodding depended on one's own point of view.

During the same years, citizens who had been disappointed by the failure of the city manager movement in 1950 could take heart from the continuation of what the *Oregonian* called "a line of municipal reform that had been bubbling for a decade or more." An impressive array of reports by legislative study commissions, the City Club, and the Public Administration Service all pointed to shortcomings in city government. A Committee for Effective City Government revived the city manager idea in 1957-1958 with support from the League of Women Voters, Junior Chamber of Commerce, Young Democrats, the *Oregonian,* and the *Oregon Journal.* Determined opposition from Bowes, Schrunk, and labor unions con-

Left: *Dorothy McCullough Lee, mayor from 1948 to 1953, tossed out a baseball to start a Portland game. Lee served in the Oregon House of Representatives and Senate and was a city commissioner before her election as mayor on an anti-gambling platform. (OHS)*

Facing page, top: *Ice hockey players, shown here in 1945, competed with baseball for fans' interest. The hockey teams went through several name changes, becoming Winter Hawks by the early 1980s. In the 1970s professional basketball began to dominate the local headlines for sports fans. (OHS)*

Facing page, bottom: *A public accustomed to American aerial feats in World War II began riding airplanes in greatly increasing numbers after the war. Air controllers, shown here in 1948, were needed to control the Portland traffic. They were, from left, William Palmer, Bernard Bastord, and Ralph Bateman. (OHS)*

vinced Portlanders to turn down the proposal by a margin of 7,000 votes. The same groups backed a proposal for a strong mayor charter in 1966, but that also went down to defeat. Portlanders were at the least consistent in their opposition to a strong executive for their city government.

It was fear of failure that aroused Portland from its hibernation. As early as 1953, the *Oregon Journal* had posed the question: "Big league city or sad sack town?" The recession of 1958-1959 had a painful impact on real estate development and underscored the weakness of downtown businesses. Retailers in the central core bounded by Burn-

side, Jefferson, and Twelfth did less business in 1960 than they had immediately after the war. The number of people coming downtown for movies, doctor's appointments, and shopping had dropped by a third. The census of 1960 brought another disappointment when it recorded a small loss of population within the city limits (373,628 to 372,676). Population for the entire metropolitan area was up only 16 percent for the decade—just half the growth rate of booming Seattle.

With its relatively slow growth overall, no one would have described postwar Portland as an "exploding metropolis" like San Jose or Los Angeles. In the sedate Portland style, however, more and more residents chose to load their station wagons and head for a house in the suburbs. Clackamas County added 26,000 residents in the 1950s. Washington County added 31,000. Eastern

Left: *Jane Powell was a former Portland resident whose career was followed closely by the Rose City populace. Television had started making inroads into family attendance at films when this 1955 musical, "Hit the Deck," was released, but times were still good for downtown theaters. Courtesy, The Columbian*

Below: *Multnomah County Fair was crowded with fun-seekers in August 1961 at Gresham, a community that experienced rapid post-war growth. The fair later was moved to Multnomah County Exposition Center, in Delta Park, sharing a multi-purpose area with other events. (OHS)*

Multnomah County from the city line to the Sandy River was the most popular destination with a gain of 50,000. The under-engineered lanes of the Banfield Freeway gave "east county" the area's first limited access freeway as it crept inward from the town of Fairview to Union Avenue and helped to attract families to new subdivisions in Parkrose, Powellhurst, Rockwood, and Gresham. The first generation of shopping centers along 82nd Street and 102nd Street and the commercial ribbons along the arterial roads served the needs of auto-oriented suburbanites and set a direct challenge to downtown businesses. The total suburban population in the three counties surpassed that of the City of Portland in 1962.

An intangible factor that prodded Portland into action was a change in the population mix. Portland was an aging city at mid-twentieth century. Despite the influx of young workers during the war years Portland had far more than its share of retirement-age residents. The median age in the city in 1950 was over 35, compared to 30 for the United States as a whole. By the early sixties, however, a steady decline in the number of elderly voters reduced the power of the group most likely to vote against tax increases. In their place came the most rapidly increasing group of Portlanders, men and women in the ambitious years from the late teens into the early thirties, who were likely to see the benefits of an active local government.

The key step in Portland's revitalization was the use of the federal urban renewal program to remake the southern edge of downtown. Portland planners had toyed with urban renewal in the early 1950s but found little support in the unadventurous political climate. In 1956, however, members of the Planning Commission and City Council took the plunge and designated fifty-four square blocks of the South Portland neighborhood as an urban renewal district. Their intention was to clear the land for a planned coliseum. The federal government awarded a grant in May 1956.

Portland's politicians had long neglected the public. East-side Portlanders

Unemployed men have long loitered on Skid Road around Burnside Street. In recent years the territory available to them on the west side of the Willamette has shrunk because of the construction of new buildings. Courtesy, Fred DeWolfe

A crowd milled inside the giant Forestry Building to view an exhibit following the building's rededication in 1952. The log building was a relic of the Lewis and Clark Exposition of 1905. It was destroyed by fire in 1964. (OHS)

had complained for decades that city buildings were always located on the wrong side of the Willamette for the majority of citizens. The old feud heated up in 1956 when an east-side businessman led a petition drive to put the location of the coliseum to a vote. In May and again in November, voters defied the advice of downtown businessmen, politicians, and newspapers and voted for construction east of the river. But federal administrators, who had been persuaded by the city's plaintive portrait of South Portland as a hopeless slum in need of clearance, refused to transfer their grant to the east side. When the new Development Commission was organized in 1958, it had an urban renewal site but no idea what to do with it. Not until 1960, when the Oregon Highway Department decided to swing the loop of Interstate 405 *south* of the renewal area, was it clear that the south end could successfully be considered part of the downtown.

There is no doubt that South Portland was simultaneously an eyesore and a real neighborhood. The eighty-four acres inside the project boundaries were a jumble of junkyards, marginal businesses, and abandoned storefronts that had lost their usefulness with the disappearance of streetcar and interurban service. Most of the area's buildings were survivors from the nineteenth century, and 60 percent were officially substandard. Rundown apartments and narrow streets were an annoyance to commuters and housewives heading downtown from the southwest hills. At the same time, many residents remembered the days when South Portland had been the first stop for Italian and Jewish immigrants, with the shops and social organizations that eased the transition to American life. The Development Commission evacuated 2,300 people before the bulldozers arrived. A third were over sixty years old; two-thirds lived alone or as couples without

THE RIVERS AND THE PORT

Like other river cities, Portland is a working city built around a working river.

On a typical Portland day, half a dozen ships load at the docks and terminals that line the Willamette from the city center to its confluence with the Columbia River. Auto carriers or container ships cast off from new terminals on the Columbia itself. The ships carry such cargoes as grain, wood chips, lumber and logs, scrap metal, and merchandise that has arrived on barge tows down the Columbia-Snake river system, or on freight trains and trucks from Oregon's farms, forests, and orchards.

From the city's bridges and bluffs, Portlanders can see a waterfront lined with grain elevators and flour mills, chemical tank farms, cement plants, shipyards, factories, and warehouses. With more workers in wholesaling, finance, trade, and transportation than many cities of its size, Portland is a regional commercial metropolis. Sales agents, shipping clerks, and insurance brokers who handle the paperwork for this riverfront enterprise overlook the river from downtown offices. Although not all employment is directly tied to the river trade, 70 percent of the jobs in the city of Portland and 50 percent in the metropolitan areas are located within a mile of either the Willamette or Columbia.

Besides serving as a center of Portland's industries, the Willamette also enhances the city's visual ambiance. The river flows high in the winter and spring, carrying a runoff that is twice as great as that of the entire Colorado River basin. By summer's end, when the snow has melted from the Cascades, the river has slowed enough for fishing and canoeing. Whether high or calm, the Willamette cuts an open space through Portland's center that sets off views in both directions. Looking down from the hills west of downtown, the river appears as a seam which joins the two halves of the city together.

Like other river cities, Portland is conservative in both social values and politics. It is a city content to have its pace set by the flow of its rivers and the cycle of their seasons.

Facing page: *The crew of the Hassalo poses circa 1900. (OHS)*

Top, left: *The La Rochefoucauld docks at the Pacific Coal Company. (OHS)*

Top, right: *A steamboat passes under the Steel Bridge in 1912 while it was under construction. (OHS)*

Above: *The small fleet of the Shaver Transportation Company was arrayed near the foot of Washington Street in 1897. (OHS)*

Left: *A tugboat tows a log raft past oceangoing vessels in this early 1960s view. (OHS)*

133

Left: *Crowds turned out for a Portland Air Terminal airshow in 1958. The airport east of the site of the city of Vanport had been developed on low, flat land near the Columbia that had been a special favorite of golf course developers. (OHS)*

Left, below: *Nurses were an attentive audience at an observation clinic at the University of Oregon Medical School. A major medical complex was developed on Marquam Hill, comprising Veterans Administration and Oregon Health Sciences University facilities. (OHS)*

Facing page: *Even before Vietnam demonstrations, protests were part of the Portland scene. In October 1962 "Women for Peace" joined students in protesting the U.S. blockade of Cuba. (OHS)*

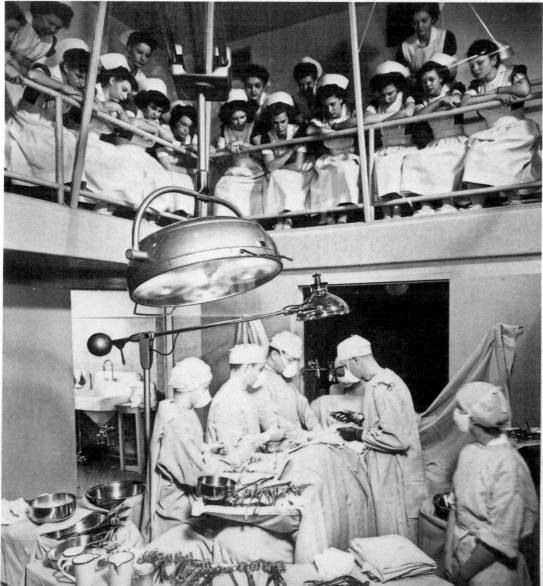

Above: *Whites and blacks joined in a 1963 "march of mourning" on N. Williams Avenue following the killing of civil rights leader Medgar Evers in Mississippi. (OHS)*

Left: *Members of the Albina Neighborhood Improvement Association broke ground in 1964 during a tree-planting drive. (OHS)*

children. Nearly all depended on cheap rents in crumbling hotels and apartments and found companionship in informal neighborhood networks.

The successful start of the "South Auditorium" renewal project made it easy for City Council to extend the boundaries north to Market Street in 1966 and to designate another forty-eight-acre renewal zone to assist the expansion of Portland State College. Compared to the architecturally bombastic Aztec temples and concrete launching pads built in urban renewal areas all over the United States, the plan for South Portland, prepared by the firm of Skidmore, Owings and Merrill, warrants at least a B-plus for handsome urban design. The plan follows the hillside contours with small parks, gardens, and walkways that preserve pedestrian scale. The new office towers and high-rise apartments work with the site rather than overwhelm it. The Lovejoy and Forecourt fountains flow, in a seemingly natural pattern, across the sloping site. The Portland State campus uses the South Park Blocks to link the urban university to its city.

The east side of the Willamette also witnessed a spectacular change in the early 1960s. In a warm morning drizzle on August 1, 1960, Mayor Terry Schrunk snipped a 100-foot ribbon to open the Lloyd Center shopping mall. Governor Mark Hatfield watched 700 homing pigeons explode from their cages to carry news of the opening to twenty-nine northwest cities. Lloyd Center was the climax of a dream by California oil millionaire Ralph Lloyd, who had begun to buy up Portland east-side real estate in the 1920s with the vision of building an alternate downtown close to the concentration of population. Despite suspicion from downtown businesses and banks, Lloyd opened a Sears store and dug the foundation for a hotel before the Great Depression put his plans on hold. But he continued to acquire land until he owned nearly 100 blocks in northeast Portland at his death in 1953.

Over the next three years the Lloyd Corporation unfolded plans for a massive shopping center only five minutes from the center of Portland. Downtown merchants watched the announcements with dismay and tried to agree on ways to ease their parking problems. Their reactions were mixed with worry about downtown decline and anger over the east-side vote on the coliseum. Financing for the shopping mall came not from local banks but from the Prudential Insurance Company. The Lloyd Corporation broke ground in April 1958, and opened the mall twenty-seven months later. *Business Week* in 1960 noted that Lloyd Center's 1.2 million square feet of rentable space and its eighty-plus stores gave Portland the nation's largest urban shopping center, a distinction that, of course, lasted only a few years. *Time* called it a "consumer's cornucopia" for the 595,000 people within a twenty-minute drive.

For the better part of a generation, Portland was a city that could not quite make up its mind between east side and west side, between growth and stagnation. City Commissioner Bill Bowes summed up the problem in 1943 when he remarked, "I hear people say that they long for the day when Portland can return to what it was before our present industrial progress." Bowes for one had no interest in looking backward: "We are standing at the doorway of a new Portland and a great opportunity." Other Portlanders took fifteen or twenty years to reach the same conclusion. The *Oregonian* announced the start of a Portland building boom in 1958, but the real importance of the Lloyd Center, the Coliseum, and Portland Center towers was to show that the sober city on the Willamette was again ready for change.

The Fremont Bridge, newest of the spans crossing the Willamette River, broke with tradition in its soaring style. Traffic congestion through Portland was eased considerably by the bridge. This 1973 view is toward the east and Mt. Hood. (OHS)

CHAPTER VII
THE MOST LIVABLE CITY

Portland is not one of the nation's most livable cities by accident. During the past two decades, city leaders and residents have replanned and rebuilt the older parts of the city for another generation of use, while constructing a new suburban environment for a quarter of a million new residents.

Much of the city's success has been due to its willingness to experiment. In the last two decades government has taken a leading role in Portland's revitalization. Between 1968 and 1972, for example, local politicians and business leaders cooperated with the Oregon legislature to establish a new set of public agencies to tackle the problems that faced the entire metropolitan area. The results were the Tri-County Metropolitan Transportation District (or Tri-Met), the Metropolitan Service District (Metro), and an expanded Port of Portland that absorbed the old Portland Docks Commission.

Within the city, citizen groups and downtown businesses cooperated on formulating a downtown plan that introduced sophisticated concepts for the functions and future of the city's core. At the same time, active and often angry neighborhood associations shifted much of the initiative in local planning to the neighborhoods themselves. Citizen planners were less interested in comprehensive development schemes than in preserving the advantages and values of individual districts.

Portlanders chose a new generation of leaders to implement the ideas about planning and development. As a County Commissioner and then County Executive, Don Clark led the way in adapting traditional Multnomah County government for modern times. Lloyd Anderson, Connie McCready, Neil Goldschmidt, Charles Jordan, and Mildred Schwab brought new ideas to Portland City Council. As city commissioner (1971-1972) and mayor (1973-1979), Goldschmidt, in particular, capitalized positively on the surge of citizen activism and used it as a foundation to implement a range of new programs. Under his administration Portland gained a national reputation as a city pioneering new directions in public policy.

Portland's new vitality was rooted in its ever evolving resources. New people, new politicians, new industries, and new customers for established businesses gave new life to a maturing city.

Americans tend to assume that livable cities are small cities, and many Portlanders like to be told that they live in an overgrown town. In fact, a city is truly livable only if it is *big enough.* To give all its residents the opportunity to realize and utilize their abilities, a city must offer an adequate base of public and private resources. Residents benefit by the opportunity to interact with others of different backgrounds and cultures. A city needs to be a certain size to be able to provide support for higher education and the arts. It also needs to be large enough to offer a variety of jobs and to develop the sophisticated business services that promote economic innovation and spinoff industries.

The threshold population for a truly

Far left: Neil Goldschmidt took office in January 1973 as the youngest mayor of any major U.S. city. He left the Portland post in 1979 for a job as U.S. transportation secretary, but returned to the area in 1981 as an executive of Nike. Courtesy, U.S. Department of Transportation

Left: Charles Jordan arrived in Portland in 1970 to head the Model Cities program, and in 1974 was picked as the first black on the City Commission. He was elected to later terms, and left in 1984 to become parks and recreation director of Austin, Texas. Courtesy, City of Portland

Left, below: After serving as an airport and later as a World War II shipyard, Swan Island became a major part of the Port of Portland. This 1960s scene shows a new shipyard repair and dry dock at lower left, and other facilities. Courtesy, Pacific Power & Light Company

livable metropolitan area is a million or two—the size range of Denver, San Diego, Seattle, Minneapolis, or Vancouver, British Columbia. Portland passed the million mark in population in late 1969. The four-county metropolitan area had 822,000 residents in 1960, 1,007,000 in 1970, and 1,240,000 in 1980. Subdivision sprawl and rush-hour traffic tie-ups are the obvious signs of this 50-percent increase in population. Just as significant is a new sophistication about everything from music and theater to city planning and politics.

One key to the boom of the later 1960s and 1970s was the revitalization of Portland's role as a river city. The port lost business to Seattle in the 1960s when the Docks Commission failed to modernize shipping facilities and ignored the growing market for containerized cargo. Under the persistant prodding of Governor Tom McCall, city leaders agreed to merge the Docks Commission into the Port of Portland in 1970 as an economic development measure. In 1973, the legislature expanded the port to serve Washington and Clackamas counties as well as Multnomah.

These decisions helped Portland in the last fifteen years to regain ground lost to its West Coast rivals of Seattle, Tacoma, and Oakland. Terminal 6 is now a major container dock. Japanese imports such as Hondas and Toyotas make Portland the largest auto port on the West Coast. Dry dock No. 4, opened in 1978 to serve Alaska oil tankers, is the largest on the coast and the third largest in the world.

The energetic Port Authority has helped the city to benefit from the growing importance of American trade with the Pacific Rim. United States commerce with foreign nations out of West Coast ports increased from 17 percent of the national total in 1970 to 24 percent by 1983. Every month ships

Left: *Dredges were essential in deepening the Columbia and Willamette rivers so that larger ships could reach Portland. This picture shows the cutting edge of a dredge, lifted out of the Columbia about 1965. The Army Corps of Engineers has had charge of river clearing. Courtesy, The Columbian*

Left, below: *This aerial of the Willamette River before construction of the Fremont Bridge shows the trainyards at lower left and right center. Swan Island, site of a Kaiser shipyard during World War II, is at upper right. Courtesy, Portland District, U.S. Army Corps of Engineers*

leave Portland for Melbourne and Singapore, Kobe and Yokohama, Penang and Pusan, Hong Kong and Taiwan, Callao, Valparaiso, and Panama. They arrive in Portland carrying steel, petroleum, palm oil, autos, and general merchandise. They depart with wheat, lumber, wood chips, and even frozen french fries for McDonald's restaurants in Tokyo. The real value of Portland trade in constant dollars tripled between 1966 and 1983.

A remarkable expansion in local electronics industries has also contributed to the Portland boom. Companies like Tektronix and Electro-Scientific Instruments originated in empty storefronts and warehouses in southeast Portland in the early 1950s. Symbolizing the transition from one industrial era to another, Electro-Scientific operated for several years out of the facility that was once the knitting mill for the company that evolved into Jantzen sportswear. As business grew, electronics companies migrated to vacant land in Washington County. Spinoff companies like Floating Point Systems and local plants of other national and international electronics

firms such as Intel and Wacker Siltronics came to Portland in the 1970s. By the early 1980s, the Portland area's "silicon forest" on the west side of the Willamette employed an estimated 25,000 assembly line workers, electronic engineers, and software writers.

The city can look forward to further growth in high technology. A recent study published by the U.S. Department of Labor showed that high-tech jobs accounted for 10 percent of *all* of Ore-

Above: Freeways circle downtown Portland in this 1974 photo by photographer Lewis Clark Cook, looking north. Willamette River bridges pictured, starting in the foreground, are Marquam, Hawthorne, Morrison, Burnside, the Steel Bridge, Broadway, and Fremont. (OHS)

Left: Portland State University is at left, and Broadway curves in the foreground looking north from near the edge of Portland Heights in 1975. Some of the results of the urban renewal effort started in the 1960s are visible at the right and center. Courtesy, Portland Chamber of Commerce

gon's nonagricultural job growth from 1975 to 1982, ranking it sixth among all fifty states in relative growth of the high-tech sector.

Portland's role as the economic capital of western Oregon and the Inland Empire is as important now as it was at the turn of the century. Today, it is a city of diversified industries and services—bankers, freight forwarders, insurance agents, wholesalers, and major law firms. Medical and architectural professionals draw patients and clients from hundreds of miles away. Portlanders working with such major corporations as Louisiana Pacific and Tektronix or with the Bonneville Power Administration make decisions that affect the future of the entire Northwest. Under pressure from the national recession of the early 1980s, Mayor Frank Ivancie tried to build on the city's strengths with economic development as the central theme of his administration.

Like many cities, Portland's growth as a regional metropolis has brought a boom in downtown building, but it has been a boom with a difference. Portland serves as a remarkable example of how

Above: *Indians from several tribes are among minorities residing in the Portland area. Some of the descendants of the native Americans practiced traditional dance steps at their encampment at a park near the Willamette River in 1979, against a downtown backdrop. Courtesy, Ted Van Arsdol*

Left: *Waterfront Park, renamed in 1984 in honor of former Oregon governor Tom McCall, has been the setting each year for celebrations and the Fun Center of the Portland Rose Festival. Portlanders played along the Willamette River at this 1982 Fun Center. Courtesy, Ted Van Arsdol*

to plan for new development without turning a downtown area into a high-rise ghost town that comes alive only from eight to five. Some officials believe that the downtown plan adopted by City Council in December 1972 was the result of a lucky convergence of circumstances. By the late 1960s the ugliness of the waterfront, the shortage of downtown parking, the decline in bus service, the competition of suburban shopping centers, and the shortage of municipal office space were long-standing problems. What was new, however, was the willingness of business and political leaders to consider new ideas and to think creatively about ways that a solution to one problem might also help with others.

Government, business, and citizens worked together to organize a downtown plan during 1970, 1971, and 1972. The initial impetus came from a business group known as the Portland Improvement Corporation, which represented major local corporations, utilities, and downtown investors. Governor Tom McCall and Portland City Commissioners Lloyd Anderson, Frank Ivancie, and Neil Goldschmidt made key decisions that contributed to downtown revitalization. At the grass roots level a Citizen's Advisory Committee gathered ideas from more than a thousand Portlanders through public meetings, questionnaires, and neighborhood groups. It was the Advisory Committee that made variety, activity, and people the interlocking foundations of the plan. Portland's goal was to design a downtown that was everybody's neighborhood—a district that would offer something for workers, shoppers, pedestrians, bus riders, the young, the elderly, commuters, and permanent residents.

The transformation of the Willamette riverfront is the most obvious change from the Portland of 1965. The old *Oregon Journal* building was razed in 1968. The two-block building situated east of Front Street between the Morrison and Hawthorne bridges had been a white elephant from the day it opened in the early 1930s as a public market. Demolition opened up views of the river and raised hopes for a riverside park. When the Fremont Bridge completed a new freeway loop around downtown in 1973, Portland was able to close the old Harbor Drive expressway and rip up the six lanes of concrete that had divided downtown from the river. The replacement has been Waterfront Park, renamed in 1984 to honor Governor Tom McCall, who had initiated the movement to dispense with Harbor Drive. The South Downtown Waterfront redevelopment project south of the Hawthorne Bridge is an extension of Waterfront Park. With a marina, esplanade, and more than 500 units of new housing, it will add to the life and vitality of Portland's rediscovered riverfront.

The Transit Mall is a Portland innovation that has encouraged development of a high-density office corridor running north and south along Fifth, Sixth, and Broadway. The mall evolved from a suggestion for single bus lanes during an early downtown planning session in 1971. Today, buses are the dominant transportation on two of the most important downtown streets. The Transit Mall has cut air pollution, speeded bus service, and simplified bus transfers. Since the mall opened in 1977, it has served as a model for similar plans in cities from Denver to Ottawa.

Portland's downtown office spine is crossed by a retail axis along Stark, Alder, Morrison, and Yamhill. Mayor Goldschmidt himself made a number of trips to Seattle in the mid-seventies to convince Nordstrom's, a major retail chain, to open a new downtown store covering a full block. Businessmen Bill and Sam Naito, who played a key role

Above: *East of Portland, Women's Forum Park commands this dramatic view of Crown Point and the Columbia River. Courtesy, Frank M. Redmond*

Left: *The south side of snow-clad Mt. Hood towers over Highway 26. Courtesy, Gregory Lawler*

145

Above: *Mt. Hood rises above vivid autumn colors on Larch Mountain. Courtesy, Frank M. Redmond*

Left: *The forest emerges from fog in Columbia Gorge. Possible ways of conserving the gorge have been frequently discussed. Courtesy, Frank M. Redmond*

Above: *Stretches of the Willamette River are tranquil and untouched. Courtesy, Frank M. Redmond*

Left: *Balch Canyon in Forest Park is a lush remnant of Northwest wilderness. Courtesy, Frank M. Redmond*

Facing page: *Tanner Creek Falls rushes along boulders in Columbia Gorge. Courtesy, Frank M. Redmond*

Left: *The sun sets on the Willamette River in Champoeg State Park. Courtesy, Frank M. Redmond*

Below: *The Columbia River moves placidly at dusk. Near Portland, the river is used extensively by boaters and other recreationists. Courtesy, Frank M. Redmond*

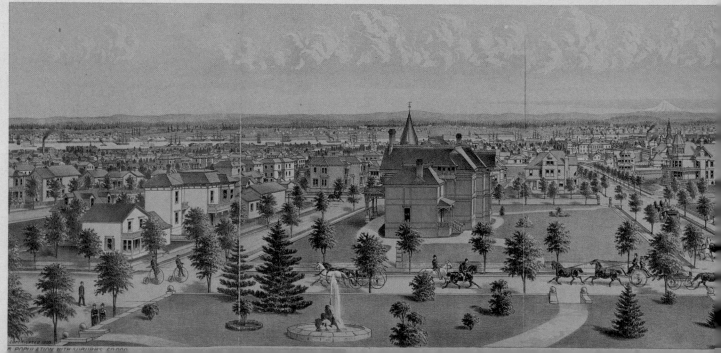

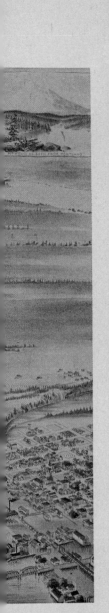

Facing page, top: *The long neck of land at the junction of the Willamette and Columbia rivers has been known for a long time as the Peninsula. Portland occupies the lower center, East Portland is at right, and Vancouver is in the distance, at upper center, in this 1890 sketch. (OHS)*

Left: *Construction of railroads helped spur a boom in public and commercial buildings. The impressive new Chamber of Commerce building was started shortly before the depression of the 1890s. Its ornate tower is shown in this 1891 sketch. (OHS)*

Facing page, bottom: *Residential streets with palatial homes extended below Portland Heights, west of the downtown area in the 1880s. This semi-parklike scene from West Shore magazine looks east toward the Willamette River, with Mt. Hood in the distance. (OHS)*

Below: *Henry Villard started construction on Hotel Portland, but the job of completion was left for George Markle, Jr. (OHS)*

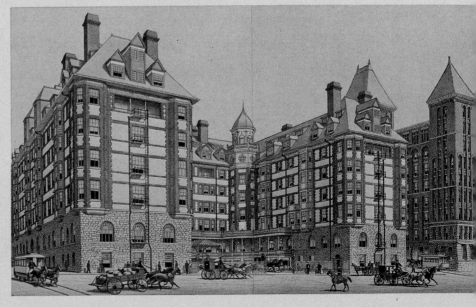

MAKE EVERY MINUTE COUNT for PERSHING

UNITED STATES SHIPPING BOARD
EMERGENCY FLEET CORPORATION

FLEET WEEK

0   4697

WELCOME SAILORS
August 3-9, 1936

Portland Traction Company ◆ Weekly $1.25 Pass
August **2-8**, 1936
◆ INCLUSIVE ◆
Form 301
(See Other Side)

Facing page: *World War I brought prosperous times to the Portland area as jobs increased, but most yards in the lower Columbia area closed after the war. (OHS)*

Left: *Searchlights probed night skies and more than 7,000 sailors swarmed ashore to visit Portland during Fleet Week in 1936. A special pass was issued for Portland Traction Company riders. (OHS)*

Below: *New shipyards were built during World War I and existing yards were expanded to meet the need for "a bridge of ships" across the Atlantic. Posters and slogans were displayed to encourage workers to greater efforts. (OHS)*

Facing page: *Native American traditions are preserved at gatherings such as the Delta Park Indian Pow-Wow in 1978. Courtesy, Frank M. Redmond*

Left: *Tribes of a different sort gather at the Annual Highland Games and Clan Gathering in Portland. Courtesy, Frank M. Redmond*

Below: *The Clackamas County Fair in nearby Canby draws bronco riders from all over. St. Paul and Molalla also host popular rodeos. Courtesy, Frank M. Redmond*

Facing page, top, far left: *Strollers enjoy the Japanese Gardens in Washington Park. Courtesy, Barbara Gundle*

Facing page, top left: *Portlanders choose the perfect jack-o'-lantern on Sauvie Island. Courtesy, Frank M. Redmond*

Facing page, bottom: *Lake Oswego has the look of the Northwest. Courtesy, Frank M. Redmond*

Left: *A hiker reaches the 8,000-foot level of majestic Mt. Hood. Courtesy, Frank M. Redmond*

Below: *A hiker rests in the Mt. Hood Wilderness. Courtesy, Frank M. Redmond*

Facing page, top: *A couple share a sunny afternoon in the Shakespeare Garden at Washington Park. Courtesy, Frank M. Redmond*

Facing page, bottom, far left: *Autumn leaves carpet the walkway in the Park Blocks. Courtesy, Gregory Lawler*

Facing page, bottom left: *Nearby Columbia Gorge is the site of spectacular views such as this one. Courtesy, Barbara Gundle*

Left: *Spring is a riot of color in the Crystal Springs Rhododendron Garden. Courtesy, Gregory Lawler*

Below: *Crystal Springs Lake comes to life with blooms. Courtesy, Frank M. Redmond*

Above: *Sauvie Island features rural alternatives to city living, such as this houseboat community. Sauvie Island's farms, wildlife sanctuary, and popular recreations are just thirty minutes from downtown. Courtesy, Barbara Gundle*

Left: *Visitors enjoy the spectacular International Rose Test Gardens. Courtesy, Frank M. Redmond*

in revitalizing historic Old Town as a shopping area during the 1970s, turned an abandoned department store into the Galleria, a vertical downtown shopping mall. Pioneer Courthouse Square opened in the spring of 1984 on the block occupied previously by the grand Portland Hotel. Pioneer Square provides Portland with a central public plaza in the heart of the retail district. The Morrison Street project between Third, Fifth, Morrison, and Taylor will add shopping, office space, and a hotel and extend the retail core to the Yamhill Historic District and the river. The Banfield light rail line, to be opened from downtown Portland to Gresham in 1986, is designed to tie this whole retail district together with streetcars that loop along Morrison and Yamhill streets.

The near east side—also to be served by light rail—is as much a part of Portland's central area as the old downtown. From the industries around the Southern Pacific rail lines to the south,

through the Produce Row warehouse district and the Coliseum-Lloyd Center area, to the Union Pacific yards and Swan Island, the east-side corridor provides jobs for about 65,000 Portlanders. The stores, hotels, and office towers in and around Lloyd Center constitute a substantial downtown area in their own right.

Downtown Portland in the 1980s is bigger, brighter, and more businesslike than it was twenty years ago. Its white collar workers occupy millions of square feet of new office space and downtown employment totals more than 80,000— up from 50,000 in 1960. At the same time, the city has taken major steps toward its goal of establishing an active and varied downtown that reaches out to the rest of the city. The high-rise boom has destroyed a vital community that housed the elderly in the Lownsdale district and now threatens to displace Skid Road residents north of Burnside, but it has complemented other revitalization plans. Office work-

A wide-angle lens took in the fountain in front of the Civic Auditorium in 1971, before trees and shrubs had grown. The auditorium is at left and St. Mary's Academy at the right, in the distance. Courtesy, The Oregonian

As shown here in 1971, the Ira Keller Fountain in the Civic Auditorium Forecourt had an almost pastoral feeling shortly after its completion. In the background is old St. Mary's Academy. The area has been almost completely transformed by urban renewal since the fountain was dedicated in 1970. Courtesy, Fred DeWolfe

ers on their lunch hours utilize new parks and patronize new restaurants and established retailers. The increased numbers of business visitors justify new hotel construction. More jobs and more after-hours attractions are gradually making downtown sites attractive for new middle-income housing.

Downtown development has complemented the increasing volume of business in the suburbs. Taken together, suburban Washington, Clackamas, and eastern Multnomah counties surpassed the city of Portland in total population in the mid-1950s and in retail sales in 1972. The number of jobs located in the suburbs matched the number inside Portland's city limits in the early 1980s. Projections for the next decade indicate that the largest number of new jobs will be created in a west-side crescent from Wilsonville through Tigard and Beaverton to Hillsboro. Northern Clackamas County along I-205 and both shores of the Columbia, from Rivergate to Troutdale on the south and Vancouver to Camas on the north, also offer land suitable for industrial development.

Portland preserved and "recycled" its older neighborhoods as its ring of suburbs grew. Despite rapid growth in Multnomah and Washington counties after World War II, a substantial 60 percent of the population within the city limits of Portland in 1970 lived in houses built before the war. By the mid-1960s, residents showed an increasing interest in neighborhood rehabilitation. Government assistance spurred neighborhood improvements. A city code compliance program targeted Irvington and University Park, with their blocks of bungalows dating to the beginning of the century. Another program was the Albina Neighborhood Improvement Project, aimed at refurbishing housing in a section of Portland's black community.

As previously noted, a minor revolution in neighborhood planning came about because of a score of largely self-defined community organizations that began to fight vigorously for change in the late 1960s. Many of these organizations were started to resist freeway construction or plans for urban renewal. By the early 1970s, active neighborhood associations and planning committees had

Freeways crowded out residences and other development in some parts of the city as highway officials sought to keep pace with traffic needs. This recent view from Burnside Bridge shows roadways east of the Willamette, and the high rises of the Lloyd Center area. Courtesy, Ted Van Arsdol

begun to define their own agendas and force recognition from politicians and planners. On the east side, neighborhood mobilization began in 1967 and 1968 with efforts to provide local input for planning federally assisted programs. Northeast Portland neighborhoods helped to plan and implement a Model Cities program that forced many public agencies to rethink the racial bias in their programs and policies. Portland Action Committees Together (PACT) helped to organize half a dozen neighborhoods in southeast Portland to participate in anti-poverty programs. Southeast Uplift was a locally organized equivalent of Model Cities serving the entire group of southeast neighborhoods that had developed in the first half of the century, including several low-income communities.

The neighborhood movement gained its most articulate spokespersons among middle-class "colonists" of the physically deteriorated neighborhoods of the west side, who united to fend off urban renewal bulldozers. The Northwest District Association was formed in 1969 to deal with the proposed expansion of Good Samaritan Hospital which would have intruded into residential blocks. The group worked with the city's Planning Bureau from 1970 to 1972 to develop an alternative plan that would preserve Northwest as a high-density residential neighborhood of Victorian houses and vintage apartment buildings of the 1920s. Today, Northwest is Portland's most cosmopolitan neighborhood, with a mix of the elderly, students, second-generation immigrants, and young professionals.

The Hill Park Association was organized in 1970 to fight the possible obliteration of the Lair Hill neighborhood, whose location just south of the downtown urban renewal zone made it an attractive target for land clearance and apartment development. After the Johns

Landing development, converting abandoned industrial land along the Willamette 1.5 miles south of downtown into offices, trendy shops, and riverbank condos, was unveiled in 1971, the Corbett, Terwilliger, and Lair Hill neighborhoods joined in the development of their own district plan to preserve old working-class neighborhoods for a new generation.

The cooperative effort between the Planning Commission and the Northwest District Association was the catalyst for giving neighborhood groups an officially recognized role in city decision-making. City Council established the Office of Neighborhood Associations in 1974 to provide support services for local organizations through central and district offices. Neighborhood associations must be open in membership and record minority as well as majority opinions. In return, city officials have learned to listen carefully to neighborhood opinion. The Planning Bureau notifies neighborhood associations of zoning change requests and has worked with individual communities on district plans and rezoning proposals to preserve residential environments. Activists in Lair Hill and Ladd's Addition persuaded the city to designate their neighborhoods as Historic Conservation Districts. Other community groups have been increasingly involved in local economic development and self-help efforts aimed at establishing affordable housing and local jobs.

The vitality of Portland's community business districts has complemented the preservation of many of its residential neighborhoods. The Sellwood and Hawthorne districts have become successful specialty shopping areas. The Hollywood and Northwest districts are serving new generations of local residents. In the face of competition from new shopping malls, the North Portland Citizens Committee secured a grant from

Facing page, top: *Mt. Hood is a dominating backdrop for downtown. Portland Hilton is at the left, the tower of the old First Congregational Church is in the center, and the forty-story First National Bank building is at the right in this 1970s view looking east. Courtesy, Oregon State Highway Travel Section*

Facing page, bottom: *Northwest Portland, near W. Burnside Street, has remained largely residential. The Elliston Apartments is one Victorian survival in the neighborhood, at 425 N.W. 18th Avenue. A horse-and-buggy ride was a quick way to town when the building was constructed. Courtesy, Ted Van Arsdol*

the federal Neighborhood Reinvestment Corporation for revitalizing the St. Johns neighborhood business district. By 1982, the success of the pilot project in St. Johns had helped to persuade federal officials to make neighborhood commercial revitalization a national priority.

The neighborhood revitalization movement also played an important part in one of Portland's major political upsets. When tavern-owner and businessman William E. "Bud" Clark decided to challenge incumbent mayor Frank Ivancie in the May 1984 primary, few experts gave him a chance to win. Clark's last elective office, after all, had been as treasurer of the senior class at Portland's Lincoln High in the late 1940s. In fact, years of activity in Portland neighborhood associations and community service programs had given Clark both name recognition and access to a network of volunteer political workers. While Ivancie misjudged his own

campaign strategy and failed to shake an image as ally of the downtown business establishment, Clark made quiet gains to emerge with a stunning victory in which he carried 235 out of 291 precincts. Clark's combination of fiscal conservatism and political populism appealed both to an older generation of neighborhood businesspeople and the new generation of neighborhood activists.

Portland's natural landscape puts its own unmistakable stamp on the city's character. Since the late 1960s, Oregon has pioneered in the conservation of the natural environment. In 1983, the Conservation Foundation reported that Oregon ranked fifth among all the states in its commitment to environmental protection. The state's system of land-use goals adopted in 1974 has guided local planners toward decisions to meet social and environmental goals. Traveling journalists give Portland high marks as one of America's cleanest and most en-

vironmentally conscious cities.

For the typical Portland resident, a protected environment has meant a usable recreational network of parks, rivers, and mountains. Within a 90-minute drive, Portlanders are able to enjoy the beaches and headlands of the Pacific shore, the steelhead streams of the Coast Range, the trails of the Cascades and Columbia Gorge, and the ski slopes of Mount Hood—including the country's only late-summer skiing, at Timberline Lodge. Closer to home, Portlanders canoe on the Willamette, sail on the Columbia, jog through the city's fine park system, and generally make use of the area's outdoor opportunities. It seems appropriate that the Jantzen, White Stag, and Nike sportswear companies are based in the Portland area.

When not exercising, many Portlanders are afflicted by a sports mania known as "Blazeritis." The National Basketball Association's Trailblazers are the city's only major-league sports franchise, making the team indispensible to the civic ego, for it is a symbol that Portland is itself a "major-league city." The Blazers have sold out their home *seasons* for more than a decade. Their high point was the 1976-1977 season, when Bill Walton led the unheralded Blazers to a sweep of the powerful L.A. Lakers in the playoffs and a hard-fought victory over the Philadelphia 76ers in the championship series.

Portland's recent decades of increasing livability have also seen the development of institutions for education and the arts. With 700,000 visitors annually, the Washington Park Zoo is gaining a national reputation for Northwest American exhibits and specialized research and the breeding of elephants, primates, and penguins. The Portland

Housing projects sprouted in many parts of the outlying areas near Portland in the postwar era. This scene is in a section of Beaverton, a suburb where pressure for more schools and other civic facilities accompanied the residential expansion. (OHS)

Art Museum and the Northwest Film Study Center are important cultural resources. Conductors Lawrence Smith and James DePriest have helped the Oregon Symphony mature into a major regional ensemble. Since its first season in 1971, Chamber Music Northwest, held on the Reed College campus every June and July, has become a leading national music festival. The Portland Performing Arts Center, partially opened in the fall of 1984, was developed through a combination of tax money and private contributions. It will feature new 450-seat and 900-seat theaters and a refurbished movie palace with 2,750 seats that was built originally in the 1920s. The center is complemented by downtown movie houses, the Oregon Historical Society, the Art Museum, and Portland State University, creating a cultural focal point for the city on the southwest edge of downtown.

The arts have flourished in part as a result of the expansion of higher education in the Portland community. Among private colleges in the area, Reed College was recently ranked one of the top ten liberal arts colleges in the country in a poll conducted by *U.S. News* magazine; Lewis and Clark College ranked fourth among regional liberal arts colleges. Portland State University is one of Oregon's three major universities. It plays a vital role in the fields of engineering, business, international studies, and urban and public affairs.

More than 140 years have passed since Lovejoy and Pettygrove tossed their penny into the air to give a name to the new settlement on the Willamette. Over those decades, Portlanders have made their share of mistakes, but they have also managed to build one of the country's most attractive and livable cities. The challenge for the future is to do as well.

Portlanders care about their city. They worry about their neighborhoods,

about access to the Willamette, about the preservation of parks and views, and about the impact of new development. They may disagree about specific political issues, but they participate actively in political campaigns and elections. Citizens who invest their time and energy can make their voices heard, whether they've lived in Portland for just a few years or a lifetime. The inscription on the Skidmore Fountain at First and Ankeny tells us that "good citizens are the riches of a city." Portland's greatest strength is that its residents take the message seriously.

An elk statue was presented to the city in 1900 by D.P. Thompson. The unusual Portland Building, designed by Michael Graves, is now a background for the statue and fountain. "The Coming of the White Man," another statue provided by Thompson, is at Washington Park. Courtesy, Ted Van Arsdol

PORTLAND'S DOWNTOWNS

Portland has already outgrown two downtowns in the course of its history. And a third has been under construction since the 1960s. Each of the city's downtowns has been bigger, and taller, than the last, as the city's commercial and professional activities demanded more and more space.

The first downtown, started in the 1850s, was built in a long strip parallel to the Willamette River by early merchants and real-estate speculators. After 1871, horsecar lines made First Street between Davis and Salmon the main business thoroughfare. From the mid-1860s through the 1880s, as the city's growing economy demanded more business space, downtown property owners replaced flimsy wood buildings with an elegant city of cast iron. The typical mercantile building was a three- or four-story masonry shell with an elaborate facade of cast iron. Detailed pillars and pilasters, capitals, cornices, and medallions imitated carved stone and turned ordinary buildings into "commercial palaces."

By the end of the 1880s, nearly 200 cast-iron fronts were attached to Portland's downtown structures. The twenty that still remain have survived nineteenth-century floods and fires and twentieth-century neglect. Most are now protected within the Skidmore-Old Town and Yamhill historic districts, designated by City Council in 1975 and recognized on the National Register of Historic Places. Restored buildings in both districts now house fashionable shops, restaurants, and offices. The heart of this first downtown (and of Portland's

Left: *Even the great flood of 1894 couldn't douse the enthusiasm of Meier & Frank's loyal clientele. Courtesy, Meier & Frank Company*

Below: *Streetcar tracks and bricked pavement were widespread in the earlier business district. The view is on S.W. First Avenue between S.W. Alder and S.W. Morrison streets, looking north. Courtesy, Fred DeWolfe*

Facing page: *A passerby takes note as pedestrians stop in 1913 at one of the drinking fountains donated by wealthy lumberman Simon Benson. He thought they would help keep people from going into saloons for drinks. Courtesy, Fred DeWolfe*

present historic districts) was the corner of First and Ankeny streets. The New Market Theatre, built for Captain Alexander Ankeny in 1872 according to the design of W.W. Piper, was the hub of Portland in the 1870s and early 1880s. A drive-through market was on the first floor; a theatre lit by a hundred gas jets and a cafe were on the second. A few steps away was the Skidmore Fountain, built with a bequest from pioneer Stephen Skidmore for the refreshment of "horses, men, and dogs." Within a short walk were the Board of Trade, the telegraph office, and the docks of the Oregon Steam Navigation Company. Since the mid-1970s, the crafts fair of the Portland Saturday Market along Ankeny Street has brought thousands of residents back to the very center of Portland's first downtown to admire the fountain, the New Market Theatre (restored in 1983), and the other buildings that recall the nineteenth century.

The second downtown began to develop uphill from the Willamette after the great flood of May 1894, which made Third and Fourth streets look like safer sites for investment than First. New electric trolley and interurban lines also used Third Street and generated such traffic jams that the city's first traffic officer was stationed at the corner of Third and Washington in 1901. A scattering of dark stone office buildings in the ponderous style of the Romanesque revival stand along Second and Third streets as reminders of Portland's taste at the end of the century. Some of the better examples include the Hazeltine Building (1893) at Second

and Pine and the Dekum Building (1892) at Third and Washington.

While the first downtown covered only about fifteen acres, the second downtown covered 120 acres by 1930 and provided four times as much office space as had been available at the start of the century. The Lewis and Clark Fair triggered this downtown expansion. A new generation of architects pillaged European architectural design to create classical banks, a French baroque hotel, an English Renaissance li-

brary, and office structures vaguely resembling Italian palazzi. The favorite new material was white or tan glazed terra cotta. Both technically and aesthetically, it was an excellent choice for facing Portland's new steel-frame skyscrapers and department stores. It was economical, fireproof, light in weight, and light in color. As downtown soared into the air with sixteen buildings of ten stories or more at the end of World War I and another eight by the end of the 1920s, terra cotta surfaces helped to re-

Above: *Horse-drawn wagons still competed for business downtown, and movie admission was only five and ten cents about the time World War I broke out. The Oregonian clock tower was still a notable feature, seen here at right center. Courtesy, Webfooters Postcard Club*

Left: *A "big-eared kid" named Clark Gable worked in the necktie department of Meier & Frank's store in 1922 before he began acting in the Astoria Stock Players Company and eventually found fame in Hollywood. Courtesy, Meier & Frank Company*

Facing page: *Some buildings shown in this scene looking west on S.W. Oak Street are still in use today. The section is north of the urban renewal which transformed a considerable part of Portland starting in the 1960s. An ice wagon is parked at right center of photo. Courtesy, Fred DeWolfe*

flect light onto the city's narrow streets.

Streetcar systems replaced the horsecar lines of the first downtown and established the center of the enlarged business district. Trolleys entered downtown from the east along Morrison Street and from the west along Washington. The core of Portland's retail district lay between Morrison, Washington, Third, and Tenth streets. Merchants built new department stores within this trolley loop, especially Meier and Frank; Olds, Wortman and King; and Lipman, Wolfe and Company. Besides the retail core, the larger downtown—bounded by the railroad depot, the civic auditorium, and Twelfth Street—housed half of Portland's business firms in the 1920s, as well as distinct entertainment, finance, and government centers.

Downtown changed little during the Depression or the two decades after. It was not until the 1960s that a third downtown of steel and glass broke the boundaries of the pre-war business district. The Portland Center Renewal Project marked the beginning of the new construction boom, which pushed the border eight blocks south. Dozens of mid-rise and high-rise buildings were built during the 1970s and early 1980s to accommodate more than 80,000 downtown workers. Most of the new offices line the southern end of the Transit Mall and portions of the waterfront. By the end of the 1980s, this third downtown will have the focus Portland has lacked for decades. The city's public center, Pioneer Courthouse Square, which covers the block where the grand Portland Hotel stood from 1890 to 1951, is an American version of the European town plaza. The Morrison Street project, covering three of the four blocks between

Above: *The Masonic Temple constructed in the 1900s is among prominent downtown landmarks. Many public events are held in the building. Courtesy, Ted Van Arsdol*

Left: *Many special events and the regularly scheduled Saturday Market help draw crowds downtown. Arts and crafts and food vendors set up shop at the Saturday Market on weekends. Entertainers are also on hand, such as the musician shown here serenading two young girls in 1974. Courtesy, Ted Van Arsdol*

Facing page: *Arcs of lights once spanned S.W. Third Avenue. This view is from S.W. Morrison Street looking north, with Owl Drug Company at right and a newsstand at lower left. Corner drugstores and newspaper stands are among downtown features that have disappeared over the years. (OHS)*

spectacular is the controversial city-county office building by post-modern architect Michael Graves, who used its surface as a paint store sampler. Overall, the strength of downtown lies in its variety, which allows it to serve the needs of different groups within the city—high-powered business-people and elderly shoppers, joggers in Waterfront Park and pensioners in residential hotels, patrons of stylish restaurants and students at Portland State. Downtown is the one part of Portland that is everybody's neighborhood.

Fifth, Third, Morrison, and Taylor, will further reinforce the retail center.

Today's downtown Portland is an eclectic mixture of nineteenth-century buildings and modern high-rises. Architects are now bringing more color into downtown structures, with surfaces of black and pink glass, red brick, and glittering aluminum in addition to tan concrete. The most

Far left: *Mt. Hood provides an imposing backdrop for this sailboat on the Columbia River. Courtesy, Frank M. Redmond*

Left: *The Soldiers Monument on Lownsdale Square is silhouetted against the setting sun. Courtesy, Frank M. Redmond*

Below: *Balloonists work to get aloft during the Folkfest at the annual Neighborfair in Waterfront Park. Courtesy, Frank M. Redmond*

178

Facing page, top: *The sternwheeler* Columbia Gorge *is a reminder of the days when such craft were predominant on the Columbia and Willamette rivers. The excursion vessel, built for the Port of Cascade Locks, is moored at Portland during the winter. Courtesy, Ted Van Arsdol*

Facing page, bottom: *This dulcimer player and his audience braved uncertain weather at Artquake in 1983. Artquake, a celebration of the visual and performing arts, opened on the Transit Mall but later moved its booths, exhibits, and shows to the Park Blocks. Courtesy, Barbara Gundle*

Left: *A flower wagon was a mobile business at Pioneer Courthouse Square shortly after its completion in 1984. Events scheduled at the square help make it a major focus of interest and activity in the downtown. Courtesy, Ted Van Arsdol*

Left, below: *Portland's Old Town features distinctive shops and restaurants, and brick courtyards for lingering. Courtesy, Frank M. Redmond*

Left: *Picturesque old monuments mark Riverview Cemetery and frame Mt. Hood. Courtesy, Frank M. Redmond*

Facing page, top: *Rooster Rock State Park in Columbia Gorge is a wonderful place from which to watch the sun set over the Columbia River. Parks and scenic viewpoints are important facets of the Columbia Gorge. Courtesy, Frank M. Redmond*

Facing page, bottom: *A notable reminder of Albina's past is a residence at 4314 N. Mississippi Avenue. It was restored as part of the trend toward refurbishing inner city homes. Courtesy, Ted Van Arsdol*

181

Above: *Modern sculpture provides a dynamic focal point for the Portland Transit Mall downtown. Courtesy, Frank M. Redmond*

Above left: *The skywalk at the Willamette Center becomes a dramatic urban space. Yamhill Market and Waterfront Park are neighboring attractions. Courtesy, Frank M. Redmond*

Left: *Mt. St. Helens rises beyond the east bank of the Willamette River. The peak in neighboring Washington began erupting in 1980, scattering ash through the Portland area. Courtesy, Barbara Gundle*

Facing page, top: *Port-
land's 1983 skyline frames
Mt. Hood. Courtesy,
Gregory Lawler*

Facing page, bottom, far
left: *Pioneer Courthouse
Square provides a variety
of interesting views. Courtesy,
Ted Van Arsdol*

Facing page, bottom, left:
*The Rose Festival fleet
arrives in 1982. Courtesy,
Frank M. Redmond*

Right: *The Bank of Cali-
fornia tower forms part of
Portland's sleek new downtown skyline. Courtesy,
Frank M. Redmond*

Below: *People throng the
lively Fun Center at Wa-
terfront Park during the
1982 Rose Festival. Cour-
tesy, Gregory Lawler*

Above, left: *New housing has been built along the river downtown at McCormick Pier. Courtesy, Barbara Gundle*

Above: *The distinctive Portland Building adds a lively aspect to the downtown skyline. Courtesy, Barbara Gundle*

Left: *A barge pulls a timber raft down the Willamette River in 1984. Courtesy, Gregory Lawler*

Facing page, top, right: *The battleship* Oregon *was a floating museum at Portland, and the marine park was named for the famous Navy vessel. Courtesy, Frank M. Redmond*

Facing page, top, far right: *Portland's skyline glows in the sunrise. The skyline has been greatly altered by urban renewal dating back to the 1960s. Courtesy, Gregory Lawler*

Facing page, bottom: *High rises tower against the sky near Portland State University, as seen from the Stadium Freeway looking northwest. Urban renewal started in this area and has moved north in the downtown section. Courtesy, Frank M. Redmond*

Left: *The south Park Blocks and Portland State University are ablaze in fall colors. In the distance are the West Hills. Courtesy, Frank M. Redmond*

Below: *Rain never dampens a parade-goer's enthusiasm in Portland, but it makes a high window the best vantage point from which to watch. Courtesy, Gregory Lawler*

Left: *Canadian destroyers dock at the seawall during the Rose Festival in 1982. Courtesy, Frank M. Redmond*

Below: *Flowers are used to cover Rose Festival floats. The festival dates back to 1907, but rose show tradition dates back even further, to 1889. "For you a rose in Portland grows," was a long-time booster slogan for the City of Roses. Courtesy, Gregory Lawler*

Above: *Activists staged a protest sit-in at the Trojan nuclear plant at St. Helens in 1977. Courtesy, Barbara Gundle*

Right: *A bike rider flips high in the air at a demonstration in Pioneer Courthouse Square. Courtesy, Ted Van Arsdol*

Far right: *This view across the Willamette River shows the construction of Portland's new downtown in the early 1980s. Courtesy, Don Eastman/Earth Images*

Massive decorative doors were a favorite of architects in Portland commercial projects shortly before and after the turn of the century. This sketch shows the entrance of the Chamber of Commerce building, on S.W. Stark Street between S.W. Third and S.W. Fourth avenues. The building was razed about 1934. (OHS)

CHAPTER VIII
PARTNERS IN PROGRESS

"Heads!" Portland's name may have been decided by the flip of a coin in 1845, but subsequent decisions and the growth of Portland have depended on much more business acumen than the random turn of a penny. From horse-drawn "Stumptown" to jet age "PDX," Portland entrepreneurs and institutions have been an integral force behind making the Rose City what it is today, one of the most livable cities in the nation.

Other towns aspired to be the metropolis of the Willamette, but this young village of Portland attracted men such as Captain John Couch who, in the 1840s, declared Portland was the Willamette River's true head of ocean-going navigation, promoted this fact to other sea captains, and settled here to help the harbor grow. A second advantage came in the early 1850s, when Stumptown's leaders and merchants banded together to form the Portland and Valley Plank Road Company to construct what became Canyon Road, tapping the fertile Tualatin Valley, and linking Twality farms with Portland docks and oceangoing commerce.

The town grew steadily, attracting a diverse group of merchants, hucksters, and dreamers. Gold discovered in California in 1848 translated into a swelling, eager neighboring market for previously isolated Webfoot merchants who soon discovered mining the mines was far more lucrative than sifting through the gravels of icy High Sierra streams. In the 1860s gold was found in eastern Oregon and Idaho, making Portland "the town that gravity built," as lumber and foodstuffs drifted down the Willamette and gold poured down the Columbia.

As Portland became the financial and trade center of the region, railroad baron Henry Villard took note. In 1883 Portland became the terminus of "the most stupendous scheme yet undertaken on the American continent," Villard's Northern Pacific Railroad, the Pacific Northwest's first transcontinental rail link.

Though the struggles of the city may be familiar, we tend to overlook those "Empire Builders" who struggled with it. These civic leaders made their way to Oregon by hitching a yoke of oxen to a covered wagon or buying a steerage ticket for America in Europe. They crossed the continent on some of the West's earliest railroads and sailed around the Horn. Later immigrants packed their worldly belongings in a pickup truck bound for Oregon or flew in by jet. Some were born here. The streets weren't paved with gold, but those who persevered gave Portland some impressive credentials.

The organizations whose stories are detailed on the following pages have chosen to support this important literary and civic project. They illustrate the variety of ways in which individuals and their businesses have contributed to the city's growth and development. The civic involvement of Portland's businesses, institutions of learning, and local government, in cooperation with its citizens, has made the community an excellent place in which to live and work.

PORTLAND STATE UNIVERSITY

Few thought tiny Portland State College had a chance of even appearing on NBC's prestigious "College Bowl" in the mid-1960s, let alone win. But when the Portland State team answered that last toss-up question of these intellectual Olympics and the final buzzer sounded, they had crushed their fifth straight opponent by a whopping 415 points to 60. The team broke every record set on the show and retired undefeated, putting unheralded Portland State on the national map of scholarly excellence.

The success of that 1965 "College Bowl" team is symbolic of the high academic standards and quality education of what is today a much larger Portland State University, a major institution in the state's system of higher education. But the road to accreditation hasn't been a

The Vanport flood of 1948 destroyed the earliest campus of Portland State University. However, the waters of the Columbia could not drown the "college that would not die," and classes reconvened within a matter of weeks.

cakewalk for this college.

Founded as a temporary facility after World War II, Portland State bucked long odds against survival to earn a national reputation as "the college that would not die." Today it continues to shape the minds of Portland's future community leaders in the stimulating diversity of an urban setting.

Although Portland State is now a major university with over 15,000 students, its roots go back to 1946 when the State Board of Higher Education established the small Vanport Extension Center on the site of today's Delta Park to meet the unprecedented demand for higher education by returning World War II veterans. Of the 221 students who attended classes that first year, 94 percent were veterans with an average age of twenty-eight. Many were married with children, and found the vacant wartime housing units of Vanport convenient residences.

Vanport offered primarily freshman and sophomore courses from other state system schools. Although evening extension classes had been offered in the city by the State System of Higher Education since 1918, no day classes were available until after World War II. When second-term registration closed at Van-

Lincoln Hall was the first downtown facility for Portland State. The college moved into this old high school building in 1952, and the structure is still used today by the School of Performing Arts.

port, more than 1,400 students were enrolled.

The close-knit faculty and student body held a joyful second anniversary celebration of the Vanport Extension Center on May 21, 1948, during which a huge rock bearing a plaque commemorating the event was donated by Delta Tau Rho and dedicated at the base of the flagpole. Nine days later the campus was gone—literally swept away by the flooding Columbia River that gushed through a nearby dike. The homes and possessions of many students were lost, and even the rock bearing the plaque disappeared beneath the fifteen-foot floodwaters on that Memorial Day 1948 when Vanport, the nation's largest wartime housing project and Oregon's third-largest city, was obliterated.

Some had fought the growth of Vanport from the beginning, and the school's opponents in Salem thought the flood would wash away any dreams of the institution being anything but a temporary stopgap to cope with the short-term swollen demands generated by the GI Bill of Rights. But these opponents hadn't counted on the enthusiastic pride, support, and cooperation of the faculty, students, and community who saw the need for an urban state college.

Four days after the flood 1,000 students gathered at Grant High School to hear assistant director Phil Putnam vow there would be summer classes, "somehow, somewhere." By that fall the college had moved to new quarters at the Old Oregon Shipyard administration building. The rock with the plaque was rescued from the muddy debris by Delta Tau Rho and rededicated at the new campus the following spring.

Floodwaters threatened the second site in 1949 and 1950 but failed to discourage students who had fought in the war and were impatient to make up for the lost wartime years. "The college that would not die" found a new site in 1952, moving into the old Lincoln High School building fronting the graceful, tree-lined Park Blocks between Southwest Park and Broadway at Market Street. The well-traveled plaque-bearing rock was again moved and dedicated. It was the rock's final

Today's campus is modern and up to date, with many open areas for study between classes.

Portland State's 15,000 students attend classes on a campus that blends easily into downtown Portland. A green belt of trees and grass cuts through the center of the campus.

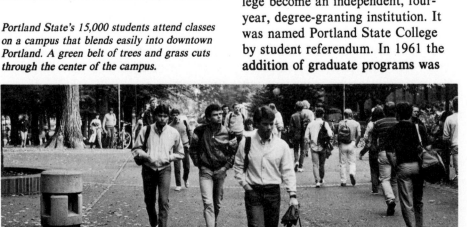

move. A permanent college grew up around "Old Main," as the stately white-columned, brick building was affectionately referred to for many years.

In 1955 efforts by then-Senator Richard Neuberger helped the college become an independent, four-year, degree-granting institution. It was named Portland State College by student referendum. In 1961 the addition of graduate programs was

authorized; in 1968 they were expanded to include doctoral programs. This growth prompted another name change, this time to Portland State University in 1969.

In the 1950s Portland State officials envisaged a campus encompassing four city blocks along Broadway, expanding south from Old Main, but PSU was destined to grow well beyond those bounds. Today Portland State's campus occupies twenty-eight buildings in a 28-block area built around the Park Blocks, a landscaped greenway area reserved for pedestrians and bicyclists.

PSU is an integral part of the community and enjoys the many benefits of being located in the state's major metropolitan center. At the edge of campus the university merges easily into downtown Portland. The areas immediately surrounding the campus contain student housing, shops, taverns, and restaurants that primarily serve the university. Commercial and governmental centers, as well as cultural and entertainment resources, are within easy walking distance of campus.

Portland State's urban setting also benefits the state's system of higher education and Portland's business community. One-half of all college-age Oregonians live, work, and search for jobs within a bus ride of PSU.

The major academic units of Portland State University are the College of Liberal Arts and Sciences and the professional Schools of Business Administration, Education, Engineering and Applied Science, Health and Physical Education, Performing Arts, Social Work, and Urban and Public Affairs. Bachelor of arts and bachelor of science degrees are available in a wide variety of fields from the academic college and professional schools. Master's degrees are offered in a number of disciplines, and the university offers six doctoral degrees.

THE OREGONIAN

The great unveiling came on December 3, 1850. Several leading men of the waterfront village of Portland held an inaugural party in a print shop on the second floor of a little frame building on the northwest corner of Front and Morrison streets. Ceremoniously taking hold of the edges of a sheet on the press, they lifted it to learn the name of the town's first newspaper—*The Oregonian.*

Its publisher and editor was Thomas J. Dryer, a 42-year-old native of New York State who had followed the gold rush to California.

Designed by Portland's leading contemporary architect, Pietro Belluschi, the Oregonian Building at 1320 Southwest Broadway has been the paper's headquarters since 1948.

Four other papers had preceded Dryer's new weekly in the Oregon Territory, but *The Oregonian* has survived them all to become not only the Pacific Northwest's largest newspaper but Oregon's oldest continuing business.

Three years later Dryer hired a seventeen-year-old printer named Henry L. Pittock, and in 1860 Dryer sold him the paper. As publisher, Pittock remained one of the two dominant figures of *The Oregonian* until well into the early years of the twentieth century.

The other was Harvey W. Scott,

who at the age of twenty-seven was Portland's first city librarian when Pittock made him editor of *The Oregonian* in 1865. Steeped in the ancient and modern classics, Scott penned clear, scholarly, hard-hitting editorials that kept *The Oregonian* in the front rank of American newspapers. During his forty-year tenure, *The Oregonian* espoused free trade, sound money, and the Republican party.

Pittock made his paper a daily, the *Morning Oregonian,* in 1861, and added a Sunday edition twenty years later. In 1892 he moved it to a new building. The structure was nine stories high and was topped by a three-story clock tower, at the northwest corner of Sixth and Alder streets.

In the 1920s and 1930s *The Oregonian* struggled for circulation with a younger rival, the feisty *Oregon Journal,* but in the boom years of World War II it surged ahead to stay.

The paper moved to its third home, a seven-level full-block building bounded by Southwest Broadway, Sixth Avenue, Jefferson, and Columbia streets, in 1948.

Two years later the Pittock and Scott heirs sold *The Oregonian* to S.I. Newhouse, owner of a group of newspapers based in New York. *The Oregonian* weathered a bitter strike that began in 1959, and in 1961 Newhouse bought the *Journal.* In 1982 publisher Fred A. Stickel consolidated the news and editorial staffs of both papers to create an expanded *Oregonian.*

To meet its growing production needs, the Oregonian Publishing Company, between 1972 and 1975, constructed and progressively occupied a separate press and distribution building on the full block bounded by Southwest Taylor and Yamhill streets and Sixteenth and Seventeenth avenues.

The Oregonian Publishing Company's production building at Southwest Sixteenth Avenue and Taylor Street was constructed in 1975 to handle the paper's growing press and distribution needs.

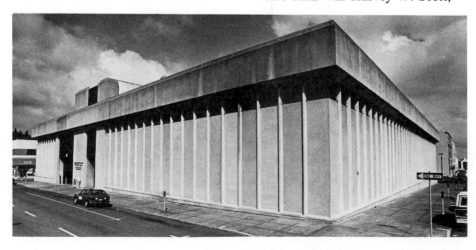

GOOD SAMARITAN HOSPITAL AND MEDICAL CENTER

Everyone praised Bishop B. Wistar Morris' desire to erect Good Samaritan Hospital and Orphanage in the booming 1870s frontier metropolis of Portland, but the local press was critical of the remote site selected. Those papers were concerned over a need "to prevent the worthy physicians from using other than sound speech....as they conveyed their patients over ruts of unknown depths and plowed land to their destination."

But Bishop Morris envisioned Portland's future growth more accurately than many of his day. The distant property purchased from Captain George Flanders is now the busy intersection of Northwest Twenty-third Avenue and Lovejoy Street.

Founded as the Episcopal Hospital of the Diocese of Oregon, Good Samaritan opened its doors "to all regardless of race, color, creed, or religion" in 1875. The original H-shaped frame facility began operation with fifty beds and a staff of five, and even in bad economic times Bishop Morris pronounced the hospital policy to be "that one-fourth of its work must go to the poor and needy."

In 1887 the University of Oregon Medical School was founded on the site "in a pasture shared with three cows." Dr. Simeon E. Josephi was appointed dean of the school, a position he held for twenty-five years, and classes were commenced in an abandoned grocery store moved to the site.

Three years later the first formal school of nursing in the Pacific Northwest was founded at Good Samaritan by the much-loved Emily Loveridge. Upon her 1930 retirement, one reporter said of her, "Hundreds are living today who owe their ability to kick and cuss to the care given them of this good samaritan."

Good Samaritan celebrated the

turn of the century by erecting its first brick structure in 1900, and continuing its course as a pioneer in the field of medicine. In 1921 it built Wilcox Maternity Hospital, the city's

The Good Samaritan Hospital of the 1870s was "in the belt of timber which skirts the city and only reached by a circuitous route of a small path through the woods."

first maternity hospital. The first EKG machine used in Portland was installed at Good Samaritan in the early 1930s, and in the next decade it brought in the first EEG machine and equipment to be used in the Pacific Northwest.

During the 1970s Good Samaritan expanded in clinical-care program areas, research activity, education, and facilities, including the West Wing

patient tower, outpatient areas, emergency department, and chapel.

Continuing its heritage, the Right Reverend Matthew P. Biglardi, Bishop of the Episcopal Diocese of Oregon, is chairman of the Good Samaritan Board of Trustees, a 22-member body that sets policy for the medical center. Chester L. Stocks is executive vice-president of the medical center and is a nationally recognized leader in the hospital industry.

In the 1980s this highly successful medical center continues to move forward by initiating many new programs of treatment, rehabilitation, education, and research. Programs such as Good Samaritan's Comprehensive Cancer Program, Senior Health Services, Diabetes Program, Heart Services, Children's Program, outpatient clinics, and laser surgery have already ushered in the medical center's second century of health services to the community.

Across from the hospital's main building, the rising Neurological Sciences Center will house forty-two clinical programs and twelve research projects along with the Oregon Lions Club's Sight and Hearing Foundation and the Devers Memorial Eye Clinic.

PACIFICORP

No insurance company would underwrite her maiden voyage from New York to Portland, and all the experts of the day predicted that she would be incinerated at sea, but in August 1880 the world's first electric ship, Henry Villard's steamship *Columbia,* cruised safely past the "Graveyard of the Pacific" and entered the Columbia River. On board were 115 incandescent lamps sparkling throughout the ship—the first electric lights ever installed outside of Thomas Edison's Menlo Park laboratories. Henry Villard, Northern Pacific Railroad baron and president of the Oregon Railway and Navigation Company, had scored another coup in his incessant effort to publicize both Portland and the Northwest.

Those first twinkling globes inspired the spread of electric power production in the Northwest, and by the end of the 1880s small power plants were operating in Astoria, Pendleton, The Dalles, and Walla Walla. These scattered companies joined together in 1910 to form the nucleus of the Portland-based Pacific Power & Light Company, which celebrated its seventy-fifth anniversary in 1985. In the course of those seventy-five years, the firm has grown from generating only 10,600 kilowatts in 1910, to the sale of about twenty-four billion kilowatt-hours today, and has moved far beyond being a company that only generates electricity. Pacific Power & Light's entry into the fields of satellite communications and coal, silver, and gold mining have given the company both national and international impact. This growth has reached the point where Pacific Power officially changed its name to PacifiCorp in June 1984 to better reflect that it is no longer totally an electric utility company. The electric utility segment continues, however, to serve customers as Pacific Power.

It started back in 1909, when Seattle's Sidney Z. Mitchell, president of the New York-based Electric Bond & Share Company, organized American Power & Light Company to consolidate several small power companies in Kansas, but his real interest remained in the Pacific Northwest. Mitchell had been involved in the region since the 1880s, and in 1885 was granted exclusive agent rights for Thomas Edison's products in the Northwest.

Twenty-five years later Mitchell's interest returned to the Northwest, and in 1910 four scattered rural

This rugged Pacific Power & Light Company line crew used hand-operated gear on an early line truck, helping to bring electric service to customers.

power companies struggling to stay in business were brought together by his firm to create Pacific Power & Light. Guy W. Talbot was named president of this combination of the Yakima-Pasco, the Walla Walla-Pendleton, The Dalles, and the Astoria systems. This gave PP&L 10,780 customers in fourteen towns and rural areas of Washington and Oregon, but during its first year of operation the firm had to build 200 miles of transmission lines to link together its scattered holdings.

It was recognized that the success of the company was linked to the prosperity of agriculture in its region, and the company's farm agents drove many miles on the dusty roads of eastern Oregon and Washington's

Palouse to help farmers build electric brooders and pump-irrigation systems. One circuit was long known as the "Moo Cow" line because it powered some of the first electrified dairy barns in the nation. In small towns, meter readers carried newfangled gadgets called electric irons under their arms to demonstrate the invention's convenience to skeptical housewives.

The acquisition of small electric companies throughout the hinterlands of Oregon and Washington continued well into the 1920s, but the metropolis of Portland, the company's headquarters, remained outside the power realm of PP&L. This changed in 1925, when Northwestern Electric Company joined Pacific Power as part of American Power & Light, a holding company. Northwestern Electric was a small utility operating in the Columbia River Gorge when, in 1913, it obtained a 25-year franchise to operate in the city of Portland and buck heads with the Portland Railway, Light & Power Company. The first inroad was made by running a 66,000-volt transmission line from Camas, Washington, across the Columbia River, and down the south bank to Portland.

By 1925 Northwestern Electric had 34,500 kilowatts of generating capacity at three locations, including two in Portland—the Pittock steam-generating station downtown and the Lincoln steam plant on the Willamette River just south of city center. It served one-third of Portland's customers and businesses.

With all of its plant additions over the years, Pacific Power was in a good position to serve new loads, but new markets for electricity now had to be created. At a 1925 sales and service convention, president Guy W. Talbot and vice-president and general manager Lewis A. McArthur spoke on the growing necessity for sales activity on the system due to

the firm's increasing power surplus. Vacuum cleaners, ranges, washers, and irons were discussed. However, the device that caught everyone's fancy was demonstrated by the Electro-Kold Corporation, which promoted household refrigeration units to convert domestic iceboxes to electric operation. The firm claimed that an electric refrigerator saved enough in what would have been paid for food spoilage and ice to pay for itself. Sales were slow at first, but in 1929 over 900 were sold as the idea began to catch on.

Through the increasing sales of electric appliances, the number of kilowatt-hours used by the average home doubled in five years, reaching 997 in 1929 and 1,170 in 1930. This was a far cry from the days in 1910

The Public Service Building in downtown Portland has long been the headquarters for Pacific Power. The lighted sign on the top, no longer in place, was once a well-known landmark.

when some companies provided a home with only a single sixteen-watt bulb and kept it lighted for seventy-five cents a month. A globe for the front porch cost an additional twenty-five cents.

The expanding company was on the rise, and by 1925 was experiencing growing pains. Pacific Power had shared leased offices in the Failing Building with Portland Gas & Coke since 1918, and newly acquired Northwestern Electric's offices were squeezed into the Pittock Block. This need for more space led to the deci-

sion to construct what was to become the Public Service Building. Within a year distinguished Portland architect A.E. Doyle had perfected the building's plans and construction had begun. The day before the building's January 3, 1928, formal opening, a Portland *Telegram* headline read: New Edifice Enchanting to Visitor's Eye.

For many years the red-capped stately white tower ranked as the tallest building in Oregon. This Portland landmark later was crowned by a flashing red and green Pacific Power sign visible at night for several miles. Airplanes flying into Portland used the lighted building as a beacon to the Swan Island Airport, and the structure was so well known that Pacific Power superimposed the building's image on photos of the company's dams to give people an idea of how high the face of a dam was.

Three of Pacific Power's most significant hydroelectric dam projects were built between the years 1929 and 1956, during the utility's development of the Lewis River in south-

western Washington. These dams not only generated power and controlled flooding; the lakes formed by their backwater have become prime fishing, boating, picnic, and swimming spots for thousands of Portland-Vancouver residents. These pastimes have been encouraged by the development of Pacific Power's recreation areas, which provide facilities for the public, including a salmon fishery enhancement program and hatchery.

Beginning in 1947 a series of mergers led to a phenomenal growth for the company. That year Pacific Power & Light formally merged with Northwestern Electric, which provided direct access to the Portland market. As a result of the process, Portland remains the only city in the United States to be served by two investor-owned power companies.

Another merger occurred in 1954 with the Mountain States Power Company, an acquisition which added a vast amount of territory from Montana to the Pacific to the PP&L system. Included in this transaction were two local telephone operations in Lebanon, Oregon, and

Pacific Power's vast coal resources, acquired in the 1950s, gave birth to PacifiCorp's mining and resource development subsidiary in 1977. NERCO is now among the top ten producers of coal, gold, and silver in the United States.

in Kalispell, Montana.

That small start has grown into what is now Pacific Telecom, Inc., an 89-percent-owned PacifiCorp subsidiary, providing local telephone service requirements to some 156 exchanges in six northwestern states plus parts of Alaska and Wisconsin. The sixth-largest telecommunications company in the land, Pacific Telecom also handles virtually all long-distance telephone needs for Alaska. In 1982 Pacific Telecom launched its own satellite—the only non-Bell telecommunications company to have a satellite capable of "seeing" all fifty states.

With that merger also came service territory in Wyoming, where Pacific Power built its first coal-fired power plant. The first unit was completed in 1958. In preparing for its new role as a user of coal, the company began in the mid-1950s to acquire coal reserves in Wyoming and Montana as future fuel sources. The size of the coal reserves and the increasing interest in coal as an energy source gave birth to Northern Energy Resources Company (NERCO) in 1977 as a wholly owned subsidiary of Pacific Power (now PacifiCorp). NERCO now operates ten mines in six states and has become the nation's tenth-largest coal-mining company. The firm is also engaged in the mining and processing of gold and silver for refining into bullion, with one of its properties in Nevada being the largest open-pit silver mine in the United States. NERCO is also involved in oil and gas exploration and development in the West.

The last major merger was announced in 1960—the company's fiftieth-anniversary year. In early 1961 shareholders approved the merger with the California Oregon Power Company, which then served 93,000 electric customers in southern Oregon and northern California.

Pacific Power & Light Company is proud of its history and its role in the community, especially its heritage of leaders who, in the words of PacifiCorp chief executive Don C. Frisbee, were "dynamic, visionary men who backed dreams with action." Frisbee points to Paul B. McKee, head of PP&L from 1932 to 1952, as being symbolic of the firm's leadership. McKee personified the spirit of entrepreneurship and the private enterprise system but was always realistic. Even with the public power overtones in connection with the federal government's proposal to construct the Bonneville Dam and other dams on the Columbia River system, McKee's realism made him a supporter of the laudable system of river improvements and helped make the dams on the Columbia possible. McKee's contributions to the community also included being one of the

founders of both the Community Chest and the United Fund. Former chairman of the board Glen Jackson is offered as another "prime example of unselfish efforts for this community and region," and an "example rather than an exception" of the role PP&L's leadership has played in the community.

Pacific Power & Light has also encouraged and made possible energy conservation for Portland residents beginning in the 1970s and introduced the nation's first zero-interest weatherization program for home owners. The company continues to encourage energy conservation, while

Getting a fifty-foot pole into a hole was accomplished with muscle in the earlier years— a job now done by a power truck.

focusing on applications of electricity in residential, commercial, and industrial sectors that will save customers energy—and dollars.

In its seventy-five years of operation, Portland-based Pacific Power & Light Company—now PacifiCorp— has moved from serving the "Moo Cow" line and peddling electric irons door to door, to relaying messages via satellite across North America. Today the three major divisions of the company—Pacific Power, Pacific Telecom, and NERCO—can boast of having assets hovering around the $5-billion mark. Its electric division alone covers a territory of 63,000 square miles, serving 662,000 customers in six western states with power supplied by thirty-three hydro-generating stations and four major coal-fired power plants.

FRED MEYER

Throughout the land, a routine grocery shopping trip in 1920 required an itinerary and tough shoe leather. There were stops at the baker's for bread, the butcher's for meat, the grocer's for sugar, and probably a visit to the farmer's market for fresh produce. Additional items meant additional stops at specialty stores. A young Portland coffee merchant named Fred Meyer wondered why shoppers couldn't be offered all these goods under one roof—his roof.

Fred Meyer's notion of complete one-stop shopping was a new concept in the United States, but the idea caught on, grew, and multiplied. We take this and many other Fred Meyer innovations for granted today, but Portland's merchandising pioneer revolutionized the industry, and when he died in 1978 the firm he had founded as a visionary young man in 1922, and personally guided for fifty-six years, was ranked forty-fifth in sales among *Fortune* magazine's fifty largest retailing companies.

Frederick Grubmeyer was born in Brooklyn, New York, in 1886. At the age of twenty-two he changed his unappealing moniker to Fred G. Meyer and headed west to Portland after a brief stay in the goldfields of Alaska. In Portland he sold coffee, teas, spices, and other grocery items door to door from his horse-drawn wagons.

Meyer soon opened the Java Coffee and Mission Tea companies in the public market at First and Washington, that era's riverside hub of the city. He also became a landlord, subleasing space to others, and as different specialty food operators moved out, he took over their operation. But the city was growing, and merchants were flocking uptown to

Here, in 1947, Fred Meyer poses with some of his MY-TE-FINE line of products, which still go through rigorous quality control to ensure that, though less expensive, they are comparable to anything on the market.

Yamhill Street around Third and Fourth avenues. Meyer joined them, but envisioned the town's continued westward expansion and took an option on the southeast corner of Fifth and Yamhill. Here, he tried something that no one else had ever done.

He conceived the idea of a grocery department store—an establishment that would house a grocery department, meat department, fruit department, coffee, tobacco, a delicatessen, and more all under one roof. Later a laundry and cleaning department, shoe repair, clothing, and an optical department were added, and one-stop shopping was born.

More shocking innovations followed. In the days of weekly or monthly accounts and home delivery, Meyer opened Portland's first cash-and-carry grocery store. This was coupled with "self-service"; rather than dealing with clerks, signs instructed novice customers to "Serve Yourself and Pay Cashier." Shoppers loved this convenient novelty.

In those days most bulk foods, such as sugar, dry beans, rice, and spaghetti, were kept in large sacks or bins. Upon request, it was scooped into a sack, weighed, and given to the customer. To enhance the self-service concept, Meyer opened a prepackaged food store, across Yamhill from his Fifth Avenue store, where he weighed and packaged bulk items in advance—a one-pound unit of this, five pounds of that. Eventually,

Fred Meyer opened the first self-service drugstore in the world at Sixth and Alder streets in downtown Portland.

all his stores used prepackaging, and others soon followed suit. Meyer supplied self-service shoppers with baskets to carry their purchases, then baskets on wheels, which evolved into today's familiar shopping cart.

During the Great Depression Meyer's longtime policy of buying Oregon products, selling them inexpensively, offering discounts and coupons, plus his entertaining promotions endeared his store to the public. He prospered to the benefit of all, promoting locally grown products and hiring new employees in those troubled years of vast unemployment.

There were restaurants in his stores from the beginning, and the 1960s saw the opening of the first Eve's Buffet in the Fifth and Morrison store. Named for his beloved wife and business partner, Eve, it grew to become, at one time, the largest restaurant chain in the state.

The expansion of Meyer's operation began in 1930 with the opening of his Hollywood store at Northeast Forty-first and Sandy Boulevard. As his first suburban store, it offered free parking for automobiles, which were fast becoming an increasing factor in marketing activity. This was followed by stores in Salem and Astoria. From 1939 to 1941 Meyer moved into the neighborhoods of Walnut Park, and Rose City, as well as uptown, with the stadium branch on West Burnside. Meyer also devel-

Fred Meyer's original grocery department store on Fifth and Yamhill was the first of its kind in the nation and parent store of the present chain serving the Northwest.

oped a knack for gauging future transportation corridors, buying property in those areas, and building when residents inevitably began arriving. Both the Gateway store and the Barbur Boulevard store were somewhat in the "boondocks" when Meyer bought the land, but then came the Banfield and Baldock freeways which lured residential growth around these stores.

Fred Meyer died in 1978 at the age of ninety-two, and in 1979 noted historian E. Kimbark MacColl spoke of him in his book, *The Growth of a City:*

"Starting with literally no capital and no formal education, he built an empire that should exceed one billion

dollars in sales during 1979. He left an estate of more than $125 million, with nearly the entire amount bequeathed to a charitable trust, the income to be used for religious, charitable, scientific, literary, or educational purposes."

That one small cash-and-carry store on the corner of Fifth and Yamhill has blossomed into a chain of over 100 Fred Meyer stores today. Beginning in the 1960s acquisitions were made that spread the company into new markets within the state of Oregon, Seattle, Washington; northern Idaho; and Montana. A 1984 merger added thirty-one new stores in five more western states. Fred Meyer went public in 1960 but once again became a privately owned company in 1981, managed by the same top-management people who headed it for many years. And Fred Meyer's vision of one-stop shopping continues to grow, with the addition of new departments such as home improvement, Garden Centers, Nutrition Centers, Pant Kingdoms, fine jewelry, soft goods (formerly apparel), and Photo Sound departments, as well as expansion in the manufacturing and processing area.

Fruit was just one of many departments under one roof, a new concept pioneered by Fred Meyer in 1922.

203

OMARK INDUSTRIES

Ted Smith, chairman and chief executive officer.

A lowly timber grub worm, gnawing its way through a Douglas fir log in the soggy Northwest forest one day in 1945, helped revolutionize the world's timber industry, taking it from the days of two-man whipsaws to the mechanized techniques of today. Next to that fallen tree sat logger Joe Cox, intently studying the skill of nature's most efficient woodcutter. Cox, a tinkerer always on the lookout for that better mousetrap, was mulling over a problem vexing him for a decade—how to design a chain for chain saws that would make them practical to use.

Cox's introduction to the crude power saws of the day came in 1935 when a lumber company he and his brother were working for handed them one of the newfangled contraptions. The mechanical beast weighed 150 pounds and was powered by a twin Harley Davidson engine mounted on pushcart wheels to give it mobility. Joe knew it had plenty of power, but thought it peculiar that it "couldn't fell a tree as quickly as my kid brother and I could." They ran it into a shed and went back to their trusty saws.

Power sawing was a great notion, Cox thought, and the only problem

seemed to be the chain, a scratcher chain designed for the power of men rather than machines. For ten years he experimented until that grub worm gave him the answer. The worm was equipped with two sharp left- and right-hand cutters mounted on each side of its head, which chipped their way through the tough native wood. Joe Cox thought if he could mold the worm's cutter design in steel, chain saws just might be practical to use.

He was right. In 1947 Cox formed Oregon Saw Chain Corporation and hired four employees to work in the basement shop of his southeast Portland home to produce saw chain that flew through wood by chipping it away rather than slowly scratching through it. And when lighter engines were developed, Oregon Saw Chain's influence on efficient timber harvesting became one of the reasons people can afford a new home.

That cottage industry grew to become Portland-based Omark Industries, a diversified international corporation with seventeen manufacturing plants in four countries and 4,100 employees creating products that are sold in over 100 countries. Today annual net sales are over $300 million.

Oregon Saw Chain, Omark's largest division, has grown to become the standard of excellence for the forest industry worldwide. It has put the state on the map by making the word "Oregon" synonymous with state-of-the-art equipment for timber harvesting—literally millions of pieces of metal are shipped throughout the world with the word "Oregon" stamped on them.

Omark's international headquarters, located in Portland, is a big jump from that first shop in Joe Cox's basement, which the firm outgrew after only one year of operation.

In 1948 Oregon Saw Chain moved

into a garage seventy feet square, and the output from this modest new facility resulted in a 200-percent increase in sales. Another landmark of that year was the hiring of employee number 16, John Gray. The 34-year-old Gray was just out of the Harvard University Graduate School of Business, but the firm's new assistant general manager garnered no "perks." His first office chair was a nail keg. But Gray stuck with the company and watched it move into a 22,000-square-foot plant on Southeast Seventeenth Street two years after he came aboard. The employees now numbered seventy, and new

John D. Gray, vice-chairman.

products were being manufactured—depth gauges, saw bars, file holders, sprockets, and wedges. In 1951 annual sales topped the million-dollar mark. Gray saw good things on the horizon, and when he learned of Joe Cox's intent to sell the company in 1953, he pulled together enough cash—and pledged a royalty—to purchase it.

John Gray no longer sat on nail kegs, and in the years ahead would shepherd the company's growth by some 80,000 percent. In 1955 a new plant, constructed on McLoughlin Boulevard, tripled the size of the old 22,000-square-foot facility, and because of its ongoing diversification, the name of the company was changed to Omark, adopting the name of a small fastening company it had acquired in 1957. That year also witnessed a battle of the saw chain titans; the winning of two 1957 patent infringement suits against McCulloch Corporation and Sabre Saw of Canada made Omark number one in the saw chain industry.

Omark was dealt a good hand, but it didn't stand pat. In 1959 John Gray signed Edward "Ted" Smith as Omark's export manager to move the company into the international marketplace. That year the firm acquired 26 percent of the stock of Sporting Arms, Ltd., an Australian concern that manufactured construction powder-actuated fastening tools. The company began growing inestimably under the leadership of Smith, now chairman (elected in 1983) and chief executive officer (since 1973).

In 1965 the firm moved into its new award-winning plant in the Omark Industrial Park. By this time the influence of Ted Smith was vividly apparent. Omark now consists of four divisions operating worldwide: Oregon Saw Chain (still its leader), Hydraulic Materials Division, Sporting Equipment Division, and Cutting Tool Division. These divisions produce everything from the world's finest saw chain to gun sports equipment products, cutting tools, timber-harvesting equipment, fastening devices for railroad use, and cutting

Oregon Saw Chain Corporation, the predecessor of Omark Industries, first operated out of the basement of Joe Cox's modest southeast Portland home. © Mather Corporation, 1975

products for the home handyman and backyard gardener.

But the leadership of Omark has done even more than give Portland international prestige. Vice-chairman

Omark Center is Omark Industries' new world headquarters in the John's Landing area of Portland.

John Gray has been largely responsible for some of the city's physical betterment, as well. The location of Omark's world headquarters is significant—Portland's John's Landing is now a pleasant area of waterfront condominiums, crisp-looking office buildings, and a large renovated group of tidy shops and restaurants.

It wasn't always so attractive, however. In the 1960s this was an area of dilapidated industry and decaying buildings on the banks of a polluted Willamette River, which was disparagingly dubbed "Carp Valley." It would have continued in this direction but for architect John Storrs' dream to clean up the riverside neighborhood. Storrs realized he couldn't tackle the renovation by himself, so he enlisted the support of Omark's John Gray. He knew that Gray had the position, finances, vision, and staying power to see it through.

It seems vision and staying power have been hallmarks of Omark Industries ever since that day when Joe Cox finally found his better mousetrap.

MARSH & McLENNAN

Logging was anything but a risk-free venture for both company owners and workers of the Northwest woods in the early 1920s, and the firm of Marsh & McLennan came west to protect this and other vital, growing Oregon industries. Founded in Chicago in 1871, the insurance brokerage and risk management firm of Marsh & McLennan has served America's growth for well over a century.

During its history the firm has participated, through its clients, in virtually every major technological and economic development up to the most recent explorations of space. Today the broadly based billion-dollar company is the world's largest insurance broker, and operates globally. In 1980 Marsh & McLennan acquired British broker C.T. Bowring & Co. (Insurance) Ltd., giving the firm direct representation at Lloyd's of London.

Donald R. McLennan's commitment to professionalism was legend. He went so far as to once spend thirty consecutive days and nights riding the routes of the first two transcontinental railroad lines into the Pacific Northwest to learn the

Marsh & McLennan entered Oregon in the early 1920s and has represented Oregon lumber and logging companies from the beginning.

operations of the businesses he was insuring. He also became an expert on many other emerging industries of the nineteenth century and their technologies, including the telephone and the telegraph.

Henry N. Marsh pioneered the concept of the U.S. insurance broker as a buyer for clients rather than a seller of insurance. Intimate with the top brass of corporate America, flamboyant Henry Marsh involved his firm in almost every important enterprise during the early decades of industrialization.

Marsh and McLennan merged in 1904, and the firm was named Marsh & McLennan two years later. Portland representation was initiated

in 1921 by Mann-Titus Steamship agents, and the first Portland office under the name of Marsh & McLennan was established in 1927. The firm insured local lumber and logging companies from the beginning, including the Brooks-Scanlon Lumber Co. of Bend, Oregon, taking over its general property and casualty insurance.

In 1932 Marsh & McLennan started active production of Oregon business, which would grow to cover Portland's major utilities and most ambitious construction projects. In 1951 the firm moved into the Commonwealth Building, and in 1970 established new offices in the Georgia-Pacific Building.

The historic claims covered by Marsh & McLennan over the years include the staggering losses of Portland General Electric, Pacific Power & Light, and home owners following the 1962 Columbus Day storm; damages inflicted by sudden ice storms; and claims due to the eruption of Mount St. Helens in 1980. Perhaps the firm's oddest policy was one taken out by Pacific Power & Light during the construction of the Hilton Hotel across the street from its headquarters building in the 1960s. The utility's officers viewed with alarm the deepening chasm being excavated for the hotel's foundation and the possibility of their building toppling into the pit. The company took out catastrophe insurance through Marsh & McLennan, a policy better known today as PP&L's "hole insurance."

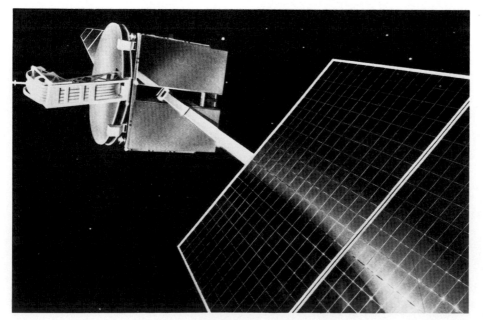

Marsh & McLennan Portland entered the space age with its coverage of the 1982 launching of Pacific Telecom's communications satellite.

PORTLAND GENERAL ELECTRIC COMPANY

In 1889 the first long-distance transmission of electricity in the nation coursed through fourteen miles of wire between Portland and the falls at Oregon City. Four years later the nation's first electric interurban railway carried passengers between these same two points. Electricity was ushering in an energized new era of technological advances that would benefit everyone, and Portland General Electric was in the vanguard.

When P.F. Morey, president of United States Electric Light & Power Company, Portland's first electric company, gazed upon the cascading waters of the Willamette River Falls at Oregon City, he visualized a more efficient means of producing power than steam-plant generation. Morey incorporated the Willamette Falls Electric Company in November 1888, and constructed Station A, a wood-plank dynamo house on stilts out over the falls on the east bank of the river. One year after Morey tapped the falls' potential energy, electric street lighting blossomed throughout Portland.

Soon, other small companies began crowding around the falls, eliminating the possibility for anyone to expand facilities. In 1892 these firms

merged to form Portland General Electric Company, and elected Morey as president. The new enterprise immediately expanded by constructing a 50- by 250-foot concrete powerhouse on the west bank of the river near the fall's canal and locks. In 1894 three 400-kilowatt alternating-current generators were installed in Station B to further electrify the community.

By 1907 PGE joined with Portland Railway Company, the city's electric streetcar system, and the electric interurban lines of the Oregon Water Power and Railway Company to form the Portland Railway Light and Power Company, later renamed the Portland Electric Power Company (PEPCO). A reorganization of PEPCO in 1946 led PGE to separate from the organization, and Portland General Electric has operated as an independent corporation since 1948.

Since that time PGE has been an eager participant in the Northwest Power Pool and the Columbia River Basin network of dams for power, navigation, flood control, and irrigation, a project that has been hailed as one of the greatest achievements of the electric utility industry. While PGE operates eight hydroelectric plants and five thermal plants in western and central Oregon, its crowning generating achievement was the completion in 1975 of the Trojan Nuclear Plant, which was built economically and has served the company well. PGE owns two-thirds of this plant, which has an output equal to that of its entire hy-

They were called dynamos, and in the summer of 1890 these six generators in Station A produced a first for the power company—the first long-distance transmission of alternating current in the United States.

Portland General Electric Company's 1.1-million-kilowatt-capacity Trojan Nuclear Power Plant, located near Rainier.

droelectric-generation system.

Portland General Electric Company proudly points out that its power generation system has led to residential rates that are only 55 percent of the national average. This Portland company provides service to about 40 percent of the state's electric customers in a compact region encompassing only 3 percent of the state's area, and it continues as a leader in the most highly electrified region of the United States.

RIEDEL INTERNATIONAL

In 1915 a 24-year-old, of German descent, named Art Riedel walked out of the soggy western Washington forests in search of steadier work than the boom-and-bust trade of a logger. Riedel found a more reliable income on the waters of the powerful Columbia River, starting work as a deckhand aboard a U.S. Army Corps of Engineers' dredge.

An opportunity came in 1930 when the thrifty former logger went to work for the Portland Dredging Company as general superintendent and also purchased 25 percent of its stock. Owning one-fourth of a fledgling enterprise, whose major assets consisted of two 2-cubic-yard bucket dredges and a 75-horsepower gasoline tugboat, couldn't guarantee immediate fortune, but it was a start.

By 1936 Riedel, in the midst of the troubled Depression years, made his biggest plunge. With his entire life savings of $6,000, he bought the remaining 75 percent of the dredging company. The next year, with two partners, Riedel branched out to form Willamette Tug and Barge, and in 1938 the two firms merged under the latter company's name.

During World War II Willamette Tug worked for local ship-repair contractors in the war effort, using the company's collection of old tugs, barges, and floating cranes, "more a fleet of rotten wood," Riedel Jr. recalls. With the danger of a postwar depression looming on Portland's horizon, Riedel Sr. saw a new opportunity to keep the old river equipment busy, and in 1946 the Sand and Gravel Division was formed.

The start of the 1950s found Willamette Tug and Barge still in the doldrums, and Arthur Riedel, Sr., seriously ill with cancer. The partners were considering a shutdown on the sand and gravel and concrete business. It was during these bleak times in 1953 that Arthur "Art" Riedel, Jr., a senior at Stanford University School of Engineering, came home to take control of the corporation's helm for his ailing father. Under the guidance of Art Riedel, Jr., the firm acquired some new equipment and "set out to diversify the company so it would not be dependent on any single profit center," Riedel Jr. recalls.

The vision of Arthur Riedel, Sr., has grown to fruition through his son and the efforts of a very talented group of people. The multifaceted Riedel International, one of the largest marine and heavy construction companies in the world, includes the largest fleet of dredges in North America, the largest sand and gravel concrete company in the Pacific Northwest, and a fleet of marine construction and transportation equipment that is one of the largest in the world. Riedel's Environmental Services Division has cleared up all types of hazardous chemical and oil spills, restored and decontaminated underground water, and removed hazardous substances including carcinogenic agents. The environmental emergency teams are ready for dispatch to job sites twenty-four hours a day anywhere in North America, but they're ready to respond worldwide when needed from bases in Europe and Asia.

As Art Riedel, Jr., states, "There are two distinctions that set us apart from other organizations: One is fast access to our hands-on management team twenty-four hours a day worldwide, and the other is our talent at 'imagineering.' We are always looking for new ways to put our talents work."

Art Riedel, Jr.

PORTLAND BOTTLING COMPANY

During the dry years of Prohibition, orange, grape, and root beer were favorite legal beverage flavors, and persistent Greek immigrant Andrew Hrestu annoyed his customers when he slipped little green bottles of a newfangled lemon-lime concoction into cases of conventional soda flavors. Cynical grocers often responded, "Hey, what's this? Take these with you and give me some grape instead."

That was in the 1930s, and Andrew and George Hrestu's Portland Bottling Company was finding it difficult to introduce 7-Up to the conservative palates of Portland. Today Hrestu is chairman of the board of Oregon's oldest active soft drink bottling company, and the oversized 7-Up bottle glowing atop his northeast Portland plant is a community landmark.

Louis and George Hrestu immigrated from a small town in Greece just before World War I, and in 1917 seventeen-year-old Andrew followed his brothers, arriving in Portland with just $7.50 in his pocket. Louis, the older brother, was active in a local bottling company. George and Andrew founded the Portland Bottling Company in 1924.

The fledgling operation consisted of a thirty- by ninety-foot room between Southeast Alder and Washington, a Model T truck costing fifty dollars, and only two or three employees. At first they sold pop only in their own ethnic community, to the many Greek coffeehouses and grocery stores along First, Fourth, and Fifth streets. These were bad times for the company, but the Chinese lotteries of the West Side gave gambling patrons free soft drinks, and this steady, reliable market kept Portland Bottling Company in business.

Good news came in 1933 when the Hrestus landed the 7-Up franchise and Fred Meyer gave them his first order—ten cases for his innovative Fifth and Yamhill store. The bad news was the repeal of Prohibition that same year, and with beer coming back to a parched Rose City, the brothers figured they'd go broke. However, a startling increase in demand for the soft drink mixers they bottled and a brief entry into wine bottling and beer distributing allayed their fears.

For a time in the 1930s and 1940s the Hrestus not only had the 7-Up franchise but the Pepsi and Coca-Cola franchises as well, but when World War II sugar rationing went into effect, Portland Bottling decided to use its available sugar for the bottling of 7-Up rather than the sweeter flavors.

In the decades following the 1940s Portland Bottling Company has experienced steady growth under the kindly, watchful eye of Andrew Hrestu—that once-poor teenage immigrant who makes no display of his

Portland Bottling Company found it difficult to introduce a new lemon-lime concoction called 7-Up to Portland in the 1930s, but today the firm's glowing 7-Up bottle above the plant is a community landmark.

wealth today. The firm continued to acquire new franchises, and today its 170 employees serve the three counties of the greater Portland area and southwest Washington, distributing 7-Up, RC Cola, Squirt, A&W Root Beer, Nehi flavors, Seagram Mixers, and Perrier to the thirsty residents of the area.

Young Andrew Hrestu proudly poses with his parents before he left the family's Limnas, Greece, home at the age of seventeen bound for Portland. He had just $7.50 in his pocket when he arrived, and today is chairman of the board of Portland Bottling Company.

PRECISION CASTPARTS CORP.

The ancient Egyptians used the "lost wax" method of casting metal to create beautiful, ornate gold jewelry, and Portland-based Precision Castparts Corp. has refined this craft to create highly specified metal parts for modern transportation, medicine, and national defense. Now known as "investment casting," this delicate technique was once confined to pieces less than six inches in diameter, but PCC pressed the limits of size by developing special mold materials and closely guarded casting techniques.

Spun off from Omark Industries under general manager Ed Cooley in 1953, PCC proved that pieces as large as sixty inches could be cast by the investment process and, in many cases, for less than half the cost of forging and fabricating the same item. Soon, jet engine manufacturers, working with hard-to-machine nickel-based superalloys, began to use PCC's cost-effective, proprietary method. PCC is now the dominant supplier of large-sized cast components, and one of only a handful of suppliers of medium-size parts for jet engines that use investment castings.

While aerospace parts make up the largest percentage of PCC's sales, the casting of prostheses—artificial hip, knee, and finger joints—remains an important market. The company also casts a wide variety of small industrial parts similar to the chain saw cutters that spawned the firm back in the 1940s.

In 1949 Joseph B. Cox, president and owner of Oregon Saw Chain, needed to manufacture a special cutter for his saw chain and felt the investment casting process was the best way to make it. Unable to purchase such cutters economically, Cox entered the investment casting business himself, founding a small operation on Southeast Powell Boulevard in 1949.

It was a noble experiment, but by

Manufacturing facilities for Precision Castparts were housed in one small building in 1951. Today the firm operates three separate plants in Portland as well as subsidiaries in England and France.

Ed Cooley, president, holds an orthopedic staple and stands before the world's largest titanium casting. The fan frame is used in a G.E. jet engine that powers large commercial aircraft.

1952 casting the special cutters proved impractical and was discontinued. Ed Cooley, who had been with Oregon Saw Chain as assistant general manager since 1950, began to spend more time with the casting operation, soliciting work outside the saw chain company.

On April 1, 1953, the casting division was made a separate corporation from Oregon Saw Chain, and an 8,500-square-foot plant was purchased at 8505 Southeast Thirteenth Avenue. Named Precision Castparts Corp., Cox was its sole owner and president, and Cooley was named general manager.

During 1953 and 1954 Oregon Saw Chain represented about 90 percent of the sales volume of Precision Castparts, and an internal organization and sales force was developed to permit the new corporation to become truly independent of Oregon Saw Chain. The planning paid off, and as sales grew in 1954 a decision was made to build a larger plant and to have more workers. In June 1955 a new plant on Southeast Johnson Creek Boulevard was completed and opened for operation.

That same year Cox purchased the Powder Power Tool Company, and the operations of that firm were combined in the Johnson Creek plant with those of Precision Castparts. Both were integrated as operating divisions under a new name coined for the occasion: Omark Industries.

In the fall of 1956 Cox retired,

selling Omark Industries to John Gray, the new owner of Oregon Saw Chain Corporation. The casting division was again spun off as a separate corporation, owned by Ed Cooley and two others, and rechristened Precision Castparts Corp. The firm then moved to the site of its current Portland plant.

In late 1959 PCC began experimenting with its current ceramic shell process, which allowed it to move beyond the conventional size limits of approximately two pounds per casting to today's castings of over 600 pounds. The casting process remains a version of the lost wax casting methods practiced by ancient Egyptians and Renaissance artisans, but is much more sophisticated.

Wax models of complex parts are produced through the use of sophisticated tooling, then dipped in special ceramic slurry that, when dry, forms a ceramic shell around the wax pattern. When the wax is melted from its shell and replaced by a molten metal alloy, a metal casting emerges that is an exact replica of the injection-molded wax model and needs very little, if any, exterior finishing.

PCC's innovative techniques enabled the firm to meet the challenge of the larger and more complex parts required by today's customers. This need became apparent as the commercial jet air transport industry reached maturity in the 1960s. PCC supplied this industry with castings of ever-increasing size and complexity, and today this Portland company manufactures titanium alloy and superalloy parts for almost every commercial and military jet engine in the free world.

After several years of research the 1970s brought the development and shipment of the company's first titanium castings, originally designed for the Boeing SST. PCC's titanium castings now are used widely in both military and commercial aircraft en-

Precision Castparts joined the new frontier of aerospace production with parts cast for NASA's Space Shuttle launching system.

gines. Precision Castparts was one of the nation's pioneers in titanium casting, and is the industry's leader today. PCC also moved into the prosthesis market, manufacturing these titanium and cobalt alloy human replacement parts for medical supply companies, and casting parts to surgeons' custom specifications for individual emergency cases.

As demand for PCC products grew, the firm began producing its own alloys, and has invested millions of dollars in new plant space and

equipment. By 1982 its titanium castings for jet engines and other parts grew so large that a separate facility was developed just to handle this end of the business.

PCC experienced tremendous growth in the 1970s and early 1980s. In 1980 the 160,000-square-foot Clackamas plant was built, and the firm moved into its attractive new corporate headquarters in the southeast Portland area. PCC expanded nationally and in 1976 further penetrated Europe by purchasing Centaur Cast Alloys in Sheffield, England, which now operates as PCC UK Ltd. In 1984 PCC bought a titanium casting plant in France that will be expanded to produce large parts.

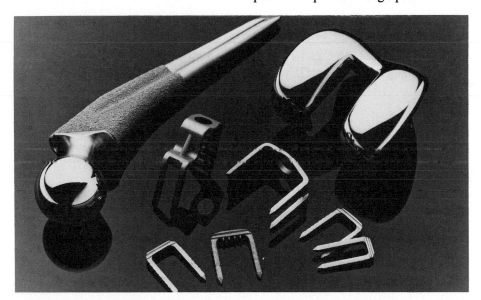

Hip, knee, and finger joints and bone staples are among the castings supplied by PCC to the medical prosthesis industry.

Parts cast by Precision Castparts Corp. soar overhead in such diverse forms as the Boeing 757 and 767, the Rockwell International B-1, and the Northrop/McDonnell Douglas F-18 fighter. The final frontier has been entered with PCC tooled up for casting parts now used in the Space Shuttle launching system.

STANDARD INSURANCE COMPANY

Leo Samuel (1847-1916), founder.

Roughriding President Theodore Roosevelt was in the midst of breaking up the monopolies and unbridled energies of the nation's "robber barons" in 1905, when Leo Samuel returned to Portland from New York a changed man. Samuel was the agent for Equitable Life in Oregon and Idaho, but early in the century an investigation by New York State's Armstrong Commission found Equitable to be one of the insurance companies operating in violation of the public trust. Why, he asked himself, should Oregonians be forced to insure themselves with eastern companies whose conduct seemed questionable at best and whose distance meant that it often took months to get a claim settled? Why not a western company? Indeed, why not an Oregon company to "keep Oregon money in Oregon"?

Samuel's musings led to the chartering of the Oregon Life Insurance Company in 1906—later to become

the first mutual life insurance company west of the Rocky Mountains. Over the years the firm grew to become Portland-based Standard Insurance Company, one of the nation's leading individual and group life insurance companies. The firm, which celebrated its seventy-fifth anniversary in 1981, began with virtually no assets in 1906, but its assets today top the billion-dollar mark. Throughout the years Standard has worked hard to live up to its slogan: "Dedicated to Excellence for Policyowners." That's what Leo Samuel had in mind back in 1905.

Thirteen-year-old Leo Samuel arrived in the United States from Germany in 1860 with an uncle who promptly deserted the boy, leaving him "one dollar and good wishes." But young Samuel also had a dream to one day publish a magazine. He began by hawking papers on the streets of New York on the eve of the Civil War, and in 1861 moved to Sacramento, California, to peddle western newsprint, sell advertising space, and eventually publish a traveler's guide for steamboat passengers. In 1871 the 24-year-old publisher moved to Portland and began publishing the lavishly illustrated and widely read regional magazine *The West Shore.* After twenty years of successful production, and with a childhood dream fulfilled, Samuel ceased publication to look for greener pastures.

After having both published and sold everything from postcards to city directories, Samuel's proven sales ability and regional contacts made him the logical choice to be

Standard Plaza, completed in 1963, played a major role in revitalizing Portland's downtown area.

Equitable Life's general agent in the area. He performed this new task with predictable success for ten years, until the findings of the Armstrong Commission gave him second thoughts about the trustworthiness of eastern financiers.

In 1905 Samuel unveiled his plan to establish the Northwest's first life insurance company to Abbot Mills, a friend and one of Portland's most successful businessmen, who gave Samuel his wholehearted support. Samuel went on to found the pioneering Oregon Life Insurance Company, with the intent of making it a mutual company in which profits would be returned to policy owners rather than company owners. But at the state capital they encountered a rude obstacle to their worthy plan. State law required the company to show a reserve fund of at least $100,000 before it could be licensed to insure a single life.

Undaunted, Samuel and Mills returned to Portland in 1906 to build the required reserve. Within weeks they secured, from among the most prominent citizens of Oregon, a list of eighty-one "guarantors," each understanding that they would receive no profit from their investment outside of simple interest. With this base the company became a reality in 1906, and when mutualization came about in 1929, the *Oregon Voter* was moved to write, "We doubt whether policyholders or the community as yet comprehend the moral grandeur of the sacrifice made by the holders of the $100,000 capital stock of our own Oregon Life Insurance Company in giving up all possibilities of speculative profit such as have inured to the benefit of successful life insurance company stockholders generally throughout the world."

During its first twenty-three years the company grew slowly but soundly under the guidance of some of Port-

An early advertisement urged Oregonians to "Keep the Money in Oregon."

land's leading citizens and financiers. By 1916 Oregon Life had ten million dollars of life insurance in force and one million dollars in assets. Expansion followed, and the company entered Idaho in 1920 and Washington the following year. In 1929, the year of mutualization, the company (now called Oregon Mutual Life), entered

Since 1929 "The Will to Achieve" medallion has symbolized the company's pioneering efforts in providing insurance for western families.

California. The solid foundation of the firm allowed it to weather the Great Depression of the 1930s and even boast ten million dollars in assets one year after the crash on Wall Street. Oregon Mutual began ranging far from its Webfoot base when it entered its fifth state, Utah, in 1944. Its name was changed to Standard Insurance Company in 1946 to reflect its broadened operation.

Standard really began picking up steam in the 1940s and early 1950s, and in 1951 the firm issued its first group insurance contract by signing on the Oregon State Penitentiary Guards and the Oregon State Police. The growth benefited policy owners with handsome dividends in 1952 when Standard announced it had reached fifty million dollars in assets. In 1963 assets jumped to the $100-million mark with one billion dollars of life insurance in force. That same year the company moved into its downtown Standard Plaza building, which ushered in a new era of downtown development.

Standard was founded to keep Oregon money in Oregon, and it has expanded this investment philosophy into fifteen western states, including recent entries into Texas, Wyoming, and Oklahoma. Future expansion may go beyond the western United States if new territory provides opportunity for gains on behalf of Standard's policy owners. Recent expansion has contributed to strong results. In 1983 the firm was able to report a net investment yield of almost 10 percent and more than thirteen billion dollars of life insurance in force.

Standard Insurance Company is proud of its heritage, and in 1982 eighty-one bricks were purchased in Pioneer Courthouse Square engraved with the names of the original guarantors to commemorate those unselfish investors who made Leo Samuel's 1906 dream come true.

213

LOUISIANA-PACIFIC CORPORATION

With all its visibility in the Portland community, many people are surprised to learn that Louisiana-Pacific Corporation has only been headquartered in the city since 1973. As a matter of fact, 1973 is the year that L-P was born, formed as a creative solution to some challenges raised by the Federal Trade Commission against another company, Georgia-Pacific Corporation. Now one of the largest Oregon-based businesses, L-P attributes much of its success to the direction of Harry A. Merlo, its chairman and president. Merlo, in turn, would be quick to credit the firm's 13,000 enthusiastic and motivated employees.

Typical of companies in the cyclical building-products industry, L-P has been subject to some ups and downs. Its first year can only be described as exhilarating. Business was terrific. The bankers provided an ample credit line. And L-P was free of FTC restraints that had hovered over many of the decisions and opportunities at Georgia-Pacific.

During its first year L-P made seventeen acquisitions, split the stock two for one, and increased earnings more than 115 percent. But, in mid-1974, the bottom dropped out of the market as rapidly as the initial success had taken hold. Curtailments, temporary shutdowns, and layoffs became a way of life. The contrast with the first eighteen months made the recession even harder to take.

The firm's response was to devise an innovative and successful communication program. It was honest, simple, and made L-P's workers feel better and look ahead, not backward. It was called "Yes We Can!"

"Sure, things look bleak," the program said, "but the means to make things better is within ourselves." It took L-P out of the recession in 1975 and, surprisingly, served the company well during the good markets that

Harry A. Merlo has been at the helm of Louisiana-Pacific Corporation since the company was formed in 1973.

followed in 1976, 1977, and 1978.

From 1979 to 1982 L-P and other forest-products companies were faced with the worst housing market in memory. L-P took advantage of the lull to gear up for the future.

Waferwood is a good example. It's a quality product that is rapidly replacing plywood since it saves the builder, home buyer, and do-it-yourselfer money and does a better job as well. L-P is the leading producer with about a billion square feet of annual capacity.

By their nature, large corporations are providers: jobs for their employees; products or services for their customers; and, with any luck, profits for their stockholders. There's a temptation to stop there, but L-P didn't succumb. Its philosophy has been to do a little more than society requires of it—to give back to its community more than it takes out.

This philosophy extends from the corporate headquarters in Portland to its plants throughout the country. More often than not, the focus of L-P's giving is on young people—from Little League sponsorship to the American Academy of Achievement and the Hugh O'Brien Youth Foundation.

The company is also oriented toward fitness and sports. In 1979 it saved the Portland Timbers soccer team from extinction by purchasing the franchise under a unique community partnership plan. Any profits from the team were pledged by L-P to six worthwhile Portland cultural and community organizations. Unfortunately, even L-P's marketing savvy couldn't save the franchise from a public not quite ready to accept pro soccer. After three seasons L-P abandoned the experiment. More recently, Louisiana-Pacific Corporation took on sponsorship of the U.S. Davis Cup team and is handling the staging of all the team's U.S. competitions.

NORTHWEST NATURAL GAS COMPANY

Gasco's familiar Linnton Plant as it looked in October 1923. One of these buildings still stands in Portland's Northwest Industrial Area.

Pounding hooves in the night kicked sparks from cobblestone streets lined by glowing gas street lamps as horse-drawn fire engines rolled full tilt to fight a roaring blaze. Water for steam to drive the engine's pump was preheated by manufactured gas, and the streets were also illuminated by the fuel. The gas came from the waterfront plant of the Portland Gas Light Company, franchised by the Territorial Legislature in January 1859, five weeks before Oregon became a state. The pioneer utility now distributes natural gas—as indicated by its modern name, Northwest Natural Gas Company—and in 1984 observed its 125th year of service.

Two Astoria merchants, H.C. Leonard and Henry D. Green, came to Portland to build a "gas manufactory." The first such plant in the Pacific Northwest, it was located on the west bank of the Willamette River near the foot of Flanders Street in 1859. Within a year flickering yellow gas lamps began brightening Portland's dark, rain-slick streets. This early gas was produced by heating coal imported as ballast on windjammers sailing into the river from Australia and Canada. Portland Gas Light Company was just that; in the earliest days of the firm lighting was the only use for the combustible vapor. Then came the preheating of water for those fire wagons and other new uses for gas, and when the firm was sold to a group of local businessmen in 1892,

its name was shortened to Portland Gas Company.

By this time service had expanded throughout the city and pipes were carrying gas on the east side of the Willamette, as well as the west. But the new owners soon experienced a temporary setback—the great flood of 1894, which put the gas works out of commission. The company's only complete service interruption, the flood prompted it to move its plant to the higher and drier ground of Everett Street.

In 1906 low-cost surplus California oil encouraged a conversion from coal-gas to oil-gas manufacture. This was also about the time gas appliances were developed—gas ranges, water heaters, and home furnaces. The West Coast's first gas furnace

was installed in the home of company president C.F. Adams.

A 1910 reorganization of the utility resulted in the familiar label, "Gasco," a contraction for the new Portland Gas and Coke Company. Demand for gas had burgeoned by 1913, and the larger plant was constructed at Linnton along the Willamette about seven miles north of Portland.

In 1955 natural gas became available to replace manufactured gas, and the next year Gasco converted its entire system to this new resource, resulting in a 17-percent rate reduction for customers. The name Northwest Natural Gas replaced Portland Gas and Coke in 1958 to reflect the change.

The first of two recent exciting developments for the company was the 1979 discovery of Oregon's first natural gas field at Mist. The second was the 1983 occupation of the firm's new offices in One Pacific Square—only a stone's throw from the embryonic coal burner on the waterfront. Northwest Natural Gas Company is the Pacific Northwest's largest gas distribution utility, in 1985, serving more than 266,000 customers in western Oregon and southwestern Washington.

This 1929 repairman advertises on his tool box the health benefits of Gasco's products.

HYSTER COMPANY

Foremen in the woods or on loading platforms would wait for a load to be engaged, then tell the winch or hoist operator to "Hoist'er." A frequent lapse in pronunciation led to these Portland-made lifting devices being dubbed "Hysters." This was in the early 1930s, and today the word Hyster is synonymous with quality materials-handling equipment worldwide.

In the 1920s Portland's Willamette Iron and Steel Company was manufacturing equipment for the ponderous steam machines that still dominated the power sources for industry and logging. Faced with changing technology and inefficient facilities, Charles F. Swigert, chairman of the board and president of Electric Steel Foundry, suggested joining with Ersted Machinery and Willamette Iron to form a separate enterprise to manufacture their products. In January 1929 the Willamette-Ersted Company was born. This firm was headed by Ernest G. Swigert. One of its first products was that hoisting winch that came to be called a "Hyster."

The business struggled through the Depression years trying to convince loggers and lumber mills that its products were more efficient than ox teams or steam "donkey" engines. The company's Straddle Truck lumber carrier was becoming common at mills, but it was believed that the carrier could stack higher if equipped with a pair of forks at the front. So, one of the earliest "forklifts" of the fledgling enterprise was a straddle carrier with forks.

By 1934 the firm was renamed Willamette-Hyster, and it continued experimenting with forklift design during the Depression, creating lift trucks with no drawings; they were simply built from available parts and handmade pieces. But soon the product's value was discovered, and its popularity spread beyond lumber

One of the current models of lift trucks loading containers dockside.

mills to docksides where early models were found to be ideal for the handling of bulky cargo.

While this was happening, inquiries began coming in for some sort of crane on wheels for more efficient handling of cargo in major ports. Experiments with "Cranemobiles" were encouraging, and Willamette-Hyster developed one called the Karry Krane, whose service to the Allies in World War II, both in industry and on docks and aircraft carriers, did more to spread the name Hyster around the world than any other single product in the firm's history.

"Willamette" was dropped from the company's name in 1944, and after World War II Hyster became active in the Marshall Plan for the economic recovery of war-torn Europe. In 1952 the firm moved into a bomb-damaged building in Nijmegen, the Netherlands, to begin manufacturing for the first time outside of the United States.

In the 1950s Hyster developed thirty-two different lift truck models, including the familiar warehousing-type lift truck, and a wide variety of other yellow-painted machines. The company began exporting in volume in the late 1960s, and by the next decade dominated the industry in many parts of the world. With the emergence of growing foreign competition, Hyster has designed and produced a less expensive line of lift trucks to be competitive throughout the world without sacrificing quality.

Hyster Company, which grew up on the banks of the Willamette River, became a private enterprise in 1984, and now operates on six continents.

The familiar Hyster warehousing-type lift truck.

BURNS BROS., INC.

None dare call one of Portland's most popular restaurants a truck stop, but the turn-of-the-century charm of Digger O'Dell's Oyster Bar and Restaurant, in the renovated historic Barber Block, is one product of Burns Bros.' efforts to revitalize Portland's East Side. While Burns Bros. began as a truck stop just across the street from Digger O'Dell's on Southeast Grand, the company now consists of eight diversified divisions, and is considered a Northwest pioneer in today's Pacific Rim trade.

Fresh out of the Navy in 1946, Art Mosely and Jack and Bob Burns selected a block across the river from the downtown area on old Highway 99E for their southeast Portland business location. The Burns Bros. Truck Stop became the first truck station in the Pacific Northwest when its nine employees began pumping gas and maintaining eighteen-wheelers in 1947.

In 1969 Burns Bros. opened one of the largest truck plazas in the United States on I-5 Freeway at Wilsonville, Oregon, to offer road weary truckers and auto travelers an oasis of creature comforts. Today the firm operates truck stops in five western states and has over 750 employees.

Burns Bros. has also gone international. Its Security Chain Company is the inventor, developer, and manufacturer of cable tire chain winter traction devices as well as conventional link chain. The firm has one plant in Clackamas, and its Korea plant has been in operation for fifteen years—one of the first joint-venture manufacturers to move into Korea from the Northwest. The Korea venture has grown into Burns Bros. International, which distributes everything from flashlights to auto parts. From its Portland offices the concern handles the worldwide importation and exportation of automo-

tive parts and accessories, with an emphasis on the burgeoning Pacific Rim trade in six Asian lands, including Japan and the People's Republic of China.

Other divisions include Automotive Jobbers Warehouse; Burns Bros. Tire Wholesalers, located in five northwestern states; Burns Western Development Division, for commercial and industrial park development;

Burns Bros.' original location on Southeast Union Avenue and Washington Street was Portland's first truck station, and, at the time, one of the most modern in the United States.

and Burns Bros. Restaurant Division, which operates eateries in five states along the West's major highways.

But the firm hasn't forgotten its roots, and in 1972 Bob Burns organized the Central East Side Industrial Council to revitalize that once-lively corridor along the east bank of the Willamette. Now, new companies are moving into this formerly run-down area to make it the "employment breadbasket of Portland."

The company's restoration of the Barber Block—the oldest commercial building on the East Side, which was designated a Portland Historical Landmark by the Portland City Council in 1978—and the establishment of Digger O'Dell's Restaurant shows the successful commitment Burns Bros. has to its neighborhood birthplace. And both the Barber Block and that first truck stop are visible from the company's nearby headquarters on Grand Avenue.

Brothers Jack (left) and Bob Burns at the 1964 grand opening of their Grand Avenue location. Beginning as a single truck station, Burns Bros, Inc., is now an active participant in the world marketplace.

PACIFIC METAL COMPANY

The year was 1876. Ulysses S. Grant was President, America was celebrating its centennial, General Custer got more than he bargained for at the Little Big Horn, and Alexander Graham Bell invented the telephone in Boston. Frederick K. Morrow and his partner couldn't compete with the headlines of 1876, but that same year in San Francisco they began the manufacture and sale of solder, Babbit metal, and type metal, and opening a branch of their firm in Portland, Oregon, was a remote possibility. However, Pacific Metal Works did move north, and it has prospered in Portland for over 100 years and has become a major force in the region's metal distribution industry, nationally an unheralded business that is larger than the U.S. airline industry. Since the 1880s it has been essential to fabrication and manufacturing in the Pacific Northwest.

In 1883 the first steam locomotive chugged into Portland over the Pacific Northwest's first transcontinental rail link. Portland was booming, and William H. Morrow, Frederick's brother, opened a Portland branch of Pacific Metal Works at Northwest Second and Davis streets to facilitate distribution to the Pacific Northwest.

In those early days some of the firm's most important products arrived from England in sailing ships

OFFICE AND WAREHOUSE
PARK AND EVERETT STREETS
PORTLAND, OREGON

In 1909 the San Francisco owners of Pacific Metal Works decided to concentrate in the Pacific Northwest. They erected a new building at Park and Everett streets in Portland.

that made the long voyage around Cape Horn and returned carrying cargoes of grain. These three-masted schooners, dropping anchor in the Willamette River, brought light-gauge galvanized steel sheet made in

Employees of Pacific Metal Works pose in front of the first Portland location, which opened in 1883 at the corner of Second and Davis.

Wales, much in demand for roofing, as well as tin and terne plate. Then came antimony from China; tin from Malaya; lead from Australia; zinc from Belgium; and sheet copper, both hot and cold rolled.

In 1888 Pacific Metal erected a one-story brick building at Northwest Second and Everett. This was initially a manufacturing facility and warehouse for imported steel and tin, but it soon served the company's complete product line for early Northwest industries—tin for the dairy industry; tin and solder for the salmon canneries of the Columbia River, Puget Sound, and Alaska, and the small operations of tinsmiths, blacksmiths, and metal shops; Babbit metal for antifriction bearing linings; type metal; and zinc for the gravity batteries of the telegraph industry.

There was also a new metal on the market that was light as a feather, but strong as steel. It was called aluminum, and some thought it was the metal of the future, but being worth more than gold at the time, it was also viewed as too expensive for practical application. Nevertheless, Pacific Metal dared to maintain a

180-pound inventory of the precious metal locked in a safe, and until after World War II the firm remained the only aluminum distributor in the Pacific Northwest. Today this "metal of the future" comprises 50 percent of Pacific Metal's total inventory, nearly four million pounds.

The 1906 San Francisco earthquake and devastating fire that followed completely destroyed that branch of Pacific Metal, and in 1909 the owners decided to concentrate the business in the Northwest. A new building was erected at Northwest Park and Everett streets in Portland. Four years later the California business was sold and the Portland business incorporated as Pacific Metal Works of Oregon, which was changed to Pacific Metal Company in 1922.

During its first century of service, the changing demands of customers and the emergence of many new products led to the distribution of a highly diversified inventory, with over 10,000 items in stock today. Stainless steel, building products, fasteners of all types, industrial compounds and adhesives, tools and ma-

Portland's flood of 1894 left Pacific Metal Company employees knee-deep in water. The poles were used to keep the buoyant wooden sidewalk in place.

chines for the working of metals, and even nonmetal products designed to replace metal have been added, giving Pacific Metal one of the widest and most diverse inventories of any service center anywhere.

This growth has dictated larger facilities, and in 1965 Pacific Metal opened a new, 110,000-square-foot headquarters and service center on Southwest Bond Avenue, just south of the Ross Island Bridge. Located on a fifteen-acre industrial site, it is a facility designed for future expansion. In 1971 some 3,600 square feet were added to the office to accommodate added computer services and the centralization of administrative functions.

Pacific Metal began expanding

Times have changed since this apparatus was used back in 1888 to manufacture and coil wire solder.

within the Northwest in 1947 with the opening of a 19,000-square-foot plant in Seattle, Washington, an operation that by 1962 had grown to 31,000 square feet. In 1979 a modern, 80,000-square-foot service center was completed to better serve the Seattle market. Pacific Metal moved into the Inland Empire by opening a branch in Boise, Idaho, in 1953 and another in Spokane, Washington, in 1962. The company began serving the rapidly growing Rogue River Valley area from Medford in 1968, and the Eugene-centered Mid-Willamette Valley in 1972. A Montana branch was opened in Billings in 1977, the firm's seventh.

Just as it served the embryonic industries of Oregon back in the 1880s, Pacific Metal Company continues to provide metal distribution services for a varied line of customers today, thus providing that all-important link between the manufacturers of metal products and vital Oregon industries, ranging from high-tech to commercial transportation, construction, and fishing.

219

R.B. PAMPLIN CORPORATION

The R.B. Pamplin Corporation was incorporated on August 27, 1957, by Robert B. Pamplin as a family investment company. It is operated by Robert B. Pamplin, chairman and chief executive officer, and his son, Dr. Robert B. Pamplin, Jr., president. Growth beyond its original purpose began upon the retirement of the senior Pamplin as chairman of the board and chief executive officer of Georgia-Pacific Corporation in 1976, when 100 percent of the Ross Island Sand & Gravel Company was purchased. Ross Island is a local firm which for nearly sixty years has participated in Portland's growth and development by supplying the materials needed for new construction.

Timber from the vast forests of the Pacific Northwest was the mainstay of construction in Oregon through the nineteenth century, but a new century brought new needs for the building industry. Cement had become an essential ingredient in masonry construction, and the cement used in Portland was at first brought in by ship from California. Demand grew rapidly. Oregon became a pioneer in highway construction with the "impossible" 1913-1915 construction of the Columbia River Highway from Astoria to Hood River, and the demand for paved highways increased. The 1916 Federal Highway Act and subsequent construction projects lifted the demand even higher, and engineers were finding it difficult to procure enough gravel on a regular basis for their needs from scattered quarries.

In 1926 Walter H. Muirhead, a southern Oregon cement maker, and Sneelock & Co., an aggregates partnership familiar with Willamette River sand and gravel resources, purchased Ross Island and Hardtack Island, organizing the Ross Island Sand & Gravel Company. As a result, there would no longer be a shortage of aggregates for local con-

The original Ross Island Sand & Gravel office was built in 1930 on Southeast McLoughlin Boulevard and served the firm until 1978.

struction. Ross Island is located at a place where the river widens dramatically and slows, and the river had been depositing gravel there for billions of years. Portland civil engineer W.G. Brown made several test borings for the firm in the area to a depth of eighty feet, and estimated that it contained a probable gravel reserve of nineteen million cubic yards, including six million cubic yards of sand.

Already the local leader in its field in the 1930s, Ross Island Sand &

This 1930s prototype was Ross Island Sand & Gravel's first ready-mix concrete truck.

Gravel moved even further ahead with the introduction of ready-mix concrete and cement trucks to haul its product to the construction site rather than mixing it at individual sites. The 1930s were also years of one of the greatest single demands for concrete ever known in the Portland area—the Columbia River's Bonneville Dam project, begun in 1933. World War II brought with it new uses for the company's concrete—a concrete airfield at Astoria, blimp hangars at Tillamook, and concrete for the enormously productive wartime shipyards of the area.

The growth of Ross Island Sand & Gravel has paralleled the growth of Portland, and its participation in this expansion is physically apparent. The decade of the 1950s was a big growth period for the company with the rapid development of Portland's arterial and highway system creating the need for tons of concrete. Another boom came with new construction in the lumber industry, paper mills, and industrial growth around the city. In 1953 the firm purchased K.F. Jacobson Co., Inc., an asphalt

The R.B. Pamplin Corporation's Ross Island Sand & Gravel Company was a pioneer in the introduction of ready-mix concrete and cement trucks to haul premixed concrete to construction sites. Courtesy, Ackroyd Photography Inc.

paving and road contractor, and in 1954 Ross Island Sand & Gravel became nationally known for being one of the first packagers of premixed concrete—the only thing it didn't have was water.

There was even more industrial growth and a great expansion of the interstate highway system during the 1960s. More and more concrete was being poured around Portland as the years wore on. Most of the bridges spanning the Willamette and Columbia rivers are composed of Ross Island Sand & Gravel concrete, and the downtown building boom of the past twenty years has resulted in one of the greatest demands ever.

From the buildings, fountains, and malls of the South Auditorium urban-renewal project of the 1960s, to the buildings popping up like mushrooms downtown today, the sands and gravels of Ross Island have been a major ingredient of urban growth. A good part of most of the buildings seen along Portland's skyline were once boulders, cobbles, gravels, and sand deposited by the Willamette

River ages ago and dredged up from a depth of 130 feet below the surface of the river by Ross Island Sand & Gravel—some of the deepest dredging done in the United States.

All of this dredging has, of course, taken its toll on Ross Island, and what was once a wooded isle in the Willamette has over the years taken on the shape of an atoll. But Robert Pamplin has planned a long-range rehabilitation program for the island. The old owner of the Ross Island operation had no such plans, but Pamplin intends to "restore the island to its original size, if not better, and revegetate it in a natural way." This restoration will be carried out in stages, which will continue well into the twenty-first century.

The R.B. Pamplin Corporation also owns 100 percent of Mount Vernon Mills, Inc., which consists of nine textile mills in North and South Carolina, Georgia, Alabama, and Maine. Established in 1848, Mount Vernon Mills is the manufacturer and seller of diversified types of tex-

tiles, specializing in a complete line of clothing for paper mills, mat felts, dry felts, and forming fabrics. Mount Vernon also manufactures meat wraps, tent fabric, gauze, mailbags, yarns, and paint cloth. The history of Mount Vernon Mills goes back a long way. Its Tallassee, Alabama, mill was used to manufacture rifles for the Confederacy during the Civil War, and was one of the last two still operating at the end of the war.

R.B. Pamplin was chairman of the board of trustees of Lewis and Clark College for thirteen years, and R.B. Pamplin, Jr., was chairman of the University of Portland for four years. They are also fund raisers for Western Conservative Baptist Seminary, but their involvement is not just a check-writing policy so much as a participatory involvement.

Ross Island Sand and Gravel does some of the deepest dredging in the United States, bringing sand and gravel up from a depth of 130 feet below the surface of the river.

ESCO CORPORATION

Charles F. Swigert's Electric Steel Company was formed on July 13, 1913, in a wood-frame building just outside the old Vaughn Street ball park, but it took months to install and become familiar with the first electric furnace used to melt steel west of the Mississippi. The furnace was imported, the instructions were written in French, and the measurements were in metric. The first casting was finally poured in 1914, and ESCO would continue pouring steel at this site for over seventy years and go on to become a worldwide leader in steel technology.

Founder Charles F. Swigert tackled any construction project as long as it was challenging, and the monuments to his drive included most of the early bridges that spanned the Columbia and Willamette rivers, the "impossible" piers for San Francisco's Golden Gate Bridge, and a large portion of Hoover Dam. Shortly after the turn of the century Swigert saw a growing demand for steel castings for equipment in the Northwest's burgeoning forest industries, and Electric Steel was founded to produce these hard-to-get steel castings for trolley cars, logging locomotives, and sawmill equipment.

If Swigert loved challenges, the foundry certainly provided them.

Charles F. Swigert, founder.

One day in 1916 the furnace exploded, blowing the roof off, spewing molten metal in all directions, and burning the foundry to the ground. About this time it was rumored the United States might enter World War I, and industry would have to gear up for war production. The foundry was quickly rebuilt and put back into operation before the boys were sent "over there."

In the 1920s a metallurgical laboratory was set up as the company began producing new alloy steels, but the logging industry was experiencing an economic slump, dragging Electric Steel down with it. ESCO began diversifying, and in 1926 the company's wide variety of products were stamped with the now-familiar "ESCO" trademark for the first time.

Times were hard during the Depression, but ESCO did a better job of keeping its people employed than most foundries in the nation, and in the process evolved from being a small jobbing foundry to an organization of specialists producing many special alloy steels and several new alloys known as stainless steel.

When the United States entered World War II in 1941, the Portland shipyards became as productive as any in the country, and the need for ESCO products seemed limitless. So well did the firm meet wartime requirements that it earned the Navy "E" Award for excellence six times.

In the decades that followed, ESCO grew into one of the world's leading manufacturers of steel alloy expendable products for the mining, earth-moving, dredging, crushing, and logging industries, and also produces high-integrity custom castings for the aerospace, hydroelectric, nuclear, petrochemical, and defense industries.

Today Henry Swigert, grandson of ESCO's founder, is chairman of the board, and the corporation now operates steel service centers in the western United States and has manufacturing plants throughout North America and Europe, with product development and metallurgical laboratories at its Portland headquarters.

ESCO Corporation is one of the world's leading manufacturers of steel alloy expendable products for the mining, earth-moving, dredging, crushing, and logging industries, and produces high-integrity custom castings for the aerospace, hydroelectric, nuclear, petrochemical, and defense industries.

NICOLAI COMPANY

When Roy Rogers enters his California desert home, he swings open custom-made doors with stained-glass windows picturing horses, cattle, and other western themes loved by this singing cowboy. Those doors were supplied to Rogers by the largest manufacturer of wood stile and rail doors in the nation—Portland's Nicolai Company, a business that has been ornamenting area homes since the 1860s.

In 1868 brothers Louis, Adolf, and Theodore Nicolai arrived in Portland and founded the Nicolai Brothers Company, a large lumbering, planing, and sash-and-door plant. Their first Portland location was built on the entire block bounded by Davis, Everett, First, and Second streets in 1869. From this plant the firm manufactured much of the elaborate wood ornamentation still admired on many of this city's venerable homes.

Specialization came in 1910 when Harry T. Nicolai and Peter Autzen founded the present door company on Columbia Boulevard, where they began producing quality custom-made doors. By 1927 the firm had grown to 500 employees with an annual payroll of over $700,000, and not only were their doors shipped throughout the nation, but over a

The Nicolai Brothers Company shipped custom-made woodwork from its first Portland plant, built in 1869 at the usually muddy intersection of Northwest Second and Everett streets.

million doors were sold in the United Kingdom, as well. With the exception of a brief move to Canada during the Depression, the Nicolai Company has operated at this site ever since.

The U.S. Army needed few doors to fight World War II, but the Nicolai Company contributed to the war effort by retooling to manufacture ammunition boxes, tent poles, and spool ends for the Army Signal Corps' wire reels. Following the war the firm ventured into the manufacture of kidney-shaped vanity tables, kitchen cabinets, and home portable bars, but eventually returned to its stock-in-trade and began producing quality, custom-made entrance, interior, garage, and screen doors exclusively.

Today the Nicolai family is still active in the company, which is now headed by chairman Theodore Nicolai III and president Richard C. Rieten. In 1976 Nicolai purchased the Clear Fir door plant in Springfield, Oregon, from Fibreboard Corp. Then, in 1981, the firm acquired Tualatin's Conrad Veneer, the makers of a wide variety of veneers used in furniture manufacturing. Today the 700 employees of the Portland, Tualatin, and Springfield plants produce a combined total of nearly 4,000 doors per day and forty million

Nineteenth-century employees pose proudly amid a display of their work—doors, shutters, window sashes, and intricately carved millworks. Courtesy, Oregon Historical Society (negative number 28219)

feet of veneer. The cornerstone of the country's largest door manufacturer remains intricately carved and leaded stained-glass doors.

Over 100 years of woodworking experience in Portland goes into each of the Nicolai Company's handcrafted, hand-finished doors.

Nicolai's current manufacturing complex in north Portland.

223

COLUMBIA STEEL CASTING CO., INC.

The city of Portland and Columbia Steel Casting Co., Inc., have seen many changes during the years between 1901 and today.

Columbia Steel Corporation was organized in the West by Central California industrial leaders who saw a need for heavy machinery that would be required for forest-products industries and metals mining. Logging and gold mining were active businesses during the 1920s and 1930s. Columbia products included sawmill loghauls, carriages, and buckets for gold-mining dredges. Prior to this, hydraulic water rams, early water-driven pumps, also were popular for irrigation on remote homesteads.

Around 1931 Columbia's Portland foundry was sold to A.M. Clark, an eastern industrial manager. Columbia Steel Corporation (CSC) decided it was not essential for the Portland

The firm's early 1900s facility was this 2.5-acre site, located at Northwest Tenth and Johnson streets.

foundry to supply parts to it when they could obtain castings from one of its other locations. Both the Torrance, California, and Portland foundries had supplied castings to the parent company with an identifying mark of a diamond T or a diamond P for later recognition of the supplier. Portland did not abandon this mark until 1952.

Hobart Bird, Sr., was an imaginative, energetic employee of the com-

Manganese steel dredging buckets were made by the Columbia Steel Corporation for service in the Federated Malay States, south of China in the 1920s.

pany in the years around the turn of the century. He was moved into leading roles in CSC's independent status, providing growth in the foundry's gold-mining markets in the western United States and Alaska. Bird acquired ownership of the company and was its president through the late 1930s.

During this time CSC's capacities were committed solely to making castings for the maritime industries, which during the World War II years employed over 100,000 people in shipbuilding and related industries. CSC made hawse pipes, stern frames, stern tubes, propellers, and rudder stocks for the shipbuilding programs in the area.

After the war, Bird returned to guiding CSC in restoring markets lost during the disruptive war years. His work was cut short by his death in 1946. Following the loss, his son, Hobart Bird, Jr., left the Coast Guard, where he had served as first officer on a patrol vessel during the war. He assumed the assignment of CSC president and reorganized the market pursuits and operations to take a significant place in manufacturing wear-replacement parts for the primary metals, construction, and heavy-equipment manufacturing industries.

Today the company's main offices and plant are in north Portland, situated on about 100 acres of land. It is a far cry from the old Northwest Tenth and Johnson location where the plant had been located until 1962. The main foundry bay building is 1,000 feet long. The pattern storage building alone spans more than an acre. The products are designed, proof-cast of specified material, and machine-finished in Columbia Steel Casting Co.'s complete "one-place" facility.

Today's modern manufacturing facility is located on nearly 100 acres in north Portland.

224

BLUE CROSS AND BLUE SHIELD OF OREGON

The two are now one, but for many years the Blue Cross and Blue Shield plans in Oregon were separate organizations, each with roots deep in the state's history. But in the 1970s a changing marketplace, fueled by rising health care costs, caused each to consider how it could better meet the needs and demands of those it served.

To create a more efficient and effective organization, the experience, skills, and ideas of the two independent staffs were merged on March 1, 1983, eliminating duplication of facilities and equipment and providing additional security for both subscribers and those who provide their care. Today Blue Cross and Blue Shield is by far the largest prepaid health care plan in Oregon, and is part of the nation's largest system.

Some early versions of prepaid health care plans originated in the Pacific Northwest around the turn of the century when physicians began contracting with logging camps to provide their services and perhaps those of a local hospital for a regular fee. From this "contract practice" concept, hospital associations and medical service bureaus evolved. Similar small, informal, prepaid health care programs emerged in other parts of the country, as well.

In 1929 a large-scale plan to pro-

vide hospital care for schoolteachers at Baylor University Hospital in Dallas, Texas, attracted nationwide attention. The idea was adopted in other cities and was extended to all hospitals in the community. The blue cross was adopted as a symbol for these hospital plans. In 1939 the California Medical Association formed California Physicians' Service to offer similar benefits for physician care, and Blue Shield plans were born.

The embryonic Blue Cross and Blue Shield plans arrived in Oregon when Northwest Hospital Service and Oregon Physicians' Service both were incorporated in 1941. This was just in time to participate in the

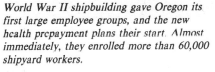

World War II shipbuilding gave Oregon its first large employee groups, and the new health prepayment plans their start. Almost immediately, they enrolled more than 60,000 shipyard workers.

health care coverage of Oregon's first large employee groups—the thousands of people working in the area's bustling World War II shipyards. Almost immediately, 60,000 shipyard workers were enrolled, initiating forty-five years of steady prepaid health-care growth for these nonprofit associations.

Today Blue Cross and Blue Shield of Oregon has more than 1,200 employees and serves the needs of 820,000 hospital-medical-surgical plan subscribers, 416,000 dental care plan subscribers, and 200,000 with vision care benefits. A special division also serves an additional 350,000 people who receive Medicare (Part A) benefits. The continuing objective of Blue Cross and Blue Shield of Oregon simply is to provide excellent service to the people of Oregon and their doctors and hospitals.

Blue Cross and Blue Shield of Oregon traces its roots to the "contract practice" of medicine in Oregon logging camps of the nineteenth century. The local doctor would contract with the owner of the sawmill to provide medical services for all employees.

JONES OREGON STEVEDORING COMPANY

William J. Jones, founder of Jones Oregon Stevedoring Company.

Stevedores such as the Portland-based Jones Oregon Stevedoring Company are a vital part of the state's bustling oceangoing commerce, and in the course of its 75-year-plus history, the firm has loaded and discharged the cargo of thousands of ships calling at Northwest ports from every maritime nation in the world. And stevedoring is no small industry in Oregon. In 1984 the longshore payroll for the Oregon area amounted to over sixty-eight million dollars, supporting the international trade that pumps several billion dollars into the state's economy every year.

William J. Jones first came to Oregon in 1908 while representing Puget Sound's Rothschild Stevedoring Co., operated by his brother-in-law, Henry Rothschild. On behalf of the business, Jones purchased the firmly established Brown and McCabe Stevedoring Company, which had been active on the Columbia River for more than thirty years. Jones acted as general manager of the Portland enterprise until 1913, when he separated from Rothschild's group and began contracting under

his own name in the Columbia River district just before World War I.

William Jones' son, Clayton, completed service as a naval officer and joined his father in 1920, at which time the company name was changed to W.J. Jones & Son. After the unexpected death of William Jones in 1921, young Clayton took the helm, managing the firm with Rowland Clapp as his second-in-command during the busy times of the Roaring Twenties. The business expanded with the local economy as new steamship lines established service between the West Coast and Europe and as trade routes were established to the Far East.

Even during the troubled years of the Great Depression, the company grew. In 1930 Clayton Jones made arrangements with his uncle, Henry Rothschild, to acquire the Brown and McCabe interests and merge them into the W.J. Jones organization. The 66-year-old Rothschild had no sons, and Jones convinced him that because there were no heirs, the family interest should be rejoined. Roths-

Stevedoring in the early 1900s (left) and the 1980s.

child agreed, and further talks led to Jones' acquisition of the Rothschild Stevedoring organization in Puget Sound. Rowland Clapp moved north to serve as president of the firm, and Roy J. Beckett joined W.J. Jones & Son as vice-president.

The death of Clayton Jones in 1956 marked the end of his personal leadership of thirty-five years, during which time the company became more firmly established and recognized as the preeminent stevedoring organization in the Columbia River area. In 1970 W.J. Jones & Son, through the efforts of Clayton Jones' son, Clayton R. Jones, Jr., acquired the Oregon Stevedoring Company, whose own history dated to 1916, and in 1971 the firm's name was changed to Jones Oregon Stevedoring Company.

Today Jones Oregon remains a "family affair." In 1976 Peter N. Beckett, son of Roy J. Beckett, became president of the firm, and today he serves as the company's chairman. In 1972, Clayton R. Jones III, currently the president of Jones Oregon, became the fifth generation of that family to work in the stevedoring business.

226

STIMSON LUMBER COMPANY

In the timber-rich forests of the Pacific Northwest, it was the habit of early logging companies to harvest a tract of timber and move on to the next. Charles Willard "Cully" Stimson had done this in Bayview and on Hood Canal in Washington, but lumbering was changing and when Stimson Lumber Company came to Oregon it came to stay. It stayed to help renew timberlands and build communities. The firm's family of owners have behind them a tradition of six generations in the same business in one of the state's most important industries, and its future looks as strong as its past.

Inspiration for a sawmill in Oregon was the large cut of Douglas fir and larch that Willard Horace Stimson purchased in Tillamook and Washington counties in 1889-1890. Forty-one years later Stimson, Willard Horace's son, built the mill in Forest Grove. However, that mill had an inauspicious beginning. The small community welcomed the employment of 250 to 300 men, but many wondered about the wisdom of opening a new mill with a depression under way.

Then, as soon as the mill was ready to start up, the great Tillamook fire of August 14, 1933, devas-

This aerial view of the Stimson Lumber Company and Forest Fiber Products Co., located in Forest Grove, was taken in 1984.

tated over 300,000 acres of timberlands, including one-third of Stimson's holdings. Before the inferno played out, 3,000 men battled the blaze. Smoke rose over 40,000 feet to dump ashes on ships 500 miles at sea. Losses were in the millions of dollars.

Stimson started the mill on logs still smoking from the heat of the fire. He and his manager, Harold Miller, knew that the damaged timber would be good for several years, and by utilizing the fire-damaged timber, Stimson Lumber Company became a model for rejuvenating the Tillamook Burn. To maximize production from the timber, the firm modified the mill several times over

the next three decades. The first change was a veneer mill to peel the damaged logs for plywood. Then they built a hardboard plant, the most modern at the time and one of the first in the country. By developing marketable panels, Stimson Lumber Company was soon a leader in the hardboard industry, and Harold Miller was called upon to serve as president of the American Hardboard Association.

Stimson's reforestation program made the burned-over lands productive again. The company built roads and removed snags to control fire and replanted with aerial seeding and with nursery stock. By 1966, when the Industrial Forestry Association endorsed Stimson's tree farm, its loggers were ready to begin harvesting second-growth thinnings.

In the 1960s Stimson Lumber Company expanded to diversify and integrate its operations. Constructed in 1963-1964, Miller Redwood followed the acquisition of timberlands there in the early 1940s, and the purchase in 1962 of Northwest Petrochemical in Anacortes, Washington, provided resin for the hardboard plant and later a redwood plywood plant in Merlin, Oregon.

Today Stimson Lumber Company's timberlands are adequate to perpetuate its mills, and tradition promises another century of operation for the firm.

Main Street, Forest Grove, 1933. Courtesy, Oregon Historical Society (negative number 15487)

THE CHAS. H. LILLY CO.

Major milestones in gardening history have been reached in the 100 years of the Portland-based Chas. H. LILLY Co. Since 1885 the firm has introduced slug bait to the United States, developed the Skagit Valley in western Washington as a major growing area for flower and vegetable seed, become well known worldwide for quality crop seeds, and emerged as the "father" of the contract system of growing seed.

The present-day Chas. H. LILLY Co. is the result of partnerships, acquisitions, and mergers throughout the firm's 100-year history.

In 1885 Chas. H. Lilly and B.G. Bogardus established a general store in their small Illinois hometown. In 1889 the partners, heeding the words of Horace Greeley to "go west," moved to Seattle and reestablished their partnership in a hay, grain, and seed business. What began as a small shop quickly grew. Within five years the business had become the largest hay and grain business in the Northwest. The Panic of 1893, responsible for many business failures, had no adverse effect on the growth of this successful enterprise. The Lilly, Bogardus Company manufactured flour for several major flour companies, including Holly and Choice Patent. Two other brands of flour were manufactured exclusively for the Oriental market. For its time, the Lilly, Bogardus Mills was considered to be the most efficient and modern.

The business continued to prosper during the 1890s. The Klondike Gold Rush of 1897 brought still more business to the operation, along with another business partner. Judd M. Elliott, a former employee of Lilly, Bogardus, had struck it rich in the goldfields of Alaska. He returned to Seattle to buy into the company, becoming vice-president. In 1900 Lilly, Bogardus became Lilly, Bogardus & Company and purchased New North-

The original Chas. H. LILLY Co. store in Seattle sold a variety of grocery items, coffees, seeds, and poultry and animal feed.

west Flouring Mills.

Prosperity brought about the need for a new facility for the expanded operation of Lilly, Bogardus & Company. In 1903 the firm built a new mill, the largest in Seattle.

Early in 1904 The Chas. H. LILLY Co. was formed as a wholesale grocery and roasted coffee company, separate from Lilly, Bogardus & Company. Later that year Lilly, Bogardus partners Bogardus and Elliott were bought out by Chas. H. Lilly, and the two ventures—Lilly, Bogardus & Company and The Chas. H. LILLY Co.—were merged, assuming the latter firm's name.

Several of the products first developed by Lilly, Bogardus and The Chas. H. LILLY Co. are still major members of the present-day product

line. Morcrop fertilizer, flower and vegetable seed, grass seed, and Go-West Slug Bait all hail back to the early days of The Chas. H. LILLY Co.

In 1928 Portlander Fred L. Trullinger, retired schoolteacher, postmaster, hardware merchandiser, store owner, and sales distributor, went to work for The Chas. H. LILLY Co. in the position of sales manager. During Trullinger's first year with Lilly, he repeatedly urged Chas. H.

Early in Lilly's history these trucks were used to deliver flour and seed.

Lilly to purchase the then-foundering Portland Seed Company, which had fallen from being a serious competitor to being a candidate for business failure. Chas. Lilly vehemently refused to purchase the seed company.

In 1929, frustrated with Lilly's refusal to buy Portland Seed, Fred Trullinger pooled his resources, left Lilly, and bought Portland Seed himself. Working through the Great Depression in its Willamette River waterfront headquarters, Trullinger turned the firm around through determination, long hours, and five-cent seed packets. This began what was to become a three-generation management and ownership of the company. In 1946 Trullinger's son, Fred C. Trullinger, became president of Portland Seed. One year earlier Portland Seed had purchased the Inland Seed Company of Spokane, beginning a series of acquisitions.

An ironic twist of history came in 1955 when, twenty-six years after Fred Trullinger walked out of The Chas. H. LILLY Co. to buy Portland Seed, his business acquired a concern three times the size of Portland Seed—The Chas. H. LILLY Co.

With these acquisitions, particularly that of Lilly, Trullinger now had a firm hold on the entire Pacific Northwest market for seed, and could tap the Willamette Valley grass seed fields to become a major producer of quality seed. The company also added a fertilizer line, including Lilly's Morcrop, and the combined seed operations made it the largest packer and marketer of flower and vegetable seeds in the Northwest.

The Chas. H. LILLY Co. headquarters on Northeast Killingsworth in Portland houses all corporate offices as well as commercial and consumer home and garden chemicals, private-label chemicals manufacturing, and a quality-control laboratory.

All the acquired companies consolidated operations under the corporate name of The Chas. H. LILLY Co. in 1963. However, the expansion days were not over. In 1970 Lilly acquired the Miller Products Division of W.R. Grace Company, a pioneer in the field of agricultural chemicals. Miller Products was started in the early 1920s in Portland. All products from The Chas. H. LILLY Co. are now marketed under the brand name "Lilly/Miller." The most recent acquisition came in 1974 with the purchase of Beale Seed Company of Ontario, Oregon.

The Chas. H. LILLY Co. moved its headquarters to 7737 Northeast Killingsworth in Portland in 1975. The Portland facilities include corporate offices, warehousing and distribution, commercial and consumer home and garden chemicals, private-label chemicals manufacturing, and quality control. Other facilities are in Spokane and Seattle.

The parallel, then merging, histories of the firm that comprise The Chas. H. LILLY Co. reflect the common ground they share—the desire to grow, to provide quality products, and to keep the West growing.

Now under the leadership of Fred L. Trullinger, its third-generation president, The Chas. H. LILLY Co. faces new challenges in a changing marketplace. But the motivations that propelled the first Fred Trullinger and Chas. H. Lilly still prevail as the firm begins its second century of growth.

In 1949 Morcrop was thirty years old. Karl Von Norman, sales manager, and Boyd Sparks, assistant sales manager, felt it deserved a celebration.

STOEL, RIVES, BOLEY, FRASER AND WYSE

The Portland law firm of Stoel, Rives, Boley, Fraser and Wyse grew up with some of the Pacific Northwest's earliest railroads and electric utility companies. Having gone through many name changes over the years, the current firm is the product of a 1979 merger of two important local law firms—Davies, Biggs, Strayer, Stoel and Boley and Rives, Bonyhadi and Smith. This merger brought together Portland's largest law firm, with a broad corporate, business, and litigation practice, and a medium-size firm with the largest utility practice in the state.

The elder firm of Davies, Biggs, Strayer, Stoel and Boley can trace its roots back to 1883, the year the Northwest's first transcontinental railroad was completed, with Portland its terminus. That year Charles H. Carey began a long career of practicing law in Portland, and represented the Northern Pacific Railroad as its Oregon counsel. Carey, who later penned some classic studies of the state's history, including the still widely read *General History of Oregon,* formed a partnership with James B. Kerr in 1907.

In 1905 Kerr came west from St. Paul, Minnesota, to represent the Northern Pacific when that railroad joined with Great Northern to construct the Spokane, Portland & Seattle Railroad (SP&S) line along the north bank of the Columbia River, providing both railroads access from Spokane to Portland. Much of his work was done in conjunction with Carey's office, a relationship that grew into a partnership two years later. Kerr went on to become one of the great land lawyers in the region and continued to handle the Northern Pacific's tangled land grant problems.

The firm of Rives, Bonyhadi and Smith grew from the partnership of Laing and Gray, formed in 1935. John A. Laing came west from New York in 1910 to represent Electric Bond & Share, which had acquired several small electric utilities in the Northwest. When these companies were merged into the predecessor of Pacific Power & Light, Laing served as vice-president and general counsel, and was joined by Henry Gray as a part of the house counsel office.

In 1935 Laing and Gray formed an independent law firm but continued to represent PP&L while working toward building a broader client base. In the 1950s the firm also represented Northwest Natural Gas and General Waterworks Corporation.

When PP&L's first rate case was initiated in 1958, the firm engaged the experienced George Rives to handle the matter; he did so successfully and was invited to join the firm in 1963. Rives brought with him a belief that the venture should further broaden its client base and reduce its dependence on PP&L. During the next fifteen years its representation expanded into business litigation, corporate representation, and antitrust work.

The 1979 merger of the two firms brought together a total of over 100 lawyers. In the past two years Stoel, Rives, Boley, Fraser and Wyse has opened an office in Beaverton to better serve its clientele from Oregon's burgeoning high-technology industries and another office in Washington, D.C., to represent its clients before federal agencies.

Charles H. Carey

John A. Laing

J.K. GILL STATIONERS

Some young men came to frontier Oregon for adventure. Joseph Kaye Gill was lured by romance. So taken was he of a Salem, Oregon, girl he met in his Massachusetts school that he twice sailed from the East Coast to Oregon to court her. J.K. Gill and the lovely Frances Willson, the daughter of a Methodist missionary who had come to Oregon in 1837, were wed in 1866.

At the age of eighty-one, J.K. Gill recollected that his mother-in-law then "owned one-half interest in a store at Salem—one side stocked with drugs, the other with books and stationery. She wished me to take charge of her half of this store, which had not been profitable thus far." Gill gave his entire attention to the shop, and succeeded to the point where J.K. Gill, "Booksellers, Stationers, and Complete Office Outfitters," is today one of the country's largest retailers of its kind with sales in excess of forty-seven million dollars a year.

In 1867 J.K. Gill acquired the stationery half of the drugstore, expanded it, and developed a book line of goods. The business prospered, and in 1868 he built a solid brick store in Salem. At the suggestion of pioneer Portland banker William S. Ladd, Gill decided to move his business to Portland in 1871, setting up shop

Founder J.K. Gill celebrates his ninety-first birthday in his office in 1931. When he died that same year, J.K. Gill was eulogized as "the dean of American booksellers and stationery dealers."

near the corner of Southwest Front and Washington. In 1922, after a series of relocations, J.K. Gill moved into its present downtown building on the corner of Southwest Fifth and Stark. This store, which has traditionally handled books, stationery, gifts, and art and office supplies, became a popular gathering place of the literary luminaries of the day. When J.K. Gill died in 1931 he was eulogized as "the dean of American booksellers and stationery dealers."

Mark M. Gill, the founder's grandson, became president in 1955 and chairman of the board in 1962, and is still active in the company as resident consultant. For many years J.K. Gill was the regional depository for sixty-four schoolbook publishers and distributor of all the books for local medical schools. The firm began expanding into shopping malls in 1965, opening the Lloyd Center

store. Growth continued, with the company adding locations first in the Seattle area with the acquisitions of the Lowman and Hanford stores and then additional locations in Oregon. The next major expansion was in the early 1970s, when J.K. Gill moved into the highly competitive California market.

Today there are forty-four J.K. Gill stores in Oregon, Washington, California, and Arizona. In 1980 Brodart Inc. of Williamsport, Pennsylvania, became the parent company of J.K. Gill. In 1982 Brodart was successful in acquiring another old-line book and stationer chain, called Burrows, with thirty-eight locations in the greater Cleveland, Ohio, area. The total number of locations represented by these two companies makes Brodart the largest book and stationery specialty retailer of its kind, with sales in excess of fifty-five million dollars.

Now based in San Diego, California, J.K. Gill Stationers has served Portland for well over 100 years and remains dedicated to the well-being of the community as an active participant in civic affairs.

The J.K. Gill store in the Clackamas Town Center, Portland, opened in 1981.

231

VIKING INDUSTRIES, INC.

The mid-1960s were youthful, halcyon days of "surfin' safaris," the Beach Boys, and "California dreamin.' " But in 1965 two young dreamers came from sunny California to drizzly Portland in a blue pickup truck with just $8,000 in their pockets to establish a trail-blazing Northwest industry.

Richard C. Alexander and Raymond S. Jarvis came north knowing most of the windows installed in Oregon were imported from California, and gambled that a demand might be created for residential and commercial windows produced closer to home. They founded Viking Industries on a shoestring, eating lots of beans and franks that first year because window glass and gas for the battered pickup seriously curtailed funds for haute cuisine.

Not only did Viking remain afloat that first year, over the past twenty years it has grown to become the producer of more insulated windows than anyone west of the Rocky Mountains. In the process, Oregon has moved from being a net importer to a net exporter of windows throughout the West.

Viking's first 6,000-square-foot plant and offices was located at 1600 Southwest Harbor Drive.

Company president Alexander, Jarvis, and a third partner, who withdrew shortly after start-up, began investing their meager operating capital by leasing a 6,000-

In 1966 Richard C. Alexander, founder, conducts a tour of the plant for his father, Clarence A. Alexander, visiting from Tennessee.

square-foot building along the Willamette River on Harbor Drive at the foot of Southwest Jefferson Street. Here, with two employees and the trusty pickup, Viking shipped its first window.

Soon, the firm had eight accounts for its thirty-four standard sizes of windows. The new enterprise was well received, and within one year business increased 300 percent.

As it expanded its designing and manufacturing of windows, Viking targeted building material dealers as its primary customers rather than contractors. Dealing in quantity, quality wasn't sacrificed. During a severe 1966 storm two houses under construction were blown to kindling, but not one Viking window cracked.

In 1968 Viking anticipated a growing demand for energy-saving windows and designed its first insulating window. It was designed not only to be energy efficient but was made reasonably priced for the typical Oregon home. The firm's insulated windows became highly popular as escalating energy costs and increased interest in energy conservation grew in the 1970s.

When power utilities began encouraging conservation by providing financial incentives for home owners to insulate their abodes, the demand for insulation products skyrocketed. Viking's proven insulated window was one of these popular energy savers, and by 1980 Viking became a major supplier for most of the energy conservation programs in the Pacific Northwest.

The company's old quarters were becoming cramped, and in 1969 the firm moved to a roomier 40,000-square-foot facility at 6430 Northeast Halsey. This, too, was soon outgrown, and in 1974 Viking Industries moved into its present sprawling 260,000-square-foot facility on Northeast 186th.

The year 1974 also saw Viking Industries venture into the export merchant and export broker business when Richard Alexander, with Hans Polstra as vice-president and chief operating officer, founded Viking International. Viking International was started to introduce domestic products to foreign markets—especially the outstanding seafoods, fruits, and vegetables produced in the Pacific Northwest.

This Viking division represents a number of Northwest food producers, and is the leading supplier of frozen potato products in the Pacific Rim, boasting 65 percent of the french fry market share in Japan. Operating out of a downtown Portland office, with branch offices in Tokyo, Japan, and Amsterdam, the Netherlands, Viking International performs a valuable service for local food producers who want to enter the international marketplace but find it untimely to start their own international division.

Viking Industries line of windows has grown from thirty-four standard sizes in 1965 to 4,500 today, and to meet the demand Viking employs the largest off-line fully automated glass cutter in the United States. During its first twenty years the firm's accounts grew from eight to 800 and the payroll expanded from two employees to more than 400. With Oregon now being a net exporter of windows, Viking maintains distribution centers in Portland, Seattle, Sacramento, and Los Angeles, with a large fleet of eighteen-wheelers shipping products throughout the West.

Viking Industries, Inc., has come a long way since that day in 1965 when its "fleet" of one blue pickup truck tooled wistfully northward along I-5 toward an uncertain future.

The present Viking manufacturing facilities consist of four buildings providing more than 260,000 square feet of manufacturing, distribution, and office space. From this facility Viking products are shipped to over 800 dealers throughout the West.

Raymond S. Jarvis and Richard C. Alexander with an early delivery truck. This truck comprised the "fleet" in 1965. Viking eighteen-wheelers now run over two million miles each year delivering to dealers and job sites throughout the West.

KNAPPTON CORPORATION

Sailing vessels were still a mainstay of commerce entering the Columbia River when the Brix brothers acquired their first steam-driven towboat, the Miler, to bring logs to their Knappton, Washington, lumber mill in 1912.

The Columbia River has served as a major river highway in the Pacific Northwest since Lewis and Clark paddled to this uncharted far corner of the continent in 1805. In the 1860s Mississippi River-style paddle wheelers plied its waters, bringing gold dust from the booming mining camps of eastern Oregon and Idaho to The Dalles and Portland. And for over seventy years the Knappton Corporation has navigated 485 miles of this flowing water highway, moving the commodities that represent the economy of this region.

Knappton has been a pioneer in river towing since 1912, when the Brix brothers acquired two steam-driven towboats to bring logs down the lower Columbia River to their lumber mill at Knappton, Washington. Soon, they were asked to move logs for other mill owners, and the Brix brothers immediately recognized the Columbia River's potential as a highway for commerce. As demand for their services grew and the cargo list expanded, the Knappton Towboat Company was incorporated in 1920 to better serve the busy trade on the Columbia River system.

From 1920 to 1979 Knappton acquired or merged eight Columbia River towing companies and obtained Interstate Commerce Commission operating authority for nearly all rivers, ports, and points on the West Coast. In 1942 the main office of the firm was moved from Astoria to Portland, where it is still based today, on the west bank of the Willamette River beneath the graceful arches of the St. Johns Bridge.

Knappton got its start by moving logs, and it still moves more rafted logs on the river than anyone else,

Knappton barging operations have been a familiar sight on the majestic Columbia River for nearly seventy-five years. Photo, Bob Graves/The Image Works

but when Peter J. Brix became manager in 1967, the firm's operation grew as never before. Under Brix, the third generation of the Brix family involved in the enterprise, Knappton expanded its operations throughout the region, bringing grain from the Inland Empire to Portland for shipment all over the world, logs for the Pacific Rim nations, and other products, including wood chips, paper products, sand and gravel, and petroleum. The firm also offers complete container barging services from the head of navigation at Lewiston, Idaho, to the lower Columbia River.

The Pacific Ocean and Puget Sound are also Knappton's highways. The firm navigates from California to Alaska. The pioneer towing company is now helping tap the resources of America's last frontier, Alaska, barging general cargo ranging from rail cars, containers, chemicals, building materials, and petroleum from the Pacific Northwest and Canadian ports.

Knappton's Ocean Towing Division has become an important link in the state's transportation network by providing barge services to the oil, mining, and construction industries.

On the river, the ocean, and the sound, Knappton Corporation is continuing a tradition of water transportation with deep roots in the region's history of economic growth.

ALEXANDER & ALEXANDER

In 1914 insurance brokers Charles B. and William F. Alexander set up shop in a Clarksburg, West Virginia, two-room storefront. That same year William F. Alexander ambitiously offered to take over and develop the Baltimore & Ohio Railroad's insurance program. The railroad company was interested in this novel proposal, but only if Alexander & Alexander opened a Baltimore office. Alexander left the B&O office, walked across the street, and rented a room. Within one hour he returned to B&O and

The Board of Trade Building, circa 1920. Courtesy, Oregon Historical Society (negative number 4289)

announced that Alexander & Alexander now had a nearby Baltimore office open for business. He got that account. That was the beginning of a firm that, through many mergers, grew to become the second-largest insurance brokerage in the world, and the largest in the United States.

Alexander & Alexander's Portland office traces its roots back to 1884, when Charles W. Sexton opened his own insurance office in Minneapolis to represent the prosperous grain, milling, and lumber industries of the area. The Sexton firm opened a Port-

land office in the Board of Trade Building in 1921 when its largest client, the J. Niels Lumber Company, expanded its operations into the dense forests of the Pacific Northwest. Another Sexton client, the Shevlin-Hixon Lumber Company, soon followed suit, and the firm was here to serve them.

In Portland Sexton became actively involved in lumber, logging, shipping, and grain operations, representing such clients as the Pillsbury Company and the pioneering Collins Pine Company. Sexton also virtually grew up with the Boise-Payette Company, a client later known as Boise Cascade. By the 1930s Sexton was one of the leading insurance brokerages for the lumber and grain industries in the nation.

Alexander & Alexander entered Portland in 1970, when it merged with the Portland, Minneapolis, and St. Paul offices of Sexton. This was one year after Alexander & Alexander had gone public, and the beginning of a growth record unparalleled in the insurance brokerage industry.

The company eventually became involved in more than 150 mergers, including the largest single merger in the industry's history. With this track record, it has developed creative approaches to risk management that have brought new products and services to its clients.

Today Alexander & Alexander has 15,000 employees worldwide, and over eighty offices in the United States alone. In 1983 the Portland office was awarded Alexander & Alexander's "Most Improved Office Award."

The brokerage's clients come in all sizes. Alexander & Alexander of Oregon affords professional services to personal and commercial accounts throughout the state. Based upon growth during the past five years, coupled with an investment in people, Alexander & Alexander is positioned to grow with Portland and Oregon in the future.

The Portland office of Alexander & Alexander was built in December 1983.

PORT OF PORTLAND

To many the Port of Portland is an enigma wrapped in a puzzle. It does go about its work quietly, making Portland the largest auto import port and the largest export seaport on the West Coast. It helped make Portland a major seaport in the nineteenth century, and this century has given the city an airport, ship-repair facilities, and has literally created thousands of acres for development and economic growth at Swan Island, Rivergate, and Mocks Landing. While the port directly employs only 700 people, it helps generate jobs for one out of eight people in the greater Portland area, and its impact on the local economy amounts to more than six million dollars a day.

The Port of Portland was established by the 1891 Oregon legislature to dredge and maintain a 25-foot-deep channel between Portland and the sea to ensure vital ocean commerce could reach this inland, fresh-water seaport. But the increasing number of cargo ships that began calling on the city overwhelmed the waterfront's few dilapidated, privately owned docks. To remedy this, the City of Portland created the Commission of Public Docks in 1910 to improve the harbor's marine cargo facilities. The result was the construction of Terminal 1 just north of today's Freemont Bridge in 1913.

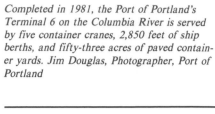

Completed in 1981, the Port of Portland's Terminal 6 on the Columbia River is served by five container cranes, 2,850 feet of ship berths, and fifty-three acres of paved container yards. Jim Douglas, Photographer, Port of Portland

Other terminals followed, in numerical order, the most recent was Terminal 6 in 1974 and expansion of this container facility by the Port of Portland in 1981.

In 1920 the federal government directed the city to look for a site for a new airport. The city turned to the port, which owned Swan Island. At this time the island was a large unused area filled in by the port's dredging operations. It seemed perfect for a landing field, and the port constructed Portland's first municipal

The Port of Portland became the first major port of call for the People's Republic of China when it resumed trading with the United States after a thirty-year hiatus. The February 1980 arrival of the Rong Cheng *marked the beginning of this two-way trade. Jim Douglas, Photographer, Port of Portland*

airport on Swan Island.

The Swan Island facility served its purpose well until commercial aviation outgrew it, and the port constructed a larger, modern airport on a parcel of dredged landfill on the Columbia River in 1940. The port was confronted with still more growing pains over the years, but successful expansion projects have resulted in today's Portland International Airport, supported by the Portland-Hillsboro, Portland-Troutdale, and planned Mulino airports to relieve the main airport of increasing smaller plane traffic.

No longer an airport by the time the United States entered World War II, Swan Island was turned over to the Kaiser shipbuilding interests, whereupon T-2 tankers were launched for the war effort at the rate of one per week. The property was returned to the port in 1948, and its ship-repair facilities were moved from St. Johns to Swan Island in the early 1950s. Major expansions of the Portland Ship Repair Yard were completed in 1979, including the addition of a fourth dry dock, the largest such facility on the West Coast.

In 1970 the port and the Portland Dock Commission merged, and the new Port of Portland, a municipal corporation, was formed. Three years later the state legislature approved expansion of the Port District to include Washington and Clackamas counties. Although publicly supported for capital improvements, the port pays its own operating and administrative costs. More growth can be expected with cargo forecasts indicating Portland's volume will increase threefold by the year 2000.

THE ROBERT RANDALL COMPANY

Robert D. Randall, founder and president.
Edmund Keene Photographers

Robert D. Randall was born in rural Minnesota during the Great Depression and grew up in a log cabin with four brothers and sisters. It is not surprising that while most kids had baseball players or movie stars for their heroes, young Randall dreamed of becoming a landlord. "When I was young, I used to think that someone who owned a fourplex was very wealthy," he says. "I always wanted to meet such a person."

Randall has done much better than those invisible landlords he worshipped as a child. The Robert Randall Company has, in fact, grown to become Oregon's largest private residential homebuilder and property management firm, averaging over fifty-four million dollars in annual gross operating revenue from 1979 to 1984.

After graduating from the U.S. Military Academy at West Point in 1956 and serving a three-year stint with the U.S. Army Corps of Engineers, Randall moved to Portland where he worked as a management trainee for Tektronix. In 1960 he entered the real estate sales and investment field, moving from an owner of small income properties, to real estate salesman, and, finally, to employee of a small investment company.

The same year, 26-year-old Randall began a one-man real estate firm that, four years later, branched out into the construction of apartment buildings rather than just buying, renovating, and renting them. Twenty units were built in 1964, and the business began growing at a staggering rate during the next fifteen years. By 1980 Randall had built, owned, and managed 15,000 units in Oregon and Washington.

Flexibility is one of the main reasons The Robert Randall Company is a survivor in the tough housing construction business. It adjusts to the changing demands of the market, be it apartments one year or suburban office buildings or single-family subdivisions the next. The Randall success formula was especially evident during the bleak years of Oregon's housing industry; from 1975 to 1976 The Robert Randall Company did twenty-five million dollars in business in the Portland metropolitan area, finishing 40 percent of the area's total apartment construction.

While the cornerstone of the business is still based on multifamily housing construction and management, the company's operations and interests over the years have grown to include all phases of real estate development. Already active in the Puget Sound area, the firm is expanding to cities outside of the Pacific Northwest. The Randall package on the move includes apartment and condominium construction and management, subdivision development and lot sales, suburban office building construction and leasing, real estate marketing and investments, and real estate financing.

In both good times and bad, Robert D. Randall is an optimistic risk-taker. A voracious reader, Randall likes to quote from Horace: "Adversity has the effect of eliciting talents which in prosperous circumstances would have lain dormant."

Constructed by The Robert Randall Company in 1982, the Village at Brookhaven II Condominium in Beaverton consists of twenty-five units of duplexes and triplexes.

WIDING TRANSPORTATION, INC.

Trains, boats, and planes are just a few of the unusual loads Widing Transportation, Inc., has hauled over the nation's highways. This Portland company has also prided itself on engineering the highest, widest, and longest loads that could be hauled legally over the interstate system. Founded by former truck driver Glenn Widing at the age of thirty, Widing Transportation now specializes in the safe transport of hazardous materials, and it has grown to become one of the largest bulk commodities carriers on the West Coast.

Starting as a teenager, Glenn Widing spent several years behind the wheel of a truck and used this experience as a springboard to become manager of two local trucking companies. In 1959 he bought Meadowlark Transportation. Meadowlark had focused on transporting gasoline and diesel fuel, but Widing Transportation expanded into hauling asphalt and oil products used in Oregon road building.

The old Meadowlark permit was a beginning, but it limited the firm to an originating point of fifty miles around Multnomah County, a permit that was soon virtually exhausted. To avoid stagnation, Widing purchased St. John's Motor Express, Inc., in 1966, a company with chemical and heavy hauling rights and men experienced in these operations. This addition of heavy-haul and the growth of both the bulk chemical and bulk petroleum divisions spurred on expansion.

This growth exceeded even Widing's own expectations, and led to the acquisition of three other companies: Evert's Commercial Trans-

port Company and Admiral Tank Lines in 1970, and Chipman Trucking Company in 1972. In 1970 Widing Transportation was given the Outstanding Hauling Job of the Year Award at that year's A.T.A. National Heavy Specialized Carrier's Conference. The winning haul involved moving a 147,000-pound, fifteen-foot six-inch cylindrical vessel on nine axles 1,150 miles from Seattle, Washington, to the Nevada desert.

But Widing has gotten away from heavy haul, and today specializes in bulk commodities transportation—chemicals, caustic sodas, acids, resins, commercial alcohols, and other hazardous, flammable, and poisonous materials. These potentially dangerous commodities are moved in heavy stainless steel tanks that could roll down a canyon without spilling a drop. Widing also has done hauling for national defense projects, atomic energy, and heavy industry. The company has five terminals up and down the West Coast, and in 1984 Portland's Widing Transportation, Inc., logged over seven million miles in the forty-eight contiguous states and Canada.

The firm hauled the Hooterville Express *from the television series "Petticoat Junction" to a new resting place beside Portland's now-demolished Hoyt Hotel.*

Widing Transportation hauled this 150-foot prefabricated steel walkway overpass structure from the Vancouver Shipyards to Interstate 5 near Tigard. Its overall length was 170 feet, making it one of the "longest" hauls in Oregon history.

LLOYD CORPORATION, LTD.

The Lloyd Center marked its twenty-fifth anniversary in 1985, but the story of the Lloyd Corporation is much more than this single noteworthy development. It goes back over sixty years to Ralph B. Lloyd's dream of building a "city within a city," acquiring land, and revitalizing a significant part of the inner city through private development without public subsidy. It is a story of livability in the center of one of America's most livable cities.

Ralph B. Lloyd, the founder of Lloyd Corporation, Ltd., began acquiring land east of the Willamette River in the early 1920s. He had tremendous confidence in Portland's future, and backed this faith with a commitment to provide the funds for his vision of unsubsidized urban renewal and planned development. And his property was no small dot on the Portland map. By the late 1950s Lloyd Corporation holdings had been consolidated to 130 blocks, extending roughly from the Willamette River to Broadway, from Sandy Boulevard to Seventeenth Street.

The acquisition and early development of what is now known as Lloyd Properties continued over thirty-five years. Initial projects were modest—clearing the land, constructing apartment houses, and developing office and light-industrial buildings. But when the plans for the Lloyd Center project were announced in 1954, it was to be the largest single development in Portland's history; and when it opened in 1960, the 1,200,000-square-foot shopping complex was among the largest centers in the United States. Its well over 100 retail outlets, open-air ice pavilion, and landscaped pedestrian malls, highlighted by seasonal flowers, fountains, and artwork by local artisans, exudes the livability of all Lloyd Properties.

Since the 1960 opening of the Lloyd Center, the firm has either an-

nounced or started a major project approximately every three years. Several Lloyd Corporation office buildings have added over one million square feet of office space to the city center, including the 1981 Lloyd Center Tower, a twenty-story, 490,000-square-foot office building. Other developments on Lloyd Properties include the 26,500-square-foot

Once a group of businesses huddled beside the waterfront, Portland's city center skyline now runs from the publicly funded urban-renewal district around the Auditorium to the privately funded projects in northeast Portland's Lloyd Properties.

Lloyd Center Courts racquetball club and the Red Lion/Lloyd Center, a 525-room hotel and convention complex.

The developed area today is approximately 7,500,000 square feet, and Lloyd Corporation is one of the largest taxpayers in Multnomah County. Approximately 15,000 people are employed within the Lloyd area boundary by the 440 retail and commercial tenants who lease space from the firm.

Lloyd Corporation, Ltd., has succeeded in enhancing a major section of the inner city that could have declined rapidly, and the firm's completed projects have stimulated the renovation, modernization, and general upgrading of surrounding commercial and residential properties.

Ralph B. Lloyd, founder of Lloyd Corporation, Ltd., whose development of the Lloyd Center and several office towers has revitalized a large area of Portland in a livable manner.

TEKTRONIX, INC.

Tektronix, Inc., is one of Oregon's brightest success stories. Founded in 1946, Tek is the state's largest private employer, and one of only a few billion-dollar companies in Oregon. It employs more than 20,600 people in its operations worldwide, and over 14,000 in the Portland metropolitan area.

Tektronix has long been known as the world's foremost manufacturer of oscilloscopes, those ubiquitous electronics instruments that test and measure electronic signals. In the 1950s Tektronix also became the leader in television test equipment, in the 1970s, computer graphics, and most recently, digital design tools.

Before World War II there was no electronics industry as we know it. Television was still in the experimental stage, and radio dominated the scene. A community of radio enthusiasts sprang up in Portland, which by the mid-1930s included two young men: Howard Vollum and Jack Murdock.

After graduation from Reed College in 1935, Vollum set up a radio repair shop in the corner of his friend Jack Murdock's radio and appliance store on Southeast Foster Road in Portland. Vollum built an oscilloscope while at Reed, and over the next five years he and Murdock dreamed of setting up an electronic instrument business. At that time the oscilloscope was a relatively crude device of limited accuracy and versatility.

The war put an end to their conversations, but not their dream. Vollum went into the Army, Murdock into the Coast Guard. In January 1946, with the war over, Murdock and Vollum incorporated their company. They produced a technically superior oscilloscope at a third the cost of other commercially available models.

Working first out of the basements of their parents' homes,

Vollum and Murdock soon moved their operation to part of Murdock's former store, and by the end of 1946 to a larger building at the corner of Southeast Seventh and Hawthorne. That year the firm numbered six; by the end of the following year it had grown to sixteen. Within four years Tektronix had 300 employees, working three shifts to meet order backlogs that often ran well in excess of six months.

But that was just the beginning, for as the electronics industry began to grow, as television caught on, and as the computer industry took off, the market for Tek products nationally and internationally grew beyond even the wildest predictions. In 1952 the company moved to larger quarters west of Portland. Adjacent to the Sunset Highway, these quarters were already too small by the day of the move. In 1956 the firm moved to its large campus in Beaverton; in the 1970s it added a site in Wilsonville and a second site in Washington

For Tektronix' tenth anniversary in 1956, founders M.J. (Jack) Murdock (left) and Howard Vollum (right) compare oscilloscopes made by the firm in 1946 and 1956. The type 511A (right), manufactured in 1946, was faster, more accurate, and less expensive than any other scopes on the market. The type 547 (left), manufactured in 1956, continued Tektronix' reputation as the world's leading manufacturer of oscilloscopes. That tradition continues today.

County. Tek now owns seven sites in Oregon and southwest Washington, has operations worldwide, and world sales of over $1.4 billion.

During the company's early years, Murdock and Vollum established the values for which Tek is famous. Modest, unassuming men, their firm reflected their style. This informal, shirtsleeves style set the tone for a business that shares its profits with its employees, operates on a first-name basis, and encourages employee education and advancement. The founders' aim was to serve customers with quality products, and run the company in a way that would serve the interests of employees and the community. In the process, the name Tektronix has become synonymous with quality within the industry and corporate citizenship in Oregon.

In 1947 the Tektronix "assembly line" consisted of the company's few employees building type 511A oscilloscopes. The firm was located near the corner of Southeast Seventh and Hawthorne in Portland. Tektronix relocated its operations to Portland's west side in 1951, and presently has over 20,000 employees in locations worldwide.

RUDIE WILHELM WAREHOUSE COMPANY
WILHELM TRUCKING COMPANY

Wilhelm Trucking began with "dappled-gray horsepower" in 1910. The old gray mares have been replaced by a large fleet of trucks that are helping to make Portland the distribution center of the Northwest.

The ceremonious retirement of Dick and Charlie, the last two dappled-gray horses owned by Wilhelm Transfer Company, was an early example of the company's progressive spirit. The familiar orange horse-drawn wagons were all replaced by the early 1920s with International trucks, making Wilhelm's one of the first firms in Portland to use motorized vehicles.

For seventy-five years now Portland's Rudie Wilhelm Warehouse Company and Wilhelm Trucking Company have been pioneers and progressive leaders in the region's warehousing, trucking, and distribution industry, helping to make Portland the distribution hub of the Pacific Northwest.

Born in 1888, Rudie Wilhelm was the son of German immigrants who operated the Wilhelm Brewery in Sellwood. He grew up working in the business, but in 1910 the 21-year-old Wilhelm saw Prohibition looming on the horizon and correctly predicted that "the brewery business would not be the place to succeed." Answering a newspaper ad, he negotiated and bought one-half interest in Noland Transfer Co., a small transfer business that consisted of two express wagons and five cayuses from eastern Oregon.

With his new bride, Angelina, Rudie built up Wilhelm Transfer Co.

at 89 1/2 Southwest Fourth Street. Working diligently and saving carefully, they were able to buy out the former owner at the rate of fifty dollars a month. Angelina was the entire office force, and Rudie followed his drays about town on his bicycle to oversee the work and lend a hand with big jobs. The main cargo was baggage, beer, shoes, and general freight. The company's reputation for honesty and reliability was well accepted.

In 1920 Wilhelm started its public warehouse with less than 5,000 square feet. Today the corporation operates nearly 750,000 square feet of warehouse space.

As the transfer company's motorized fleet grew in the 1920s, so did the demand by customers for storage space, spurring Wilhelm to rent a building on First Avenue. As demand increased, the company moved into a larger building on Northwest Eighth and Everett streets in 1925, a six-story, 70,000-square-foot facility. With this roomy addition to the business and later additional facilities, warehousing advanced in importance equal to the transfer and hauling business.

Since 1919 Wilhelm Transfer has been in the forefront in using the largest equipment available, and in the 1940s heavy-haul loads began to skyrocket in size. Loads of 200 to 300 tons were hauled by Wilhelm on some of the largest and most varied types of equipment in the West.

Wilhelm Trucking has its headquarters in the Guilds Lake Industrial Area. Rudie Wilhelm Warehouse has its offices and over 700,000 square feet of warehouse space in the Milwaukee Industrial Area.

Wilhelm Transfer Company began as a family business, and Rudie Wilhelm Warehouse Company and Wilhelm Trucking Company remain so today. Founder Rudie Wilhelm, Sr., died in 1968 at the age of seventy-nine, and the second and third generations of Wilhelms are now active in the company's management, growth, and participation in the development of Portland's distribution industry.

GRANTREE CORPORATION

Ask a Portlander about GranTree Corporation and you'll hear, "Sure, that's the company that rents and sells furniture across eight western states."

True. Except few recognize GranTree as the homegrown firm that developed to its present eminence in just two generations, both living. Starting with two ambitious young men, it rose to become one of the nation's two largest companies of its kind: renting and selling home furnishings to fit today's mobile style of living.

From those two young men, with little money but plenty of entrepreneurial spirit, GranTree today numbers 1,200 employees, 300 in Oregon, with a $24-million annual payroll, almost $6 million of it in this state.

Of the two founders, one, J.D. Manley Treece, lives on in Portland, at age ninety, hale and sharp. His son, Walker M. Treece today carries on that original enterprising spirit as chairman and president of GranTree.

Despite its sixty-six years of operation, GranTree never was one to set a course and rest on the oars. The company always has maintained itself on the cutting edge of changing technology, economics, and consumer preference.

No fewer than three times GranTree has completely shifted business focus, once propelled by competition, once by changing economic forces, once to exploit perceived opportunities. Three times the company has ascended to a rank of leadership in its field. This phoenix-like resurgence comes, says Walker Treece, from management's continuing willingness to plan ahead and adapt proactively rather than reactively.

Portland in 1919, like the world generally, was struggling to adjust to the cultural shocks of World War I. The horse-and-buggy era was gone. The airplane and auto were the hot new technologies.

Young Manley Treece, returning from naval duty, saw the auto as a great field of opportunity. He joined the late Burt B. Granning to go into the business of selling cars.

Treece and Granning opened their Automobile Public Market at Southeast Eighth and Hawthorne, the first covered auto lot in the city. At night, huge French doors could be shut to enclose the otherwise open building.

Young Treece and Granning had good success selling autos but saw the growing need for automobile time sales financing. So the partners transformed the firm into one of the first independent time sales finance companies. Other auto dealers sold cars and began bringing their financing to Manley and Burt.

By 1926 auto financing had become so big that the partners dropped auto sales. They had become the largest independent time sales financing company in Oregon.

World War II brought a second tremendous cultural impact. With it came thousands of new families and a housing shortage. The mobile home became a popular answer. The banks wouldn't finance them but Granning and Treece pioneered the time sales financing of these "new homes."

The end of World War II brought other changes. Granning sold out to Treece in 1946. In 1948 Walker Treece dropped a foreign service career in Austria, which had followed war service in Europe, to join the company in Portland following the accidental death of his younger brother, Warren.

Young Treece now perceived the need for a new direction. The powerful banks were increasingly capturing a market share of the time sales financing field. Like his father, Walker Treece quickly positioned the business to move in a new direction. Treece, as president of the Oregon Consumer Finance Association working with the superintendent of banks,

J.D. Manley Treece, one of the co-founders of the present GranTree Corporation.

counseled the legislature in updating the laws licensing and regulating the consumer finance industry. The company was off on its "second career," consumer finance.

The firm began liquidating funds out of auto finance faster than it could reinvest it in consumer finance. Walker and Manley organized a major regional commercial equipment leasing company and added an insurance agency and an industrial loan license serving small businesses.

By the late 1960s the organization had become Granning & Treece Financial Corporation, growing to fourteen offices and straining at its Oregon boundaries. For the second time the company was "first," this time the largest independent consumer and industrial financial services company in Oregon.

The Eighth and Hawthorne location served the company until 1972. After an interim move, the executive headquarters was established in 1979 at GranTree Plaza, 2501 Southwest First Avenue, anchoring the south end of Portland's beautifully developed urban-renewal area.

Before Granning & Treece could expand beyond state lines, it needed additional capital and acquisition capability, so it became a public venture in 1970.

The year 1971 brought Granning & Treece to what may have been its most significant milestone to that date. The company acquired Custom Furniture Rental with offices in Oregon and California. Here, Walker Treece employed the acquisition technique now emulated by many others. He bought Custom Furniture with stock and long-term subordinated notes to be paid out of earnings of the acquired business.

The year 1972 saw further growth with acquisition of Lease Northwest, Inc., an automotive and equipment leasing company.

A new name was needed to characterize the diversified company. The company ran a contest and ten employees suggested the logical winner, GranTree.

The unexpectedly severe recession of 1973-1974 brought GranTree to its third crossroads as interest rates rose to all-time highs, adversely affecting the interest rate-sensitive leasing and consumer finance business. Management elected to put all its manpower and resources into furniture rental, anticipating that to be a growing market, and proceeded with an orderly and profitable divestiture of all other operations.

Today GranTree has reached its third "first," being the leading company of its kind in the eight western and southwestern states and one of the two leaders in the entire United States.

Flowing with the tide of cultural change, GranTree targets its market at the largely mobile segment of today's society: students, singles sharing housing, divorced persons, military personnel, temporary business residents, and the increasing number who perceive their lives are

Walker M. Treece, chairman and president, directs the firm from executive headquarters overlooking modern high-rise apartment buildings which typify the mobile life-style of the 1980s and a preference for renting home furnishings rather than buying—a market that helped build GranTree into one of the nation's leading companies in its field.

better served by use rather than ownership of home furnishings.

The company offers a package of benefits tailored to this market, with month-to-month rentals, wide selection of contemporary furniture, exchange privileges, prompt delivery, and other services—all for modest fees.

Out of this package has grown "the GranTree Furniture Cycle." Rental furniture creates in turn rental-return furniture with a unique furniture value. The rental return draws potential buyers who often opt for the new furniture also offered to bal-

ance the merchandising of the retail discount stores.

With all this economic growth, GranTree has not neglected what Walker Treece sees as its business citizenship obligation. He, father Manley, and others in the company have, besides regular monetary contributions to human services and cultural organizations of the city, served on boards, ranging from the Shriner Hospital for Children to the Chamber of Commerce, Oregon Symphony, Center for Hearing and Speech, the Mayor's Committee to Develop Portland's Coliseum, and numerous others.

Today Walker Treece sees GranTree's growth paralleling that of the city itself. Recently he pondered: "Did the city grow and pull the businesses behind it? Or did the businesses grow and pull the city behind them? More likely they pulled together, true partners in progress."

STAN WILEY, INC., REALTORS

No silver spoons were offered Stan Wiley, and when Tish Rice, senior vice-president of Stan Wiley, Inc., Realtors, is asked what sort of background is desirable for a career in real estate sales, she cites her successful father's credentials. From 1925 to 1944 Wiley worked as a cowboy, wheat rancher, trucker, logger, grocery store owner, auto salesman, and machinist in the Yakima Valley, in Montana, and in Portland. Upon this unlikely foundation Portland's Wiley built one of the most successful and highly acclaimed real estate companies in the nation.

In the nineteenth century the Wiley family settled in the Yakima Valley, and in 1908 Stan Wiley was born near the homestead in Wiley City, Washington. Right out of high school he began a blue-collar odyssey that would lead him to Portland during World War II, where he worked as a machinist for the Pointer Willamette Trucking Company. Wiley's first venture into the real estate business came in 1945 when he joined A.D. Newman Realtors, selling a good deal of property in the area around his Moreland neighborhood home.

In 1955 Wiley and his wife, Dorothy, began their own real estate business in the downtown Portland Title and Trust Building where the couple sold thirty-two properties that first year. That figure was a far cry from the nearly 5,000 properties the firm would be moving annually in the 1970s, and for the first ten years it would remain a small operation. But by the mid-1960s the first branch office was opened in Westmoreland followed by branches in Lake Oswego, Beaverton, Halsey Center, and elsewhere as business began booming. "We never have siphoned off a lot of money," Wiley said in 1977. "That is how we were able to grow. The first ten years were slow and gradual. To this day, I

Stan Wiley, along with his wife, Dorothy, founded their real estate firm in 1955. Daughter Tish Rice (right) is senior vice-president of Stan Wiley, Inc., Realtors.

am still following that philosophy."

The success of that philosophy is reflected by the offices and honors held by Wiley. He has served as president and as a member of the board of directors of the Portland Board, as president of the Oregon Association of Realtors, and as director and member of the National Association of Realtors' executive committee. Wiley was also named Oregon Realtor of the Year in 1975. Stan Wiley, Inc., is recognized in the industry as one of the nation's leading Realtors, and was the thirteenth member of "The Dozen," a select group of twenty-four of the nation's most prestigious real estate firms.

This is also a company with a future. "I don't want this to be like many real estate companies I've known," maintains Wiley, "where when the owner is gone, so is the company." A firm believer, since the age of seventeen, in the dignity of labor, Wiley has no plans to retire. Daughter Tish Rice is senior vice-president of this family-owned Portland company, and a third generation has entered the business. From a husband-and-wife operation in 1955, Stan Wiley, Inc., Realtors has grown to 414 people today, with fourteen branch offices in the greater metropolitan area and executive quarters in Beaverton.

RIVIERA MOTORS, INC.

Ugly "Bugs" invaded Portland in 1954, but few took them seriously. Most agreed with auto magnate Henry Ford who, when offered defeated Germany's Volkswagen factory for free after World War II, is reputed to have concurred with his board chairman's opinion that "I don't think what we are being offered here is worth a damn!" Undaunted by continuing American skepticism, Knute Qvale established the Riviera Motors distributorship in Portland in 1954, and hundreds of thousands of Volkswagen sales here have proven that Henry Ford didn't always have the better idea.

In 1949 only two Volkswagens were sold in the entire United States, and Detroit automakers weren't losing any sleep over the fewer than 1,000 Bugs sold nationally in 1953. But a few men, such as 31-year-old Qvale, kept the faith, and he opened his wholesale and retail Riviera Motors distributorship on Thirteenth and West Burnside in 1954 to introduce Volkswagen to the public and to encourage new dealerships in the territory of Oregon, Idaho, and Montana. The building was leased from Joe Fisher, who, along with other prominent Portlanders, had previously been offered the Volkswagen distributorship but had scoffed at the idea of Bugs ever catching on. Fisher required a substantial lease deposit to be forfeited in case of early departure because he was certain Qvale's pipe dream would collapse in a matter of weeks.

Qvale did move out of that building before a year had elapsed, not because the Bugs didn't sell, but rather because business had increased beyond the capacity of Fisher's building. New to Portland, the homely "Beetles" were wondrous curiosities that turned peoples' heads. They were mere novelties at first, but slowly the idea of quality, price, and economy caught on, and that first year Riviera Motors sold 200 Volkswagens, making Portland one of four West Coast cities that, combined, sold slightly more than half of all Volkswagens sold in the nation.

Riviera's business boomed at its new location near the stadium at

Knute Qvale, president of Riviera Motors, Inc., and Porsche Audi Northwest, Inc.

Southwest Eighteenth Avenue and Morrison Street. The number of new dealerships quadrupled over the previous year, and Volkswagen sales increased by nearly 500 percent. Portland had fallen in love with the Bug, and soon thousands were sold annually; 160,000 Volkswagens were sold by Riviera and its sixty-nine dealerships during the 1960s alone.

In 1962 Qvale added Washington and Alaska to Riviera Motors' region and constructed a new 77,000-square-foot headquarters building in Beaverton. Riviera had begun retailing Porsche automobiles in 1956, and this division grew to become a distributing company called Porsche Audi Northwest, Inc., in 1970. The 1971 development of its 200-acre Five Oaks Industrial Park near Hillsboro created the current headquarters of Riviera Motors, Inc., and Porsche Audi Northwest, Inc., the center for wholesale sales and distribution of current Volkswagen, Porsche, and Audi automobiles, parts warehousing, distribution, service, and educational programs throughout the Pacific Northwest and Alaska. Knute Qvale's unwavering faith in the trusty, loveable, ugly Bug back in 1954 has made him the sole distributor in the region for over thirty years, and Riviera Motors, Inc., now has sixty Volkswagen dealerships and Porsche Audi Northwest has thirty-eight Porsche Audi dealerships in operation.

Riviera Motors was a pioneer in the mass importation of automobiles to the Port of Portland, today the West Coast's leading auto import port.

ALPENROSE DAIRY

Early-morning pasturelands gleaming with dew once stretched unbroken west of Portland between Hillsdale and Beaverton, and milk trucks rolling over the rural Bertha-Beaverton Highway passed few buildings along this route outside of the infrequent "whistle-stops" at Bertha Station and others. It wasn't that long ago, but times have changed. The populations of both Portland and Beaverton have overflowed their bounds and merged, the Bertha electric interurban railway station is long gone, and buildings line both sides of today's Beaverton-Hillsdale Highway. But in the midst of this swelling megalopolis, Alpenrose Dairy on Shattuck Road stands as a reminder of quieter days. Of this once-thriving pastoral dairy community, Alpenrose is the only survivor, and it has developed into much more than a dairy.

In the nineteenth century the green rolling hills southwest of Portland were dotted with dairies largely operated by Swiss immigrants. One of these pioneer dairymen was Florian Cadonau, who, in 1891,

---

Around the turn of the century Alpenrose Dairy was located near what is now Southwest Forty-fifth and Vermont streets. Milk delivery was expanded in 1930, and for the first time help from outside the Cadonau family circle was needed.

Henry and Rosina Cadonau pose with former Portland Mayor Terry Schrunk at the dedication of Alpenrose Dairy's Storybook Land, the dairy's annual Christmastime miniature fantasy land.

owned a dairy farm near what is now Southwest Thirty-fifth and Vermont, and began delivering milk in three-gallon cans by horse-drawn wagon to a restaurant in downtown Portland.

Around the turn of the century the dairy was relocated near Forty-fifth and Southwest Vermont. Henry Cadonau, Florian's son, married Rosina Streiff, daughter of the Swiss consul, in 1916. She named the business Alpenrose Dairy, after the famous little mountain flower that bloomed in the Swiss Alps.

A four-year-old Ford touring car was purchased in 1918, and converted into a delivery truck for the firm's growing list of customers. By 1922 Henry and Rosina had taken

over full ownership of the dairy business, and things began to happen.

Deliveries were expanded in 1930, and for the first time help from outside the family was needed. By 1951 there were sixty-four retail routes, a number that doubled by 1961, not counting the dairy's thirty-two wholesale routes.

A disastrous fire in 1943 almost destroyed the facility, and the next year the family purchased the Elco Dairy, the present 52-acre site which today is shown on Portland maps as

Alpenrose Park—and the mapmakers have good reason for designating the Alpenrose location a park.

Since 1956 there has been no greater thrill for a Little League baseball player than to play a championship game in Alpenrose Stadium. Butterflies flutter in the stomach of a young center fielder as he jogs out of the dugout to take his position before the green and white scoreboard and pennants flapping above the outfield wall. The crowd cheers from the grandstand. Those days of sandlots and grade school playgrounds are over. There are even lights for night games.

Under the guidance of Henry Cadonau and his son Carl Sr., Alpenrose Dairy has evolved into a family fun center, a 52-acre Alpenrose Dairyland. Near the three diamonds of the Little League baseball complex, built in 1956, is Dairyville, a replica of a western frontier town. Inside the dozens of small false-front shops are treasured antiques, a doll museum, an old-fashioned ice cream parlor, a harness store, a music shop, and other reminders of a remote era. The 600-seat Opera House contains a majestic 4,000-pipe organ from the old Portland Civic Auditorium, and elsewhere is an impressive collection of antique music boxes, nickelodeons, victrolas, a calliope, and early elec-

Anita Jean Cadonau, the founder's granddaughter, poses in the festive, snow-covered Storybook Land, a popular annual attraction at Alpenrose Dairy.

tronic instruments. Several vintage automobiles are garaged nearby.

Behind Dairyville is one of the Northwest's finest quarter-midget racing arenas, where young drivers jockey for position around the oval while dreaming of Indianapolis. Nearby is the Circuit d'Alpenrose, a high-banked, Olympic-style velodrome for bike racing, which has been the site of several National American Bicycle League championship meets.

Every Christmas make-believe, snow-covered Storybook Lane returns to Dairyville with tiny homes for nursery rhyme characters such as the Three Little Pigs, Billy Goats Gruff, and Peter Rabbit. The residents of these holiday cottages are piglets, kids, and bunnies, part of about 250 other farm animals that Dairyland keeps on hand to delight thousands of city kids year-round.

The periodic Fourth of July Americana Pageant, a costume spectacular celebrating our nation's past, is a joint effort by the dairy and Portland's Youth for Christ organization. Other events at Dairyland during the season include the Shetland Shodeo, dog shows, a Little Britches rodeo, Country Fair Day, and a frog-jumping contest. And the admission is always free at Alpenrose Dairyland.

Alpenrose Dairy has a rich heritage in the Portland community and today offers much more than "the very best" dairy products. The entry of Carl Jr., Randall, and Roderick into the business marks the fourth generation of the Cadonau family active in Alpenrose Dairy and Dairyland.

ROLLINS BURDICK HUNTER OF OREGON, INC.

In 1936 Richard M. Cole had worked two years for the General Insurance Company when he decided he would open his own agency. He realized the potential needs of the consumer but began his insurance agency modestly by sharing an office and one-half of the services of a secretary with his attorney father. It was a one-man agency, with Cole keeping his own books for accounts that in the beginning consisted of relatives and personal friends. A five-dollar All Risk ski insurance policy premium was important enough to make a personal call across town.

Portland's Cole, Clark & Cunningham was founded in the depths of the Depression, and survived the war years to become a pioneer in offering engineering, inspection services, and loss prevention while working as a participant with client companies. When this local insurance brokerage merged with Rollins Burdick Hunter in 1971, it entered worldwide markets and became part of the seventh-largest stock brokerage firm in the nation. The Portland office, however, operates as an independent subsidiary of Chicago-based Rollins Burdick Hunter to serve the mainstays of Oregon's economy.

Maurie Clark joined Cole in 1940, moving a secondhand desk into the Couch Building office and contributing his old used Chevy as the company vehicle. William Cunningham came on board in the fall of 1941, but within weeks America's sudden entry into World War II put all of the struggling triumvirate into uniform. That senior partner Richard Cole also was snapped up by the military didn't bode well for the young firm of Cole, Clark & Cunningham.

The winds of fate didn't seem to be blowing their way, but Cole hired Marshall "Duke" Brown to hold the firm together while the partners served their respective Navy, Army, and Coast Guard hitches. Brown rep-

Richard M. Cole. Photo circa 1950

resented the absentee agents admirably, and remained with Cole, Clark & Cunningham until his retirement in 1971.

After the war Cole, Clark, and Cunningham regrouped, moved their offices into the Title and Trust building on Southwest Fourth Avenue, and spotted a need for an insurance agency that was geared to industry. The firm began offering attractive industrial packages to companies burdened with several different types of insurance. The package offered by Cole, Clark & Cunningham included liability, property damage, fire, workman's compensation, and group life, accident, and health all handled by a single agent.

Cole and Clark were both Portland natives who had worked in the logging and lumber business and were familiar with Oregon's forest-products industry. The firm offered its package to companies such as Willamette Valley Lumber (known today as Willamette Industries), and Roseburg Lumber (today the largest individually owned sawmill, plywood plant, and particle board plant in the world). The Portland office has represented these companies to this day.

In the 1950s the firm expanded into a wide spectrum of Oregon's

traditional economy—canneries, fruit growers, heavy manufacturing, transportation, and shipping. Cole, Clark & Cunningham's representation of scores of logging and lumber businesses soon made it a leader in this valuable field.

With industrial coverage a key objective, the firm also hired personnel to head its engineering, safety, boiler and machinery, and life and group departments, selecting men who had spent a good number of years as field men, underwriters, fire engineers, and other specialists. The firm became an outstanding organization of experts geared to providing what Cole, Clark & Cunningham dubbed

Maurie Clark. Photo circa 1950

"protectioneering" insurance: protection through the application of engineering industrial insurance problems.

The protectioneering service helped industrial management buy, build, and protect property wisely, and reduce the hazards of fire and accidents by assisting clients in inspecting for safety. This service was most valued in the forest-products industry, where the firm worked closely with various government departments regarding fire laws. Frequent inspections helped check for fire hazards and assisted clients in fire prevention

and equipment. Cole, Clark & Cunningham's forest fire prevention billboards along the state's highways were familiar sights, common sense, and good advertising, and the firm's name became eminently recognizable.

Now known as Rollins Burdick Hunter of Oregon, Inc., since the 1971 merger, the company has continued expanding into new fields of Oregon industry. One example is its specialization in helicopter logging and heavy lift risks which operate around the globe. The firm's clients include some of the largest businesses of this type in the world.

Rollins Burdick Hunter of Oregon plans to expand with the economic growth of the state, both new and traditional. This runs the gamut from new high-tech, aviation, marine, and heavy industries to the venerable and still-major industries that helped build the state, such as lumber, logging, agriculture, and paper manufacturing.

In 1984 the firm moved into its new quarters in the newly erected

Pacwest Center with W.D. Johnson as president and chief executive officer. Of Rollins Burdick Hunter's forty-four offices nationwide, the Portland facility is the firm's third largest with well over 100 employees. Operating as an independent subsidiary, Rollins Burdick Hunter of Oregon, Inc., is building on the solid Portland foundation laid by Cole, Clark & Cunningham. Only the name has changed.

In 1980 (from left to right) the late L.A. Pierce, former president; Maurie Clark; Richard M. Cole, chairman; and Dick Johnson, president, admired the redwood plaque presented to Cole, honoring forty years in the Portland insurance industry.

During the 1950s and 1960s Cole, Clark & Cunningham's forest fire prevention billboards were familiar sights along the state's highways.

LEUPOLD & STEVENS, INC.

The crack of a rifle echoed in the hills as a deer bounded through the brush unscathed. Marcus Leupold, an accomplished local pianist and son of the founder of Leupold & Stevens, vowed he could make a better scope than the one mounted on his rifle that luckless day in the late 1940s. Leupold returned to the Portland plant and did just that. Today Leupold & Stevens, Inc., is famous as the company that manufactures some of the finest aiming devices and mounts for sports guns in the world and as the first company to make handgun and archery scopes for target shooting.

The Leupold scope is a quality product that is preferred by sportsmen, hunters, and target shooters worldwide. Founded in Portland in 1907, and now operating in Beaverton, Oregon, Leupold & Stevens also produces and distributes superior binoculars for hunters, football fans, and opera patrons.

Sports optics are a major segment of Leupold & Stevens business, but the other side of this $30-million-per-year company is a field in which the firm has been a leader for over seventy-five years. As the trailblazing producers of stream flow and water level recorders, the hydrographic instruments of Leupold & Stevens measure water levels and flows in the reservoirs, rivers, and lakes of ninety-two countries around the globe. Here, too, quality has long been an essential component, and some fifty-year-old units are still in use along several river basins.

German machinist apprentice Fred Leupold immigrated to the United States at the age of sixteen to escape a rigid Old World economic system that he saw give unearned privileges to the ruling class. That was in 1891, and after working for a Boston surveying instrument manufacturer, searching for adventure and fortune in Alaska during the 1898 gold rush,

The founders of Leupold & Stevens, Inc., are Fred Leupold (top), Adam Voelpel (bottom left), and J.C. Stevens (bottom right).

and gratefully returning to his old job in Boston, Leupold moved to Portland in 1907. There, joined by his brother-in-law Adam Voelpel (later changed to Volpel), an avid outdoorsman from the forests of Russian Poland where his father had been a gamekeeper for a Polish count, Leupold began the business of manufacturing and repairing surveying instruments.

Leupold and Voelpel soon had three employees working in their business on the fourth floor of the old Phoenix building at Southwest Fifth and Oak. However, the delicate trade of manufacturing precise surveying equipment was hindered by downtown street vibrations shaking

the building. As a result, the company moved into a quiet residential location next to Leupold's home on Northeast Seventieth Avenue. Here, it gained a reputation among local engineers as the maker of accurate, dependable, quality products, but with a limited product line it was becoming apparent the company needed an inventor to design products to meet a wider need.

That inventor knocked on their door in 1911. John Cyprian Stevens was born near Moline, Kansas, in 1876. He received a degree in civil engineering from the University of Nebraska and spent eight years in water studies for the U.S. Geological Survey.

Stevens knew firsthand the needs of the working hydrologist and made inventions to fit those needs. His first invention was a water recorder for use in remote locations that required checking only a few times a year rather than once a week as the eight-day, clock-type recorder demanded.

Armed with plans for even better instruments, Stevens went in search of a firm with the ability and foresight needed to build and market his

Invented in 1910 by J.C. Stevens, this Stevens Type A Recorder was the first of a long line of measuring devices the firm has marketed worldwide for over seventy-five years.

visions. Stevens, the inventor Leupold & Voelpel needed, walked into a shop tailor-made for his needs. He sold them on his innovative recorder ideas, and Leupold and Voelpel eagerly produced and marketed the device. Realizing the importance of Stevens' inventive genius, he was asked to join the firm as a partner, and the firm became Leupold, Volpel & Co.

Along with the company's surveying instruments, there emerged a worldwide market for Stevens' product line in the 1920s and 1930s. Recorders and surveying instruments were shipped throughout the world to such places as India, Russia, Scandinavia, Canada, Japan, and Central and South America. The need and demand for its products remained even during the grim years of economic depression, and no employees were released during the 1930s.

Stevens went on to receive seventeen patents for water and rainfall recording devices—some ahead of their time, such as the Telemark. Developed in 1937, the Telemark was a float-operated measuring device designed to relay the level of a lake or river through the telephone system. Creative genius such as this eventually led to today's Stevens Memomark III Encoder, which relays water-level data via satellite for flood forecasting in remote areas. The Stevens hydraulics line has grown to include the sewage-flow meters required by many cities and states to meet antipollution legislation.

By 1941 the company had outgrown its East Side residential quarters. Renamed Leupold & Stevens after the 1940 death of Adam Volpel, the firm moved into a new building at Northeast Forty-fifth and Glisan just in time to participate in the national war effort of World War II, making instruments for the Maritime Commission's Liberty and Victory ships. When this facility was out-

Introduced in 1946, the Leupold riflescope is a precision, computer-designed instrument with delicate accuracy under the most abusive conditions. Leupold & Stevens is America's dominant manufacturer of sports optics.

grown in 1968, following the rapid growth of its sports optics line in the 1950s and 1960s, the firm moved into its current facility on Meadow Drive in Beaverton.

Fred Leupold died in 1944, and management responsibility passed to his sons, Marcus and Norbert, and to J.C. Stevens' son, Robert, all of whom learned the business from the ground up by starting in the shop. When the second generation of family leadership retired in 1983, Werner Wildauer took the helm. President and chairman of the board Wildauer began his career with Leupold & Stevens in 1958 as a machinist in the shop, worked his way up through the ranks, and today heads America's dominant manufacturer of sports optics.

The United States is still a net importer in this field—eighteen million dollars worth of rifle scopes alone were imported in 1983—but Wildauer and Leupold & Stevens want

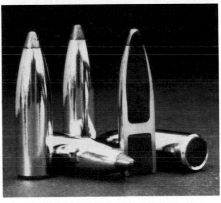

In 1969 Leupold & Stevens became affiliated with Nosler Bullets. The highly regarded "trophy-grade" bullets are manufactured in Bend, Oregon, and marketed by Leupold & Stevens.

to return the technological leadership in consumer optics to this country. Over the years the firm has proven this goal is within reach through innovation and by using only the most up-to-date production equipment, subjecting its products to severe quality-control tests, and by making its 500 employees proud of their work, funding their advanced education, and encouraging them to climb the corporate ladder through quality performance.

ST. VINCENT HOSPITAL AND MEDICAL CENTER

Not all of Oregon's "Empire Builders" were cast from the same mold as the gilded woodsman atop the state capitol in Salem. Oregon's first recognized architect and one of its leading early-day artists in the medium of wood was Mother Joseph of the Sacred Heart, a pioneer humanitarian who personally designed and ornamented the region's earliest hospitals and schools.

Mother Joseph, with four other Sisters of Providence, founded and operated the Pacific Northwest's first hospital, St. Joseph, at Fort Vancouver in the Washington Territory in 1858. Fortified by her faith in God and her compassion for the poor and neglected, she went on to establish a network of hospitals, schools, orphanages, homes for the aged, and shelters for the mentally ill.

Among the hospitals she established was Portland's St. Vincent Hospital, founded in 1875. That institution was Oregon's first hospital, the cornerstone of the progressive medical center that St. Vincent is today, and one of the first among the Sisters of Providence health centers caring for millions in the West.

Though Mother Joseph had launched the region's first hospital in Vancouver, she long hoped for a much-needed facility in rapidly expanding Portland, the metropolis of the region. In 1874 four Sisters of Providence from Montreal led by Mother Mary Theresa were sent west to help make this dream come true.

While Mother Joseph was gifted not only in design, construction, and woodworking, but in fund-raising and administration, Mother Theresa also brought impressive financial and administrative skills. Other sisters had contributed their experience in Canadian hospitals, and all were prepared to provide the long hours of hard physical labor that would be required to pioneer St. Vincent Hospital.

Truly a legend in her own time, Mother Joseph of the Sacred Heart established St. Vincent Hospital and made monumental contributions to health care, education, and social works in the Northwest. A statue of Mother Joseph is in the National Statuary Hall, Washington, D.C.

What was first needed was a site on which to build. Father F.N. Blanchet, archbishop of Oregon and pioneer missionary of the 1830s, and Mother Joseph were offered a fine site in East Portland, but the land was offered by transportation baron Ben Holladay who was feuding with West Side business interests. It

Oregon's first hospital, St. Vincent Hospital opened in 1875 and grew rapidly with the community.

seemed an offer that couldn't be refused, but Father Blanchet had hoped for a hospital on the West Side, and Mother Joseph was troubled over joining with Holladay, who had a reputation as a ruthless businessman.

The dilemma lingered, and Mother Joseph went to the cathedral on Southwest Third and Stark to pray. Inside, she was inspired to drop her precious medal of St. Vincent in the poor box, asking the good saint to decide what was best.

A few weeks later, while she was celebrating the Feast of St. Vincent de Paul in Vancouver, a letter arrived informing Mother Joseph that the Portland St. Vincent de Paul Society had just offered an excellent site on the West Side and $1,000 to begin work. Holladay's offer was declined; St. Vincent Hospital would have a West Side address.

The donated site was just west of Couch Lake on the block bounded by today's Northwest Twelfth, Thirteenth, Marshall, and Northrup streets. As she had done in Vancouver, Mother Joseph burned the midnight oil designing and listing specifications for construction. Under her personal on-site supervision, a formidable three-story building arose on the lot, and after considerable cleaning and scrubbing and furnishing and equipping, St. Vincent Hospital opened its doors to the public on

July 18, 1875.

During its first year of operation, St. Vincent admitted 320 patients; 52 people were cared for in their homes; and 718 visits were made to ill persons. In keeping with the sisters' policy of turning away no one in need, 82 charity patients received care, and 1,050 free meals were served to the poor or temporarily unemployed, with no questions asked.

Funding for such an openly charitable institution remained a problem. This was partly alleviated by the sisters' periodic fund-raising tours throughout Portland and the Willamette Valley, efforts made difficult by a skeptical, overwhelmingly Protestant population. The tours that proved most lucrative were those led by Mother Joseph into the far-flung gold mining camps in eastern Oregon, Idaho, and Montana. The stories of sisters entering the dark mine shafts, of the long horseback rides, and of confrontations with highwaymen, Indians, and grizzly bears, are the stuff of legend.

The hospital grew. By 1882 there were thirteen sisters and twelve employees to serve the increasing number of patients. But Portland was growing as well, and not in a way beneficial to the hospital. The site of St. Vincent, once remote from the city, was by the 1890s surrounded by noisy sawmills and smoke-belching industry. The hospital was also "bursting at the seams" with patients, and a decision was made to move.

In 1892 the cornerstone was laid for a larger St. Vincent Hospital on Northwest Westover Road on the lower slopes of the hills west of Portland. The proposed move to higher ground was dramatically justified when the huge flood of 1894 inundated most of Portland's business section, and floodwaters lapped at second-floor windows of the hospital.

The new hospital building on a

high slope of the West Hills was dedicated on July 14, 1895. Designed by Mother Joseph, it was a six-story, Gibraltar-like structure jutting out from the hillside with a 275-bed capacity. It became one of the best-planned and -managed medical centers in the nation, and it grew steadily to keep abreast with the times and the latest medical techniques.

St. Vincent Hospital and Medical Center's tradition of caring continues for future generations.

Wings were added over the years, and the facility became something of a landmark.

In the early 1960s it became increasingly apparent that St. Vincent once again was taxing its physical capacity, unable to expand to keep abreast with the future. After many serious and extensive studies, the

Owned and operated by the Sisters of Providence, St. Vincent Hospital and Medical Center has been located at 9205 Southwest Barnes Road, Portland, since 1971.

Portland West Hills/Beaverton area overlooking the broad Tualatin Valley was selected as a new site for a multimillion-dollar medical center that was opened in 1971.

Today St. Vincent Hospital and Medical Center epitomizes the advanced technology, skills, innovation, and training of modern medicine. The hospital is recognized as one of the leading cardiac centers in the Northwest. During the final third of this century, St. Vincent has established such progressive programs as day surgery, a walk-in clinic, occupational health, home care, hospice services, labor-delivery-recovery suites, chemical dependency treatment, wellness classes, and management services for assisting smaller hospitals.

Although a major medical center with a sizable staff, the hospital is not too big to remember the individual. It is in the spirit of St. Vincent de Paul that St. Vincent Hospital's people strive to offer compassionate service. The dignity of the individual, respect for life, and service for everyone without regard to ability to pay are all part of the Sisters of Providence's and St. Vincent Hospital's tradition of caring, a tradition that goes back over 125 years in the Pacific Northwest.

PENDLETON WOOLEN MILLS

The Friendly Scout, *an artist's rendering used extensively in Pendleton advertising.*

Thomas Kay arrived in Oregon in 1863, and for over thirty years he ranked as an outstanding textile manufacturer in pioneer Oregon, rising from an obscure mill-hand position in England to one of the most prominent woolen mill men on the Pacific Coast. But it was Clarence Morton Bishop, tutored by his grandfather, Thomas Kay, who brought an idle woolen mill back to life and for sixty years shepherded it to its present position as a respected name in the nation's textile and apparel industries. And today Portland-based Pendleton Woolen Mills' distinctive blue-and-gold label assures buyers that they have purchased a garment with an impressive pedigree for quality and value, made in America of 100-percent virgin wool.

Pendleton, Oregon, was the center of the Inland Empire wool-growing area. It was the hub of a far-reaching network of rail lines and freight wagon routes, and wool growers benefited from its central location. In 1893 the region's first scouring mill was constructed there. However, escalating shipping costs to eastern markets inhibited the success of this eastern Oregon enterprise. To counter this problem, the scouring mill's operators built a woolen mill in conjunction with their wool-handling facility, and Pendleton Woolen Mills was incorporated in 1895.

The mill produced blankets and Indian robes and shawls that were popular on the West's Indian reservations. The Portland department store market grew as well, and when the Klondike gold fever infected the nation, bales of blankets and mackinaws were shipped to that frosty El Dorado. Unfortunately, the mill was operated by men not experienced in textile manufacturing, and limited successes were interspersed with frequent reversals. The mill finally collapsed under the weight of the recession of 1907.

By 1908 the once-ambitious Pendleton Mill had become an idle facility with broken-down machinery and a leaky roof. T.C. Taylor, one of the original incorporators of the first mill, recognized the value of the industry to the Pendleton community and worked to see it reopened. Taylor was also a member of the Oregon Legislature, and he approached fellow legislator Charles P. Bishop for support. Bishop was interested. His wife, Fannie Kay

Thomas Kay, who arrived in Oregon in 1863 and rose from a mill hand in England to one of the most prominent mill men on the Pacific Coast.

Bishop, was the daughter of pioneer Thomas Kay. Bishop's sons, Clarence and Roy, had trained under their grandfather, were graduates of the Philadelphia Textile School, and had each gained eastern mill experience.

It was agreed that if the citizenry of Pendleton would invest in a twenty-year, $30,000 bond issue at 10-percent interest, the Bishop family would put up matching equity to revitalize the Pendleton industry. On February 16, 1909, the Pendleton Woolen Mills was incorporated under the ownership of the Bishop family, and Clarence and Roy Bishop enthusiastically accepted the challenge of developing the new company. By September a three-story building was erected, new and old machinery was moved in, and the wheels began humming under the guidance of a family skilled in the textile business.

The old line of products was reintroduced to the market with an emphasis placed on the distinction of quality identified with the blue-and-gold label. Business was brisk, and in 1912 the family acquired and began operation of a second mill nearer the Portland market in Washougal, Washington.

After World War I Pendleton opened an office in Portland on the first floor of the Oregon Building at

The original mill was built in 1909.

Clarence Morton Bishop, grandson of Thomas Kay and founder of the Pendleton Woolen Mills.

Southwest Fifth and Oak streets, which served as both a showroom and an office. Around this time Clarence Bishop envisioned the now-familiar men's shirts of colorful flan-

nel and plaids, rather than the traditional ones in solid colors.

In 1922 the office in the Oregon Building became the headquarters of the expanding enterprise. A small operation in Vancouver had outgrown its quarters, and in 1924 a building was leased at Northwest Ninth and Flanders in Portland. This, too, was soon outgrown, and in 1930 arrangements were made to lease the Meier & Frank warehouse at Second and Jefferson.

This move came during the early months of the Great Depression. Through 1931 and into 1932 business was stagnant, shipments were returned unpaid, and only a skeleton force was retained even though layoffs were delayed until 1931. Reluctantly, the company was considering closing its Portland facilities and moving to Pendleton's Washougal property. This action seemed unavoidable until Portland garment factory superintendent Joseph Van Reet suggested opening a clothing outlet for sale to the public. A strong customer response enabled the firm to weather this difficult period. Pendleton was in Portland to stay,

and in 1939 it purchased the Meier & Frank warehouse it had been leasing.

After World War II business prospered in the thriving economy, and Pendleton introduced a line of women's wear. One jacket caught the fancy of the consumer, and Pendleton named it the "Forty-niner" for the year of its inception. Made of Washougal flannel in colorful plaids and patterns, the garment was especially popular from 1949 until 1957, an unheard-of record in women's wear where tastes change by the season.

By the time of president Bishop's death in 1969, Pendleton Woolen Mills had grown from eighty employees and 40,000 square feet of space in 1909, to eight manufacturing facilities, over 2,000 employees, and one million square feet of plant space. Under his sixty-year leadership, Pendleton Woolen Mills grew from revenues of $100,000 made up of only a few items to a multimillion-dollar volume comprising over 2,000 items. A fifth generation is in the business today headed by Clarence's sons, chairman Broughton H. Bishop and president C.M. Bishop, Jr., thus continuing the family traditon of woolen manufacturing.

255

WESTIN-BENSON HOTEL

Crime fighter Eliot Ness, the scourge of rum-running mobsters in black sedans during the days of Prohibition, may have been puzzled to see the letters "OH" inlaid on the door of his hotel room. Ness thought he had checked into the Benson Hotel; but it was an easy caper to solve. Those initials are still on the doors of Portland's venerable Westin-Benson Hotel today, because the city's most glamorous hostelry was christened the Oregon Hotel when it opened in 1913. But that name survived for only one year before Simon Benson, the "Northwest Lumber King," had his praiseworthy moniker attached to yet one more local landmark.

One of Portland's leading philanthropists, Benson began life humbly as the son of Norwegian immigrants. He arrived in Oregon in 1879, and began his own small-scale logging operation in the Coast Range, using borrowed oxen to drag timber out of the woods. With two partners Benson expanded his operation in the 1890s, and is credited with introducing steam donkey engines and rail locomotive equipment into the woods of the Pacific Northwest. Over the years his success, fame, and

Proudly displaying the London Grill's ninth consecutive Holiday Magazine *award for Distinctive Dining in 1965 were, left to right, Norman Bay, the magazine's Portland distributor; Peter Egner, manager of the London Grill; Joe Callihan, Benson Hotel general manager; and Ivan Runge, executive chef.*

generosity grew. Benson created the oceangoing Benson log raft, was a benefactor of Benson Polytechnic School, gave to the Multnomah Falls Benson State Park, sponsored the world-renowned Columbia River Scenic Highway, and furnished those bronze landmark Simon Benson drinking fountains for the downtown streets in the earnest belief that men could quench their thirst without entering a saloon.

In 1912, the same year he donated those temperate fountains, Benson saw Portland's growing need for a truly first-class hotel, one to rival the best he had lodged in during his trips to California and the East Coast. Benson commissioned the firm of

famed Portland architect A.E. Doyle to design a structure replicating Chicago's Blackstone Hotel.

No expense was too great for the interior. Beautiful Italian marble was imported for the lobby's sweeping

Pioneer logging operator, philanthropist, and self-made man Simon Benson spared no expense to give Portland a first-rate hotel to rival the best in the nation.

The original front desk of the Benson Hotel retained the old Oregon Hotel "OH" logo in the metalwork to the left and right.

Guests of the Benson Hotel in the 1950s arrived in style, as evidenced by this limousine on display in the hotel's Crystal Room in 1955.

Portland's last surviving graciously grand hotel, the Westin-Benson, retains the charm of a bygone era.

ied the mistakes made in operating donkey engines and constructing sea-going rafts," he later said, "I studied this hotel to learn where I could cut out waste and lost motion, and improve the service and increase trade."

Under the supervision of Benson, the hotel established itself as one of the premier accommodations of the region. Then, he recalled, "I had demonstrated to myself I could make it pay, so I sold it for an even million dollars." As that was the cost of original construction, Benson's effort was more of a civic service than an investment.

The new owners and managers, William Boyd, Sr., and Robert Keller, maintained the hotel's excellence until their retirement in 1944. That same year the facility became part of today's Westin chain of international hotels, and as other vintage

Designed by famed Portland architect A.E. Doyle, the Westin-Benson Hotel has served the city with quiet dignity since 1913.

tablishment to lose money, and took it under his capable wing to nurture its growth in 1914. He renamed it the Benson Hotel, and he personally worked for its success.

It soon became profitable because this self-made man dealt with the hotel's deficits in the same manner in which he had learned to cope with problems as a logger. "Just as I stud-

staircase, and mahogany with gold trim was selected for most of the woodwork. For the main lobby's paneling he selected Russian Cirassian walnut. Now extinct, the rare walnut was shipped around Cape Horn from the forests of the Czar. Benson was used to dealing with large lumber bills, but it is said he nearly fainted when he saw the imperial Russian invoice. The final cost of Benson's 200-room hotel was equal to a rival elegant hotel two and a half times as large, but he was after quality rather than quantity.

Never intending to run the facility himself, Benson had leased the operation to the adjacent Oregon Hotel Company. The two were known as the Old Oregon Hotel and the New Oregon Hotel. Despite its magnificence the hotel dipped into the red month after month. However, the lumberman didn't build this fine es-

When the London Grill opened in 1954 it became a trendsetter for America's hotel restaurants.

establishments fell to the wrecking ball, the Westin-Benson Hotel became *the* place to lodge for presidents, dignitaries, and celebrities visiting Portland.

The Benson's fame was enhanced in 1954 with the opening of the London Grill. Originally known as the Fountain Grill, and as the Oak Room in the 1940s, the London Grill became a trendsetter for America's hotel restaurants. A theme restaurant rather than simply a hotel dining room, its ambience launched the Benson into the spotlight. It went on to win seventeen continuous *Holiday Magazine* awards for excellence in dining, an honor given to only a handful of restaurants. It still ranks as one of the best places to dine on Portland's burgeoning restaurant scene.

In 1959 a $3.5-million remodeling and the addition of a new wing gave the hotel a total of 350 rooms and added Trader Vic's restaurant. The Benson's charming Crystal Room couldn't meet the growing demand for private parties, so a 650-dining-capacity ballroom and a series of smaller meeting rooms on the lower

level were added. These improvements firmly established the Westin-Benson Hotel as the city's finest.

Hotel manager Paul Himmelman is pleased to point out that during the establishment's entire history it

The London Grill is a "theme" restaurant rather than the simple hotel dining room, and its ambience launched the Benson Hotel into the national spotlight. Photo, Ackroyd Photographers Inc.

has had only three owners, and numbers are used to illustrate its continuing success. A guest checks in every 135 seconds, and there are 800 to 1,200 pieces of luggage handled per day. About 30,000 pieces of china and silver are washed every day, and a staff of approximately 350 earns well in excess of one million dollars per year.

Not only is the Benson Hotel Portland's last surviving graciously grand hotel, Westin is proud to claim it has managed this hostelry longer than any other hotel in the world.

And, yes, while it's officially the Westin-Benson Hotel, romantic Portlanders will forever call it, fondly, "The Benson."

A horse-drawn carriage brings general manager Paul T. Himmelman to the entrance of the Benson Hotel in 1980.

R.M. WADE & COMPANY

The covered wagons of over 6,000 pioneers rolled along the Oregon Trail to The Dalles in 1850, and one of those immigrants was seventeen-year-old R.M. Wade, who settled with his family at The Dalles. A restless lad, Wade later crossed the Cascade Mountains via the torturous Barlow Road. Moving south, Wade courted and married Anne Williams of Lookingglass, Oregon, and the young couple journeyed by stage to the goldfields of California, settling in Yreka. Here, Wade opened a hardware store to outfit miners.

In 1865 Wade moved to Salem, Oregon, and founded R.M. Wade & Company, selling hardware and farm implements. R.M. Wade & Company was the ninth company to receive *The Oregonian* 100-year-old recognition and is the only one of the nine that is still owned and run by the same family, making it one of the state's most venerable businesses.

In 1883 the company moved its headquarters to Portland, operating from a building on Southeast Hawthorne Avenue and Water Street. The firm acquired a manufacturing plant, Multnomah Iron Works, in 1920, and a principal product of this factory became a gasoline-driven drag saw, an early power saw for loggers introduced by R.M. Wade in 1914. In 1936 the factory designed and manufactured one of the first farm sprinkler irrigation systems, and today is a worldwide leader in all types of farm irrigation.

A nineteenth-century pioneer in its field, Wade has linked its programs to two crucial aspects of the nation's growth: America's western development and the agricultural revolution in soil tools and methods of crop harvesting.

R.M. Wade & Company has three divisions. One is Wade Manufacturing Company, which manufactures sprinkler irrigation and distributes it throughout the world. Headed by Edward Hall Newbegin, great-grandson of R.M. Wade, the division is located in a modern factory on fifteen acres at Tualatin, Oregon.

The Distribution Division is a wholesale company selling products for U.S. and foreign factories to dealers throughout Oregon, Washington, Idaho, Utah, Nevada, and Alaska. It is divided into three separate subdivisions: farm equipment and tractors, pumps and water systems, and outdoor power equipment. The

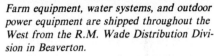

Farm equipment, water systems, and outdoor power equipment are shipped throughout the West from the R.M. Wade Distribution Division in Beaverton.

president of this division is Wade Newbegin, Jr., great-grandson of R.M. Wade.

The Corporate Division is headed by Wade Newbegin, Sr., chairman of the board, and Edward Hall Newbegin, president of R.M. Wade & Company. It is the financial center for the firm and includes the dealer flooring operation, Wade Credit Corporation.

R.M. Wade is a closely held enterprise with all ownership in the Newbegin family. Edward Newbegin married R.M. Wade's daughter, Susan, and was president of the company from 1915 to 1929. Wade Newbegin, Sr., is a grandson of R.M. Wade and was president of the corporation from 1929 to 1982. In 1982 he assumed the position of chairman of the board, and Edward Hall Newbegin became president of the firm.

R.M. Wade & Company established the R.M. Wade Foundation to honor its founder and has used the foundation income to aid agriculture education and experimentation in the Pacific Northwest.

Wade Manufacturing Company, a division of R.M. Wade & Company, is located in this up-to-date facility on fifteen acres near Tualatin.

STEINFELD'S PRODUCTS COMPANY

Henry Steinfeld (center) stands behind his prize-winning sauerkraut. Introduced in his downtown vegetable stall in 1922, Steinfeld's pickles and sauerkraut immediately caught the fancy of Farmers' Market shoppers.

The Steinfeld family has been associated with Portland for over seventy-five years. European immigrants Henry and Barbara Steinfeld were wed in Winnepeg, Canada, in 1909 and honeymooned in Portland. The newlyweds were so taken by the Rose City they moved there in 1909. The vegetables grown on the Steinfeld's North Portland family farm were sold in the old, fragrant Farmers' Market along Southwest Yamhill Street until a surplus remained of cucumbers and cabbages in 1922.

With the surplus vegetables and some recipes she had brought with her from Canada, Mrs. Steinfeld and her daughter, Elsie, made two 48-gallon wooden crocks of pickles and one of sauerkraut in the back of the family garage. Introduced downtown, the Steinfelds' pickles and sauerkraut immediately caught the fancy of Farmers' Market shoppers.

Their experimenting with cucumbers and cabbages grew to become Steinfeld's "Western Acres" Products, and today is the only major sauerkraut packer west of the Mississippi producing more than 8,000 tons a year. However, cabbage for sauerkraut is only a part of the forty-five million pounds of locally grown cu-

cumbers, cauliflower, and other vegetable products Steinfeld's ships annually throughout the West, around the Pacific Rim, and to the Middle East.

The Steinfelds' pickling business grew up around their home in St. Johns on North Allegheny. Sons Victor and Raymond grew up with it. They began working when they were old enough to pull weeds, and later lugged 100-pound sacks of cucumbers to the 5,000-gallon vats. Years later, after their father retired

from the business in 1942, the two sons' intimate knowledge of the entire process made the family business what it is today.

In 1951 the company bought a Scappoose, Oregon, plant that was transformed into Steinfeld's major sauerkraut facility. Today the site is one of the most modern manufacturing operations handling sauerkraut, relying on state-of-the-art equipment.

Steinfeld's Products Company has experienced continual growth throughout the years in spite of a disastrous fire in 1978 which destroyed the St. Johns facility. The company rose from the ashes the following year when a manufacturing plant was dedicated in South Rivergate Industrial Area.

Steinfeld's prides itself in blending improved technology and equipment with the old, proven methods of processing. It continues to make genuine dill pickles cured the old-fashioned, natural way, using good local produce and fresh spices, the way Mrs. Steinfeld did in 1922.

Ninety percent of the vegetables used by Steinfeld's are grown within a thirty-mile radius of its two Portland-area plants. Over $2.5 million in vegetables were purchased from the local agricultural community in 1984. Steinfeld's wishes to continue growing with the community, and is one of the nation's few family-held pickle-producing companies able to boast of doing just that. Third-generation members Richard, Ray Jr., James, and Jane mark another generation of Steinfelds who are active in the company, contributing to Portland's growth.

Steinfeld's extends beyond the immediate family. Many of the firm's dedicated employees have worked over twenty-five years for Steinfeld's. In fact, three generations of other families have been employed, making Steinfeld's a truly Oregon family business.

The first two generations of Steinfelds in the early 1920s. In the front row Henry and Barbara Steinfeld flank son Raymond, while standing (left to right) are William, Elsie, and Victor.

NORM THOMPSON OUTFITTERS

What do Australian glazed apricots, Welch miners' lamps, and eelskin wallets have in common? They have as much in common as King Tut's favorite board game, Columbia River salmon jerky, or Harris tweed jackets—quality. Quality and the fact that they are a mere sampling of the unique goods offered by Portland's oddly eclectic Norm Thompson Outfitters, a nationally acclaimed firm that has carved a unique niche for itself in the mail-order industry by offering a product line that contains not one item anyone really needs. Its trademark says it gives customers a chance to "Escape from the Ordinary."

The seed of this firm was most likely planted by an avid fly fisherman as he gazed into a flickering campfire. Norm Thompson was an outdoorsman who approached fishing and hunting as a fine art, and it was this spirit that inspired him to found Norm Thompson Outfitters in 1949.

Thompson began by placing small ads in outdoor magazines advertising superb flies for discriminating fly fishermen. A mailing list was built up from the response and was used to promote an expanded product line

Norm Thompson's original retail store on Northwest Thurman Street.

The firm's 1950 catalog.
Norm Thompson's Spring 1985 catalog.

that included buckskin shirts, deerskin moccasins, boarhide Wellington boots, and safari hats, for the country gentleman look.

Thompson's son-in-law, Peter Alport, also a sportsman, later took over the company, and traveled the world not merely in pursuit of sport, but in quest of the best outdoor clothing and equipment available. Disdaining mediocrity, Alport was never satisfied during his "continuous pursuit of perfection," as he called it.

A mail-order firm from the beginning, Norm Thompson began with a modest Northwest Thurman Street store, which was a showroom for the company's merchandise. But, as more and more people began coming to Portland to view firsthand the unique quality catalog items, the showroom evolved into a retail outlet.

In the early 1960s Norm Thompson began expanding its apparel line, offering more tweeds and cashmere and lambswool sweaters, all designed to stay in fashion and made to last. Not inexpensive, perhaps, but a bargain in the long run. The firm has always seen the difference between fulfilling needs and fulfilling desires, and no matter how frivolous some of

its offerings may appear, each has to function.

One of its long-shot functional offerings was the casual shape-it-yourself, Irish country hat handcrafted in cottages scattered throughout the Irish countryside. Introduced in the mid-1960s, a period when the hat business in this country was all but dead, it was offered as a dare "for those who are still individuals." It caught on as a protest against conventional headwear and what it symbolized, and it is said Norm Thompson was responsible for bringing headwear back into fashion.

In 1960 Norm Thompson brought back the warm, durable, fleece-trimmed sheepskin coat from Bulgaria to America, and was the first store in the United States to offer the now-common sheepskin automobile seat cover. Traditionally offering largely European imports, the firm is moving more toward promoting quality American goods, giving Oregon-based craftsmen national exposure, and introducing many local products, such as Oregon gourmet foods, to a national market. Portland's Norm Thompson Outfitters has proven that, be it practical men's and women's footwear, or soapstone Chinese worry balls, there's always a market for the best —if it truly is the best.

BENJ. FRANKLIN FEDERAL ASSOCIATION SAVINGS & LOAN

Business was booming in Portland during the early 1920s. Increasing numbers of ships cruised in and out of the Willamette River port, and new shops and businesses opened their doors and prospered. In these bustling economic times, a young Portland insurance man named Ben Hazen spent his spare time selling coin banks—clocks which required the insertion of a coin before they could be wound each day. These automatic reminders for saving money fascinated Hazen, and he thought they might be a good way for banks to attract new customers. But only one small savings and loan association was interested, and it lacked the money to buy the clocks.

Ben H. Hazen, founder, pictured shortly after the opening of the Benj. Franklin in 1925.

Undaunted, Hazen purchased the clocks himself and initiated a sales campaign for the firm. Hazen's sales promotion brought in far more accounts than any previous campaign for the savings and loan. This success convinced Hazen to open his own savings and loan association in 1924.

Under Hazen's leadership Portland's Benj. Franklin grew to reach the billion-dollar milestone in 1977, helped finance nearly 100,000 homes by 1980, became the largest savings and loan in the Northwest in 1982 when it merged with Equitable, and is now one of the largest in the nation.

The groundwork for Hazen's savings and loan was laid in 1924, but it was yet unnamed. Hazen's business associate, Charles F. Berg, recommended that Hazen, "Pick one with 'oomph.'" Hazen reflected on *Poor Richard's Almanac* and the thrift slogans of Benjamin Franklin, and found it an appealing theme. The savings and loan was named "Benj. Franklin," just as Franklin had signed the Declaration of Independence.

Hazen opened his doors to the public at the corner of Southwest Fourth Avenue and Oak Street on January 17, 1925, armed with only $15,300 capital and one employee, and began offering his beloved coin-operated clocks as a premium for new accounts. Again, it worked.

Like most institutions, the Benj. Franklin rode the 1920s balloon of credit and easy money higher and higher. However, the institution took a more conservative route than most during these heady economic times. When the balloon burst in 1929, sav-

ings institutions began toppling like houses of cards. The Great Depression took its toll, and seventeen savings and loan competitors failed in Portland alone.

The soundly managed Benj. Franklin was one of only two local associations that survived, and it did so by helping people. Instead of repossessing the homes of people hard pressed to meet their mortgage payments, the institution worked with each family to help them refinance and reduce their payment to an amount they could meet.

During this time, the Benj. Franklin introduced its first colonial quarters on Morrison Street. The distinctive decor included antique furniture, counter, and books; an old colonial clock; a Revolutionary War musket; and other reminders of Franklin's era. Today this elegant theme has continued to be a familiar sight in the main office and many of the Benj. Franklin branches.

World War II created both a scarcity of goods at home and high payrolls, which combined to lead people

The Benj. Franklin's first office, at Fourth and Oak, featured the woodpecker, "Nature's Systematic Savers." Hazen brought north and displayed these California telephone poles, with nuts embedded in holes by woodpeckers depositing food for the future.

to save as never before. Deposits in the Benj. Franklin grew dramatically. The postwar years were good as well, and Portlanders were wild with demand. New houses, automobiles, and goods impossible to obtain for years now could be purchased—but at rapidly inflating prices. Savings accounts dipped, and to encourage new accounts the institution offered the new Benjamin Franklin half-dollar as an incentive for savings.

The end of the war also saw the return of Hazen's son, Bob, who had been a teller before enlisting. Bob Hazen set up the GI home loan program, did appraising, and learned as much as possible about saving and lending. He served the association as a branch manager, president, and chairman of the board, and has been recognized as one of Portland's leading citizens.

Portland began expanding rapidly during the 1950s and 1960s. These decades ushered in the era of suburban land developments, shopping centers, urban renewal, and new hospitals, as Portland stretched its population boundaries into the suburbs. The Benj. Franklin began branching out to meet this growth in 1951 with the opening of its Hollywood office at Northeast Thirty-ninth and Sandy Boulevard, the first of eighty-two offices in the states of Oregon, Washington, Idaho, and Utah.

The management and employees of

This Mount Vernon-style branch in Lake Oswego represents the colonial architecture of many Benj. Franklin offices.

the Benj. Franklin became active in local civic affairs, and within a few years the association would be known for its hospital lending and willingness to help churches add on, restore, or build from the ground up. The Benj. Franklin also financed Somerset West and Charbonneau which, with their country settings and easy access to Portland, were successful in the suburban housing market.

The twenty-story Benj. Franklin Plaza headquarters, overlooking the Willamette River, was fittingly dedicated in 1976, the nation's bicentennial celebration of men such as Franklin. But, as a result of the merger with Equitable Savings, the institution nearly doubled in size, and the building could not accommo-

date all departments and employees. It was sold in 1983 as plans were developed to build a new facility on the Francis Ford property on the corner of Southeast Grand and Hawthorne. Construction started in 1984, with a completion date set for the spring of 1986.

In 1983 Dr. G. Dale Weight, a prominent New York savings bank executive, assumed the position of chairman of the board and chief executive officer. Robert E. Downie continued as president and chief operating officer.

While the Benj. Franklin is still committed to preserving the city's heritage by funding the historic preservation of old buildings, the organization is soundly in place to meet the challenges of the 1980s and beyond. The institution has helped build the Northwest and buoy its economy, channeling back 103 percent of every savings dollar into the local economy through the financing of new construction and home purchases. It continues to encourage its customers by advocating the principles of thrift by its namesake Benjamin Franklin, who advised, "A penny saved is a penny earned."

A model of the Benj. Franklin's new financial center, a landmark structure in East Portland, will feature a skybridge connecting a three-level parking structure to the main building. Construction began in the summer of 1984 and will be completed in the spring of 1986.

MEIER & FRANK COMPANY

For over 125 years local shoppers said of Oregon's oldest department store, "If you couldn't find it at Meier & Frank, you couldn't find it." Founded two years before Oregon became a state, Meier & Frank remains a retail institution in the heart of downtown Portland and throughout the Willamette Valley from Vancouver, Washington, to Medford, where its eighth store opens in 1986. But it wasn't always easy.

Aaron Meier, a 26-year-old German immigrant, came to Portland from the rugged gold camps of California in 1857. In this raw village called "Stumptown," Meier founded a retail store, based on customer satisfaction, in a modest frame building near the muddy intersection of Front Street and Yamhill Street. Meier struggled for several years, stretching his credit to the limit, as everything seemed to go wrong. "Those were trying times," his widow, Jeanette Meier, recalled in 1920. "Mostly I was fearful that Father would break down. But he never did. He always said, 'Some day, Mother, we will have the greatest store in the Northwest.'" Sure enough, he soon was moving into larger quarters.

In 1873, 23-year-old Sigmund Frank arrived in Portland. Meier was immediately taken with the young man's business savvy and made him a partner. Business went well for Meier and Frank until the worst fire in Portland history reduced twenty square blocks of the city's central business district to ashes in August 1873. The partners immediately rebuilt. In 1885 the Meier & Frank Company moved into a new two-story building on Taylor Street between First and Second. Here, they took dressmaking out of the home by introducing ladies' ready-to-wear to Portland. Disaster struck again when the great flood of 1894 inundated the first floor to a depth of over three

Meier & Frank was located on Taylor Street between First and Second from 1885 to 1898. The great flood of 1894 inundated the first floor of the store and the water reached a depth of over three feet.

feet. The store, however, stayed open for business—false raised walks and counters served customers in rowboats.

That flood may have prompted the move of Meier & Frank to the "mercantile wilderness" way up on Fifth Avenue in 1898. In the store's new five-story, half-block building, the enterprise emerged as "One of America's Great Stores," boasting two elevators and many mechanical innovations never before seen on the Pacific Coast. In 1909 a ten-story annex was added to the store on Alder Street, and in 1913 the five-story structure on Fifth Avenue was razed to make way for a new sixteen-story building, which was Portland's first skyscraper and the largest department store west of Chicago.

Meier & Frank not only survived the Great Depression of the 1930s, but helped guide Oregon through those grim times when company president Julius L. Meier was elected governor of Oregon, serving for two terms. During World War II Meier & Frank's war bond drives were cited as the "most outstanding of any department store in the United States" by the U.S. Treasury De-

The current Meier & Frank building before construction of the transit mall. The left corner of the structure was added to the original facility during the Depression, filling in the entire block.

partment and the *Saturday Evening Post.* Improvements continued after the war, and in 1950 the store installed the longest escalator system in the world.

Although the Meier & Frank Company ceased being a family operation in 1966 when it joined the May Department Stores Company, the firm remains very interested in maintaining the high degree of customer service Aaron Meier endeavored to achieve in 1857.

PATRONS

The following individuals, companies, and organizations have made a valuable commitment to the quality of this publication. Windsor Publications and the Portland State University Foundation gratefully acknowledge their participation in *Portland: Gateway to the Northwest.*

Air Filter Sales & Service
Alexander & Alexander*
Alpenrose Dairy*
Greg and Ann Austin
Blue Cross and Blue Shield of Oregon*
Boettcher & Company
Burns Bros., Inc.*
Cascade Shipping Company
Coldwell Banker
Columbia Forest Products, Inc.
Columbia Steel Casting Co., Inc.*
Dehen Knitting Co.
Emerick Construction Co.
ESCO Corporation*
Floating Point Systems, Inc.
Ford Black & Co., P.C.
Benj. Franklin Federal Savings & Loan
   Association*
Freightliner Sales & Service of Portland,
   Inc.
General Mills Inc.-Portland, Oregon
J.K. Gill Stationers*
Otto & Jean Glausi
Good Samaritan Hospital and Medical
   Center*
Grantree Corporation*
R.A. Gray & Co.
Hayden Corporation
HELLO J/R
Franklin D. Hood
Hyster Company*
David O. Johnson
Jones Oregon Stevedoring Company*
Knappton Corporation*
Koldkist-Beverage Ice Co., Inc.
Leupold & Stevens, Inc.*
The Chas. H. LILLY Co.*
Lloyd Corporation, Ltd.*
Louisiana-Pacific Corporation*
Mail-Well Envelope Company
Marsh & McLennan*
Meier & Frank Company*
Fred Meyer*
Nicolai Company*
Northwest Natural Gas Company*

Omark Industries*
Oregon Blue Print Company
The Oregonian*
Osborn & Associates, Inc.
Pacific Machinery & Tool Steel Co.
Pacific Metal Company*
PacifiCorp*
Paine Webber Inc.
R.B. Pamplin Corporation*
Otto & Marie Papasadero
Pendleton Woolen Mills*
Pepsi-Cola Bottling Co.
Portland Bottling Company*
Portland General Electric Company*
Port of Portland*
Precision Castparts Corp.*
R.E.F.U.S.
The Robert Randall Company*
Rankin, McMurray, VavRosky & Doherty
   Lawyers
Riedel International*
Risberg's Truck Line
Riviera Motors, Inc.*
Rollins Burdick Hunter of Oregon, Inc.*
St. Vincent Hospital and Medical Center*
Sonitrol Pacific
Stagecraft Industries, Inc.
Standard Insurance Company*
Steinfeld's Products Company*
Stewart & Tunno Insurance Agency
Stimson Lumber Company*
Stoel, Rives, Boley, Fraser and Wyse*
Tektronix, Inc.*
Telecheck of Oregon, Inc.
Norm Thompson Outfitters*
Touche Ross & Co.
Toyota Motor Distributors, Inc.
Utility Equipment, Inc.
   Roy Goecks
   Barbara Goecks
Viking Industries, Inc.*
R.M. Wade & Company*
Western States Chiropractic College
Westin-Benson Hotel*
Widing Transportation, Inc.*
Stan Wiley, Inc., Realtors*
Rudie Wilhelm Warehouse Company
   Wilhelm Trucking Company*

*Partners in Progress of *Portland: Gateway to the Northwest.* The histories of these companies and organizations appear in Chapter VIII, beginning on page 193.

SELECTED READING

The history of Portland has been well-served by several studies that place the development of the city within the growth of the Pacific Northwest. Dorothy Johansen and Charles Gates, *Empire of the Columbia* (New York: Harper and Row, 1967) and Earl Pomeroy, *The Pacific Slope* (New York: A.A. Knopf, 1965) are regional surveys. Gordon Dodds, *Oregon: A Bicentennial History* (New York: W.W. Norton, 1977) is the most recent state history. Samuel Dicken, *The Making of Oregon* (Portland: Oregon Historical Society, 1979) gives a geographical perspective, while a number of the essays in Thomas Vaughan, ed., *The Western Shore: Oregon Country Essays* (Portland: Oregon Historical Society, 1975) deal directly with Portland.

The Native American peoples of Oregon are treated in Stephen Dow Beckham, *The Indians of Western Oregon* (Coos Bay: Arago Books, 1977); Robert H. Ruby and John A. Brown, *The Chinook Indians* (Norman: University of Oklahoma Press, 1976); Robert H. Ruby and John A. Brown, *Indians of the Pacific Northwest* (Norman: University of Oklahoma Press, 1981); and Jeff Zucker, Kay Hummel, and Bob Hogfoss, *Oregon Indians: Culture, History, and Current Affairs* (Portland: Oregon Historical Society, 1983). Joel V. Berreman's "Tribal Distribution in Oregon," *Memoirs of the American Anthropological Association,* 47 (1937) is a useful specialized source.

For early exploration and pioneering, the journals of Lewis and Clark (various editions) are an invaluable starting point. Also see: Fred William Powell, *Hall J. Kelley on Oregon* (Princeton: Princeton University Press, 1932); Eugene Snyder, *Early Portland: Stumptown Triumphant* (Portland: Binford and Mort, 1970); Malcolm Clark, Jr., *The Eden Seekers: The Settlement of Oregon* (Boston: Houghton Mifflin Co., 1981); Howard Corning, *Willamette Landings: Ghost Towns of the River* (Portland: Oregon Historical Society, 1973); and William Bowen, *The Willamette Valley: Migration and Settlement on the Oregon Frontier* (Seattle: University of Washington Press, 1978).

The essential source on Portland's development as a community during the nineteenth century is Paul Merriam's "Portland, 1840-1890: A Social and Economic History" (Ph.D. Dissertation, University of Oregon, 1971). Harvey Scott's *History of the Oregon Country* edited by Leslie Scott (Cambridge: The Riverside Press, 1924) and Joseph Gaston's *Portland: Its History and Its Builders* (Chicago: S.J. Clarke Co., 1911) are records of the city's development by active participants in its history. Thomas Vaughan and Terence O'Donnell's *Portland: A Historical Sketch and Guide* (Portland: Oregon Historical Society, 1984) captures the spirit of the city. Other valuable studies include Glenn Quiett, *They Built the West: An Epic of Rails and Cities* (New York: Appleton-Century, 1934); Arthur Throckmorton, *Oregon Argonauts: Merchant Adventurers on the Western Frontier* (Portland: Oregon Historical Society, 1961); Charles A. Tracy, "The Police Function in Portland, 1851-74," *Oregon Historical Quarterly* 80 (1979); and Malcolm Clark, Jr., ed., *Pharisee Among the Philistines: The Diary of Judge Mathew P. Deady, 1871-1892* (Portland: Oregon Historical Society, 1975). One of the best recent studies is Ruth B. Moynihan, *Rebel for Rights: Abigail Scott Duniway* (New Haven: Yale University Press, 1983).

The physical development of Portland is traced in Thomas Vaughan and Virginia Guest Ferriday, eds., *Space, Style, and Structure: Building in Northwest America* (Portland, 1974); Richard Marlitt, *Nineteenth Street* (Portland: Oregon Historical Society, 1978); William J. Hawkins III, *The Grand Era of Cast Iron Architecture in Portland* (Portland: Binford and Mort, 1976); Al Staehli, *Preservation Options for Portland Neighborhoods* (Portland, 1974); Fred DeWolfe, *Portland Tradition in Buildings and People* (Portland, 1980); Eugene Snyder, *Portland: Names and Neighborhoods* (Portland: Binford and Mort, 1979); and Virginia Guest Ferriday, *The Last of the Handmade Buildings* (Portland: Mark Publishing Co., 1984).

Ethnic minorities in Portland and Oregon are treated in Elizabeth McLaglen, *A Peculiar Paradise: Blacks in Oregon, 1788-1940* (Portland: Georgian Press, 1981); William A. Little and James Weiss, *Blacks in Oregon* (Portland: Portland State University, 1978); Nelson Chia-Chi Ho, *Portland's Chinatown: The History of an Urban Ethnic District* (Portland: Bureau of Planning, 1978); and Tricia Knoll, *Becoming American: Asian Sojourners, Immigrants, and Refugees in the Western United States* (Portland: Coast to Coast Books, 1982).

For the last hundred years of Portland history, an essential starting point is two books by E. Kimbark MacColl: *The Shaping of a City; Business and Politics in Portland, Oregon, 1885-1915* (Portland: Georgian Press, 1976) and *The Growth of a City: Power and Politics in Portland, Oregon, 1915-1950* (Portland: Georgian Press, 1979). Carl Abbott, *Portland: Planning, Politics and Growth in a Twentieth Century City* (Lincoln: University of Nebraska Press, 1983) also covers Portland's growth over several generations.

More specialized books on the twentieth century city include Carl Abbott, *The Great Extravaganza: Portland's Lewis and Clark Exposition* (Portland: Oregon Historical Society, 1981); William Toll, *The Making of an Ethnic Middle Class: Portland Jewry over Four Generations* (Albany: SUNY Press, 1982); Charles McKinley, *Uncle Sam in the Pacific Northwest* (Berkeley: University of California Press, 1952); William W. Pilcher, *The Portland Longshoremen: A Dispersed Urban Community* (New York: Holt, Rinehart & Winston, 1972); and Ellis Lucia, *The Conscience of a City: The History of the Portland City Club* (Portland, 1966). Other specialized studies include Mansel Blackford, "The Lost Dream: Businessmen and City Planning in Portland, Oregon, 1903-1914," *Western Historical Quarterly* 15 (1984); Harvey G. Tobie, "Oregon Labor Disputes, 1919-23," *Oregon Historical Quarterly* 48 (1947); and Kenneth Jackson, *The Ku Klux Klan in the City* (New York: Oxford University Press, 1967).

INDEX